1986

I, Witness

I, WITNESS

Personal Encounters with
Crime by Members of the
Mystery Writers of America

EDITED AND WITH AN INTRODUCTION BY

Brian Garfield

Times
BOOKS

Contents

CONTENTS

Introduction

MY PUBLISHER threw a party in his penthouse overlooking the Hudson River and it was after midnight when we left. We were among the first to depart; we had a long drive home. Down on West End Avenue we found our convertible where we'd parked it (the car was too old to steal) and I was fitting the key into the door when a cold breeze sluiced in across the river and a sound, like the flutter of a sailboat's canvas, drew my attention. It was close against my ear and I had no trouble finding the source of the noise.

It was the car's convertible top—shredded into tendrils.

A vandal had slashed it. He'd cut through the canvas to steal a threadbare car-coat that we'd kept in the boot-well.

The coat was of no value. In fact the convertible top was of no value either: it was ready for replacement and we'd bought a new one; fortunately we hadn't installed the new one yet.

I knew the vandal had done us no real harm. At worst we'd have a chilly drive home.

Yet my first response to the discovery of this mindless violence was swift and stark. No need here for an essay on the American and his car; by intimate extension this act of savagery had been committed against *me:* "*I'll kill the son of a bitch.*"

The affront, the insult, the indignity, the injury—they were personal. My boundaries had been violated, my property trespassed upon. He had *no right.* "*I'll kill the son of a bitch.*"

But wait. He slashed the convertible; therefore he has a knife; likely he's accustomed to using it on substances more gelid than canvas.

Furthermore: am I not civilized? Do I lay about me in blind violence? Do I mete out capital punishment for trivial vandalisms? Do I commit vengeful murder?

Yes—but only in fantasies. Only in those gut-reactions that are too swift to be countermanded by inhibition. In that primitive self and for one broken instant of time, yes. "*I'll kill the son of a bitch.*"

Then followed the inevitable cooler second thoughts, the return of reason and inhibition and humor; a sour remark about the vandal, a wry remark about the cold trip ahead; we got in the car and drove home.

It was a trivial incident but it stands out in mind because I caught myself in that unguarded primitive moment. It was as if a camera had fired, freezing frame, capturing my momentary rage for later examination.

Picture an incensed citizen: *They've got no right. If I had my way I'd kill every one of the sons of bitches—get 'em off the streets.*

What if someone actually did?

I made from this a book called *Death Wish,* about a man who enters that moment of rage and never emerges from it.

A writer has trained his perceptions. It is not enough for the muse to speak; the writer must know how to listen. He has taught himself to see stories in everything around him. He is like an oracle who can construct a fabulous prediction from the random design of a few leaves in a cup. A bizarre footnote in the history of American crime becomes, in Robert Bloch's hands, the novel *Psycho;* a comically inept French crime becomes, in Donald E. Westlake's hands, the novel *Jimmy the Kid.*

Each of us has experienced an incident that stands out in memory; perhaps it has provided the anecdote we most often tell on ourselves. The writer makes use of such incidents; the crime writer makes use of crimes. This is a book of personal experiences. In it, each essay recounts an actual episode (usually a criminal one) as it was perceived firsthand by a witness, victim, detective, historian, reporter, or criminal who happens also to be a novelist.

An amateur sleuth journeys to Northumberland to investigate the mysterious death of a young girl murdered twenty years ago on the lonely moors. The sleuth: Julian Symons.

A private eye is summoned by a San Francisco banker. "You've got forty-eight hours to find the man or we're in expensive trouble." The private eye: Joe Gores.

A novelist in Johannesburg publishes a fanciful fictitious solution to a murder that has baffled police. Then the novelist receives a letter from the murderer: "You are right." The novelist: Peter Godfrey.

A young reporter is sent by muckraking columnist Jack Anderson to investigate certain dubious election-campaign funds. The trail leads the reporter into a steamy sewer of corruption. The reporter: James Grady.

A writer investigates a mysterious murder (or suicide?) and learns that crime and detection in reality are hardly as tidy as crime novelists like them to be. The writer: Donald Hamilton.

Several mystery writers are summoned to a press conference by the Police Commissioner of New York City. The Commissioner announces that the mystery writers have been recruited to lend their keen deductive talents to the city in an effort to solve baffling crimes. Soon one of the mystery writers finds himself in an NYPD squad car patrolling dark streets menaced by muggers and killers. The mystery writer: Hillary Waugh.

An FBI agent must deal with an informant's revelation that the United States is being invaded by invisible creatures. "They come from China and they are also making them in a paint factory in Clifton, New Jersey." The FBI agent: Tom McDade.

Those cases and many others are recounted in this book, sometimes with outrage and sometimes with hilarity. In the episodes outlined above, the writers acted *in loco* detective. Other writers played other roles. Al Nussbaum, for example, was one of the

FBI's "Ten Most Wanted" criminals because of his embarrassing success as a bank robber.

This book's publication celebrates the opening of the Second International Congress of Crime Writers, held in New York City in March 1978. The first such Congress was convened in London in 1975; the New York meeting is the first to be held in the United States.

The authors who contributed to this collection are of several nationalities, befitting the ecumenical flavor of the Congress, but all of them are members of the Mystery Writers of America, the host organization that sponsors the New York Congress. The Mystery Writers were determined to produce an extraordinary book to commemorate the extraordinary occasion. That book is now in your hands.

It was conceived by MWA's Executive Vice-President, Dorothy Salisbury Davis, and initially it was to be an anthology of fact-crime articles by fiction-crime writers—an analytic text in which famous novelists were to turn their attentions to the realities of infamous criminal cases: Jack the Ripper, Lizzie Borden, that sort of thing.

It didn't work out that way. Each author made it clear that he had a vivid personal experience—a brush with justice or injustice—that was more significant to him than any remote episode of oft-discussed criminal history.

The contributors swiped the initiative and the book; they created this volume themselves. They were daring: they came out from behind the alter-ego disguises of their fictions; they stand before us like actors without makeup or prepared scripts. Yet we have no trouble recognizing them instantly. No one but Donald E. Westlake could have written the delightful "Tangled Webs for Sale: Best Offer." In Desmond Bagley's stark eyewitness account of a political assassination we find unmistakably the same brash crisp charm that characterizes both the Bagley thrillers and the Bagley person. The first-person private eye in Joe Gores's autobiographical essay will not be an unfamiliar character to readers of Joe's detective novels. (Like Dashiell Hammett, Joe was a working San Francisco shamus before he became a professional writer.)

Each of the contributors here is in excellent company: these are writers' writers, held in great esteem by their colleagues. Among them they have won literary awards, warmed the cold hearts of critics and, along the way, perpetrated a fair number of best-sellers: *In the Heat of the Night* (John Ball), *Psycho* (Robert Bloch), *Where Are the Children?* (Mary Higgins Clark), *The Six Days of the Condor* (James Grady), the Matt Helm spy novels (Donald Hamilton), *Condominium* (John D. MacDonald), *The Tower* (Richard Martin Stern), and many more.

They are a richly varied gathering of prominent crime writers; in this book they are presented in person.

The fiction of crime and suspense deals with issues of morality.

At first glance the genre may appear to consist mainly of superficial yarns of adventure and menace. But crime writers are deceptive—it is their stock in trade—and quite often, upon closer inspection, we find them dealing (sometimes overtly, sometimes slyly) with profound concerns of good and evil. The literature of crime and suspense can provoke images and questions of the most complex intellectual and emotional force; it can explore the most critical of ethical and behavioral dilemmas.

Normally, as writers of fiction, we are free to contrive imaginary circumstances in which we can conduct such examinations and provocations in relative convenience. We're free to suit the crime to the punishment, as it were. But in this book each writer has volunteered to participate in an experiment in which his inventive mind is constrained by, and pitted against, the implacable actualities of justice and injustice.

Some of the crimes discussed in this book are infamous; others are obscure or even trivial. But each of them is a crime that has provoked, intrigued, shattered, offended, or inspired one of us to the extent that it seemed to demand publication. In that respect I believe this book is unique: it presents the writer in person—the novelist in confrontation with his raw materials.

With one long-ago exception this is my first attempt to edit an anthology. I had to grope my way through the job and several writers suffered from my inexperience because at first we weren't sure what sort of book we wanted. Several contributors worked long and hard only to have their submissions excluded because they no longer suited the book; it kept changing shape. I found it agonizing to reject those manuscripts; some of them were splendid. But they were insufficiently personal or insufficiently criminal.

Those writers, as much as those whose essays appear in the book, were exceptionally generous in their efforts to lend support to the International Congress of Crime Writers because they wrote these essays expressly for this book. It is not a pastiche of previously published works. Only two of the essays have appeared elsewhere in their present form and these two (by Julian Symons and Robert Bloch) are published intact not because of auctorial laziness but because in my opinion they suit the book perfectly without need of any revision. A few others (by W. T. Brannon, Lucy Freeman, Donald Hamilton, and perhaps two or three more) are based on books or articles previously published by their authors but the versions herein are new.

As a novelist I have no audience but myself—I try (usually without too much success) to write a book that I'd like to read if someone else had written it—and I carried that principle over into this job, soliciting and selecting essays to suit myself. To that extent the book is as personal to me as any of the essays is to its own author. Yet no anthology is a one-man show; it is the contributors, not the editor, who create its excellences. And in this case, in the task of editing the book, I have had invaluable assistance and guidance from Dorothy Salisbury Davis and from our publisher's amiable and expert editor, Marcia Magill. To them, and to those who contributed so generously of their labor—including those whose submissions do not appear here and those who were not already my personal friends whose arms were within twisting distance—many, many thanks.

—Brian Garfield
New York, 1978

I, Witness

Tangled Webs for Sale: Best Offer

Donald E. Westlake

AT THE KIND OF literary cocktail party where the only food available is seven or eight trendy variants on potato chips, I sometimes limit my drinking to dry vermouth on the rocks, as a self-protective gesture. That's what I was carrying, while roaming with less and less hope in search of at least one small bowl of peanuts, when the short lady with the lace at her wrists said, "May I ask you a question?"

"You haven't seen any cashews, have you? Possibly a bowl of fruit?"

"Sorry, no. *May* I ask you a question?"

Near to hand was a bowl of trendy potato chips; they had a rippled surface, like my stomach lining. "Yes, of course," I said.

"Tell me," she said, "Where *do* you get your ideas?"

"I am a Crime Novelist, madam," I said. "I steal them."

She laughed, but didn't go away. "Surely not," she said.

"Surely so," I insisted. The rippled chip was very dry and very salty. I sipped vermouth and said, "Tom Lehrer defined it for us all." And, in my loud tone-deaf voice, I sang, "Plagiarize! That's why the Good Lord made your eyes!"

"But not *you*," she said. Nothing would deter her, and my singing—which normally can empty a room—had attracted two or three passersby.

"Everyone," I told her, and them, "everyone steals, whether only a line, a situation, a character quirk, a setting, perhaps a murder method, a complete plot, possibly even an entire thematic substructure, a whole view of life. As we stand here gorging ourselves on potato chips, college students all over the country are writing themes in which every sentence ends with three dots, thanks to their recent exposure to Celine. And why not?" I demanded, noticing that one or two fiction writers had joined the group. "Plagiarism is merely imitation, and imitation is said to be a form of flattery. One of the better forms of flattery. I have in my time," I continued, "both flattered others and been myself flattered by those bastards treading on my heels."

"Sorry," said the short gent behind me. He picked up the chip bowl and moved around front.

"Not you. And in any case there's no point getting upset about people stealing ideas from one another. I'm finally coming to understand that no matter how hard I hustle or how lazily I dawdle we'll all get to Tuesday at the same time."

"What have *you* stolen?" demanded a fellow I recognized as a moderately known novelist reputed to be very handy with a lawsuit.

"I won't tell you what I've stolen personally," I answered, "but I will tell you of a time when I became a receiver of stolen goods; even to the point of filing off the serial numbers and reselling the stuff."

"Who'd you steal from?"

"I didn't steal. I received stolen goods."

"Who from?"

"A Hollywood movie producer."

The entire group shifted from one foot to the other. Hearing that Hollywood movie producers might be found with stolen goods about their persons was not interesting news.

The litigious novelist, however, pursued the point: "Who did *he* steal from?"

"A gang of professional criminals in France. And they had started the process by stealing from Lionel White."

The lady with the lace at her wrists said, "Who is Lionel White?"

"A very good crime novelist," I told her. "I doubt he himself knows how many of his books have been made into movies. There was *The Money Trap* with Glenn Ford, and an early Stanley Kubrick movie called *The Killing,* and—"

"Get to the point," suggested the novelist.

"I suppose I will, eventually," I said, pausing to sip vermouth. "But mentioning *The Killing* reminds me of another example of how ideas travel. That movie was based on a novel called *Clean Break*. A while later, there was a novel called *League of Gentlemen,* written by John Boland, and made into a movie—"

"—starring Jack Hawkins, with a screenplay by Bryan Forbes," suggested the short gent. He was eating all the chips out of the bowl, one after the other, like a metronome: dip-chip, dip-chip, dip-chip.

"That's right," I agreed. "In that movie, which was a comic treatment of the kind of caper story at which Lionel White has always specialized—the tough gang of professional crooks pulling off a robbery of some sort—Jack Hawkins assembles his gang by sending each man half of a five-pound note and—"

"Ten-pound note," corrected the short gent.

"Are you sure? Anyway, half a note and a paperback crime novel. He wants them to read the novel to see how professionals do it, and the novel he sends them is *Clean Break,* by Lionel White. So the notion of using Lionel White's ideas to trigger other people's ideas already exists."

The novelist said, "What does all this have to do with you and receiving stolen goods?"

"Now we've come to that," I assured him. "Among Lionel White's other books was one called *The Snatch,* which was a kidnapping novel, featuring his usual breed of hard-bitten professionals. As with many American crime novels, this was translated into French and published by Gallimard in their Serie Noir. A minor French criminal read the book, decided it was a blueprint for a practical crime, and induced a few of his criminal friends to read it."

"Wait a minute," said the short gent, putting down the empty chip bowl. "That's what Jack Hawkins did in *League of Gentlemen.*"

"Except," I pointed out, "that Hawkins and his gang used the *manner* of *Clean Break* while making up their own crime. Otherwise, John Boland and Bryan Forbes might very well have found themselves being sued by Lionel White."

My novelist friend growled low in his throat. He was drinking something as colorless as water, with a bit of lemon rind in it. Such drinkers are dangerous.

"To return to France," I said, "these criminals—"

"I love France," said the lady with the lace at her wrists. Her drink was a dark maroon in color, and it coated the glass. Had oil-spill become a popular beverage?

"France is all right," I answered, "but if you——"

"Lionel White," insisted the novelist.

"Those French criminals," urged the short gent.

"What happened next?" demanded two or three fringe members of the group. (They were, had they but known it, exemplifying not only the human need for narrative which creates jobs for storytellers like me, but also the professional need which at times drives writers to seek the answer to that question in other writers' books.)

"Well," I said, "the French criminals weren't planning to write any novels, so they didn't have to be careful not to get too close to the original story. They decided to follow White's blueprint *exactly,* doing everything precisely as described in the book." I sipped vermouth. "The book," I went on, "told them how and where to find their victim, so they did that part and it worked. It told them how to engineer the actual kidnapping, and they did *that* part and it worked. It told them how and where to keep the victim, how to make contact with the parents, and how to collect the ransom without getting caught, and everything it told them to do they did, and it all worked."

The novelist, sounding suspicious, said, "This is a true story?"

"It is. The book told them to choose an infant, because an infant wouldn't be able to identify them later, and the infant they chose was the grandson of the automaker, Peugeot. The Peugeot kidnapping became the crime of the decade in France; brilliant, audacious, professional in every way."

The lady with the lace at her wrists said, "What happened to the child?"

"Fortunately," I told her, "the book had emphasized the point that the child should not be harmed in any way. If the child were returned safely at the end of the exercise, the crime would eventually be forgotten and the police would concern themselves with other more recent outrages. But if they were to kill the child, the police—and the wealthy Peugeot family—would *never* give up, until the criminals were found. So, once they got their ransom money, the gang returned the child—in the manner described in the novel—and that was the end of it."

"What happened next?" asked two or three recent additions to the group.

"They ran out of book."

"What did they do?"

"They were left with nothing to rely on but their own teeny brains. They threw their money around in neighborhoods where they were known. They got drunk in bistros and hinted at secret knowledge in the Peugeot kidnapping. Within two weeks they were all under arrest and most of the money had been found and returned to the family."

Smiling—his chin was very salty—the short gent said, "They should have used some of the money to hire Lionel White to write a sequel."

"If he'd put that thought in the book, they would have."

The disputatious novelist said, "Where do *you* come into all this?"

"Rather later," I told him. "Let me make the point here that factual events cannot be copyrighted. It would be against the law to steal the plot or characters of Lionel White's *Clean Break,* but it is not against the law to borrow for one's own literary use the true story of a group of criminals imitating a novel. This was the suggestion brought to me back in the late sixties by a producer named Eddie Montaigne. A very nice, pleasant man, Montaigne had been the producer of the Phil Silvers TV series 'Sergeant Bilko' and of a long line of movie comedies including the Don Knotts pictures. Universal Studios had offered to finance him for a major-budget comedy, and his idea was to do a movie based on the Peugeot kidnapping. Not that he insisted on a kidnapping, and he certainly didn't want a French background. What he wanted was a story about criminals copying a book. He asked me if I'd like to do this story, and I said I would, and in our first meeting I made my principal contribution to the project, by suggesting that a *movie* about these criminals should have them imitating not a book but a movie."

"Of course," said the novelist.

I sipped vermouth. "We had a step-deal," I said, throwing in a little shoptalk to please the novelist (pleasing one's audience is *much* more important than having an opinion about one's audience), "which began with my writing a ten-thousand-word story treatment. Initially I felt I'd rather stay away from kidnapping, because if for no other reason it was too close to the truth, and after thinking about felonies for a while I came up with the substitute of counterfeiting. It seemed to me that Dennis O'Keefe had starred in any number of movies in which he was a Treasury Agent disguised as a crook so he could infiltrate a counterfeiting gang, and I thought it might be fun to cobble up a nonexistent movie out of bits and pieces of those Dennis O'Keefe epics, and make *that* the movie my own crooks would be imitating. The problem was—and it was frequently also a problem in the Dennis O'Keefe movies—there's very little that's either dramatic *or* comic in counterfeiting."

The short gent had wandered away—it's hard to keep an audience interested—but now he came back with a new bowl of potato chips and said, "Why didn't you have them rob a bank?"

"The problem with robbery, and with most other crimes," I told him, "is that they aren't *serial*. They happen and they're over with. There's no reason for the criminals to keep going back to the book —or the movie—to see what to do next. Counterfeiting is at least a serial crime, in a dull way, but finally I had to go back to the original. Kidnapping is, more than any other, a crime that takes place step by step."

"So you did the story treatment about a kidnapping," said the novelist.

I withdrew, from the short gent's new bowl, a potato chip. All the chips in this bowl were identical—medium tan, shaped like a moray eel, with a consistency suspiciously like fiberboard—as though they were all clones from some original proto-chip.

"I did two story treatments," I said, as the tasteless chip passed through my mouth, chased by vermouth. "The counterfeiting treatment was generally agreed to be a mistake, so *then* I did the kidnapping treatment, and that was generally agreed to be okay. Until, unfortunately, it got to Lew Wasserman, head of Universal, who had to approve the project before it could be slated for production."

The novelist said, "Don't tell me Lew Wasserman objected to plagiarism."

"I doubt he approves of it," I said, "at least not in its actionable forms, but that wasn't the problem in this case. The problem was, Lew Wasserman had just become a grandfather. Now, I'd altered from the true-life story—and from *Clean Break* as well—by making the victim a bright self-sufficient ten-year-old boy rather than a baby, since fearing for a baby's safety is inimical to comedy, but it wasn't change enough for Grandfather Lew. 'You can't make a comedy about a kidnapping,' he said, apparently never having heard of O. Henry's 'The Ransom of Red Chief.' In any event, that killed the movie deal."

"Is that it?" demanded the novelist. "That's the whole story?"

"Well, not exactly. In stealing ideas, the professional novelist's richest hunting ground is himself. One's own earlier work is full of potentially useful material. A quick paint job, rearrange the furniture, and *voilà!*"

"I do love France," said the lady with the lace at her wrists.

"But if you're going to Europe," I said, "you should certainly—"

"You stole from yourself," suggested the novelist.

"Granted. I would have sued me, but I settled out of court."

The short gent, dip-chipping his way through the pseudo-chips, said, "What did you steal?"

"The whole idea, lock, stock, and barrel. I'd already written two comic novels about a gang of professional criminals who are more unlucky than inept, led by a gloomy fellow called Dortmunder.* At the suggestion of my very good friend Abby Adams, I borrowed back the kidnapping story and turned it into the third Dortmunder novel, called *Jimmy the Kid*. Since what I was writing was a book, I changed the original from a movie back to a novel, and included

---

* *The Hot Rock* and *Bank Shot.*—Ed.

excerpts from that novel, which was called *Child Heist,* written by a tough crime novelist called Richard Stark, who works the same general territory as Lionel White."

The novelist gave me an unfriendly look. "If *I* were Richard Stark," he said, "I'd sue."

"Well, the fact is," I told him, *"I'm* Richard Stark. I've written any number of novels under that name about a tough professional thief called Parker,** but *Child Heist* isn't among them. It is an invented novel from a pseudonymous author appearing in a real novel from that author's real persona based on a movie treatment by the same author based on a producer's idea to use a real-life case in which actual criminals performed a crime based on *The Snatch,* by Lionel White." I drank vermouth.

The short gent said, "So the *Child Heist* excerpts in *Jimmy the Kid* are all of the book that was written? The rest doesn't exist?"

"Right."

"Will you ever write the rest?"

"Somehow I doubt it. In the first place I think I'd get cross-eyed by now, and in the second place, wouldn't it somehow complete the circle? Wouldn't I—or Richard Stark—simply wind up writing *The Snatch?"*

"Then Lionel White would sue you," the novelist told me, with some satisfaction.

"He might. On the other hand, having been at both ends of that kind of thievery, I know it takes a lot of provocation to make a plagiarism suit seem worthwhile."

"Oh, no, it doesn't," said the polemical novelist.

"It does with most of us. And we *all* borrow, all storytellers do, whether we know it or not. The books we've read, the movies we've seen, they still float in the bilge of our brains, along with our own experiences and prejudices and hopes, and sooner or later something comes out of us that we originally got from somebody else. For instance," I said, backing away from the company, "this entire conversation is nonexistent and borrowed from Tom Wolfe."

"Which one?" cried the short gent, as I moved away.

"Both of them!" I told him, and headed for the bar. "A very

** Including *Point Blank, The Split,* and *The Outfit.—Ed.*

tall bourbon," I told the chap in the white coat. "And you might as well add an ice cube."

DONALD E. WESTLAKE wrote, among other books, *Two Much* and *Enough.*

Letter from a Killer

Peter Godfrey

LATE in 1950, *Spotlight,* a popular South African weekly, was sold to new owners who resolved to convert it to a monthly, as from January 1951. The new editor-in-chief, Pieter Beukes, decided that what the revised publication needed most was an original crime feature that would command instant attention. He then made contact with me and my good friend Benjamin Bennett to see if we had any ideas on a feature.

Ben Bennett had made his name first as a newspaper crime reporter and then as the author of a number of books dealing with actual crimes committed in South Africa. I had also achieved local recognition as a writer of crime fiction. At the time, too, I was a regular contributor to *Ellery Queen's Mystery Magazine.*

Ben and I came up in very short order with a cracker of an idea. Imagine a spread across two pages the same size as the *Saturday Evening Post.* On the left, the strapline read: "Fact Crime—by Benjamin Bennett," followed by its relevant headline. The right-hand page was "Fiction Solution—by Peter Godfrey." If we confined ourselves to 2,500 words each, we would have room to fill a continuation spread, and illustrate both facts and theory with photographs from the original crime.

For the opening feature we suggested that Ben write: "Who killed Bubbles Schroeder?" My side would be a suggested solution to the really baffling mystery.

Beukes had no hesitation in deciding the Schroeder case would be a winner. It was a South African *cause célèbre,* only two years old and still a frequent talking point. The murdered girl was glamorous, beautiful, and immoral. All attempts at solving the mystery —and they had followed almost every conceivable line of suspicion thrown up in Johannesburg, a city never slow to produce and embellish a plethora of rumours—had ended in failure.

A strange coincidence was that I had known the murdered girl. She was born in 1931 in my home town, Vereeniging, a sort of expanding village where everyone in the 1930s not only knew everyone else, but even the names of farming families in a twenty-mile radius. I remember her best as a scrawny untidy kid of seven just before the war, and can recollect a friend of mine referring to her as "that Schroeder brat."

She didn't remain scrawny, as she didn't remain "Johanna," the name with which she was christened. She grew taller and curvier and practised to improve on a natural allure in the next ten years. Then she became "Bubbles" and moved to glamorous postwar Johannesburg in 1947, soon after her sixteenth birthday. Here she blossomed into a perpetual party girl. But she always remained a brat. She was popular because she was decorative and easy. Not overtly cheap in manner, always expensive in cash, she made many male friends, and kept none of them for any length of time.

August 15, 1949, was the last day in her life of eighteen years, two months and seven days.

Here is how she spent some of her last hours.

Early in the afternoon she went to the apartment of a former lover. Her reception was cool, but she helped herself with some insouciance to roast turkey and brandy, borrowed a ten-shilling note (worth about $1.25) and then some small copper coins for "bus fare." At the time she was wearing a brown coat, black shoes with cross-over straps and thick soles, and carried a purse.

A short time later she was back at another apartment in Dorchester Mansions occupied by a seventy-year-old tailor who had given her a room to sleep in. She changed her dress, then went out to meet a youth, Baxter, with whom she had spent the previous weekend. Baxter wanted her to meet his "rich friend," Arthur Porter.

(None of these names are correct. In fact, names of all innocent parties have deliberately been altered for obvious reasons.)

The trio drove out to the opulent Porter Estate in the wealthy Johannesburg northern suburb of Illovo. Porter's parents were away; in fact, apart from servants, Arthur Porter and his cousin Andy Lester were the only occupants and Lester was out on a date. There was a security guard at the gate of the estate.

Bubbles, Baxter and Porter had several drinks, followed by a dinner of asparagus, soup, chops and fried potatoes, canned peaches, and coffee. After that there were more drinks and Bubbles also ate a quantity of salted peanuts.

Just before midnight, Baxter left, and shortly thereafter Lester returned from a visit to the cinema with a girlfriend. Meanwhile the sociability of the party had deteriorated, and Bubbles was becoming thoroughly disagreeable.

Because Porter was feeling his drinks and since his car was still standing in the driveway, Lester volunteered to take her home. The car was clocked out by the security guard at 1:30 A.M.

He was back in a little over twenty minutes.

Porter was alarmed. "What happened?" he asked. "You couldn't have taken her home."

"The little bitch," said Lester. "She was impossible. She got out of the car in Oxford Road." The highway he mentioned was about ten-minutes' drive from Illovo.

Pressed, Lester went into more detail. "Soon after we left here, she asked if she could drive. You know the car's new, and I wouldn't let anyone else touch it, so I refused. Then she stretched out her leg and jammed on the footbrake. The car stalled. I gave her hell. She got out of the car and said she was going to walk home. I told her not to be a fool and to get back in. She did so, then asked me once more to let her drive.

"I told her to forget it. I was really annoyed. She jumped out of the car again, and said, 'I'm walking home. Which way do I go?'

"I told her to follow the overhead trolley-bus wires. I waited, thinking she was bluffing, but she kept on walking very fast and not looking back. I thought if that was the way she wanted it, the best thing for me to do was to go home."

Porter was aghast. "How can you let the girl walk home alone at this time of night?"

"That's what she wanted," said Lester stubbornly. "I'm going to bed."

Porter took out his own car and made a thorough search for Bubbles, but saw no trace of her. Eventually, he was clocked in back at the estate at 2:50 A.M.

The next day the two boys contacted Baxter, who went with them to Dorchester Mansions. Bubbles had not returned home, but the old tailor had much experience of her erratic habits and thought nothing of it. The boys eventually decided to consult the police. No trace of Bubbles was found throughout that day.

But early the next morning, Wednesday, August 17, African labourers discovered the body of Bubbles Schroeder in a plantation in Birdhaven, a suburb near where Bubbles had last been seen, but certainly not in the direction in which she had been walking. She lay on her back so neatly and tidily, it was obvious someone had gently laid out her body. Her clothing was undisturbed. A handful of builder's lime had been forced into her mouth, but cause of death was strangulation.

There was no indication of rape. True, one leg of her panties was torn, but the tear may have had nothing to do with the crime. Bruising and marks indicated that some form of ligature, like a scarf, had been drawn round her neck. Stomach contents indicated she had been killed very shortly after she left Lester—unless she had been what the medical examiner called "a slow digester."

The lime in her throat came from a small dump left by builders only a few yards from the body. Bubbles's coat, shoes and purse were missing.

The case had all the ingredients necessary to convert Johannesburg into one big wagging tongue of gossip.

The police had a card up their sleeve. Forensic evidence indicated that Bubbles had been seated in a car at the time of her death. Under strangulation, the human bladder always voids itself. It is even more difficult to remove traces of urine than traces of blood. So the cars of all boyfriends she had known—and a ripe cross-section of Johannesburg society they proved to be—were impounded and gone over with a fine comb by forensic experts. No positive clue emerged.

But those who knew her well did suggest an explanation for the disappearance of the coat, shoes and purse. Apparently, Bubbles had the habit, when entering a car, of draping her coat loosely over her shoulders like a cape, putting her purse on the seat beside her, and kicking off her shoes. It seemed likely that the killer, lifting her body out, let her coat slip, thus leaving it, her purse, and shoes in the car.

Lester and Porter were arrested and brought to a Preparatory Examination (the South African equivalent of grand jury). The police case was entirely circumstantial. Almost the only point at issue was whether Bubbles could have braked Lester's car in the manner described. Medical evidence and a reconstruction with a model indicated it was possible. A witness came forward with evidence that Bubbles had once stopped his car in the same manner. Lester and Porter were discharged. The case remained a baffling mystery.

But now, two years after the murder, Ben Bennett and I began to scrutinise the evidence in great detail. Ben's motives were purely those of a meticulous craftsman—to put all known facts into a logical sequence. So far our interests were identical, but I had to go further. I had to try and solve the crime—as if it were a mystery fiction.

My first postulation was—because of the negative forensic examination of all the cars involved—that the killer was a stranger, someone not yet mentioned in the case. I visualised him for a short while as X, and then without knowing why I began to think of him by the name by which British police describe an unknown criminal. I began to call him "Chummy."

Initial deductions were based on probability. For instance, I thought it more likely that at that hour of the morning he was going from the city centre towards his own home—which placed that residence in one of the suburbs lying to the north of Johannesburg. From the clues, I tried to work out what psychological and physical attributes of the killer could resolve the paradoxes of the crime. I asked myself what he had been doing in the city, why he was driving home so late, and a myriad other questions.

Somewhere in the middle of this maze, I felt a *click* of identification. From that moment on, I knew a certainty that outweighed all ifs and buts.

And the words began to flow easily from my typewriter:

I KNOW THE MURDERER

Yes, I know the murderer of Bubbles Schroeder . . .

I can see him clearly as though he was actually standing before me —a young man, around twenty-five, with broad shoulders, strong arms, and delicately sensitive fingers. No, I cannot tell you his name, his height or colouring, because he is not known to me in the flesh. Only in the mind . . .

I know he has strong arms and shoulders because no weakling could have carried the dead weight that had been Bubbles Schroeder from his car to the spot where she was found without leaving definite traces of his progress. I deduce his hands are sensitive, because the neatness with which the body was laid out presupposes a man with a tidy mind —a bookkeeper, an artist, a window-dresser—one of a dozen trades or professions where the hard work is with the head, and only delicate labour with the hands.

And because when I first read details of this case, I could not reconcile these self-evident facts with the one mark of apparently savage and unreasoning brutality—the ramming of the handful of lime down the throat of the victim—I tried to solve the mystery by *feeling* myself into the mind of the murderer. I tried to imagine his motive . . . and suddenly I knew . . .

I knew *why* he had done it, and in that instant he became three-dimensional to me. Or, rather, his mind became three-dimensional. I knew, with an utter certainty, that his actions were those of a man showing consideration for people dear to him, of a man with an awakened sex instinct, whose desires had been repressed, and who found unexpectedly that they would have to be repressed for longer than anticipated.

The picture of a man, loving his wife, whose wife was away too long . . .

And this is his story:

Normally he would have put his car away when he returned from work, but that afternoon he left it in the driveway of the guest-farm at which he was staying. He thought dimly, "I'll do it later . . . first, if there's a letter . . ."

There was. He tore it open, swallowed the first sentences in gulps, then stopped, went back over the few previous lines, and read slowly. The words said: ". . . So you see, darling, it's very difficult for me to leave in the midst of all this trouble. I can't come back by Wednesday, at any rate. In fact, I think I'll have to stay at least another week. Of course, I'll let you know . . ."

And suddenly he realised just how much he was missing her.

He put the letter in his pocket, and was turning away when he felt the restraining hand on his arm. It was Brown. "Game of bridge tonight?"

He felt, somehow, that he had to escape from the invitation. "Sorry, old man," he said. "As a matter of fact, I've just come in for a quick bite. Some friends of mine have asked me out for the evening." He added, "That's why I left the car in the driveway."

Lies . . . but he had to get away, see a show, do something different. If he wanted to get in anywhere decent he should telephone —only the phone was so darned public. If Brown happened to overhear . . . better take a chance on getting a seat.

He left early on the long ride back to town, parked his car on a lot, and bought a paper. He looked at the theatre pages. He skipped His Majesty's—he'd take her to see *Annie Get Your Gun* when she returned. *The Fallen Idol* at the Metro—probably packed out. Look at the other shows—*The Velvet Touch, Summer Lightning, The Last Days of Dolwyn, Winter Meeting*. Bette Davis. Yes, and the Empire was only a short walk. Right. *Winter Meeting* it would be.

There was only a small queue at the box-office, and after he had bought his ticket he had time to kill. He stood in the foyer, watching the people come in, scanning faces, and did not know why he was doing so. After a while he went in and took his seat.

At intermission he came out into the foyer again, and suddenly he realised why he was looking so avidly at people. In the hope of recognising someone. Anyone.

He mentally shook himself, and tried to be objective. He wondered whether it was just the bright lights that made the women seem so animated. And their escorts. Or was it just the fact that couples knew they would be alone after the show? Funny that. They *wanted* to be alone . . .

Not even the brilliance of the star could make it anything but a bad film. But there was something about it . . . a long-drawn-out nostalgia, a bitter-sweetness that plucked at him.

Coming out, he tried to shake off the mood, but he couldn't. In the foyer again there were the pretty girls, the flashy women, the suave escorts, but all with a new impatience in their actions. An impatience to go out, to go home, to be alone.

He went to a crowded café and drank his coffee slowly, looking all the time. Strangers. Only strangers.

And when he took his car off the lot, he found he did not want to start back. He rationalised. He thought he would like to stay in town, just a little while longer, just to see—it was uncanny that he, who

knew so many people, should not come across any of them. Let him
just meet one and he would be satisfied; he would then go home.

He parked his car near a brightly lit café in Kerk Street, and
remained behind the wheel, smoking, watching the people as they
passed. Town was emptying rapidly. After a long while, the lights in
the café went off. He leant forward to start his engine, but something
held him back.

It was just a hint of movement, a shadow of blackness, fifty yards
away, but it was moving toward him. A car turned the far corner, and
in the slow lightning of its headlights the shadow etched itself into the
outline, the shapely outline of a woman walking toward him.

And he knew why he had been waiting.

The woman was now on the other side of the road, and almost
abreast. He opened the door of the car so the interior lit up, put one
foot on the ground, and cleared his throat.

Without hesitation or even change of pace the woman veered round
towards him, said "Hullo."

And he saw that the shapeliness he had seen in her figure was an illusion, that under the paint her face was lined and old, and that her
eyes were as cold as ice.

He said nothing, just jerked his head away, started the car and
drove off. He did not even look back to see what she was doing.

He felt nauseated, angry with himself for what he had done. All the
same, he drove slowly, carefully watching the road and sidewalks
ahead of him. Once or twice he imagined he saw girls walking ahead
of him. The second time he suffered this illusion, he put his foot down
on the accelerator.

Tired, he thought. I'm much too tired. And I'm still a long way
from Rivonia and my bed. No chance of a girl being out now. Not so
late, anyway . . .

But near the end of Oxford Road he saw her in the gleam of his
lights, and she was signalling him to stop. He stopped.

She said, "Could you give me a lift to town?"

Of course she realised that he was going in the opposite direction,
and perhaps it was because of the greater favour involved that she
tipped her head provocatively. He was conscious only of her youth
and prettiness and the curves of her femininity beneath her tight-
drawn coat. His nostrils picked the faintest aroma of brandy beneath
the fragrance of her perfume.

He said, "Get in." He held the door open for her. She sat down,
started to wriggle out of her coat, and when he helped her he was surprised to find that he was not trembling. She hung the coat loosely
round her shoulders. With a sidelong smile she bent to unbuckle her
shoes, slipped them off, and said, "My feet are hurting. I've been walking quite a bit."

He turned the car slowly in a wide circle. "Why? Miss the bus?"

She laughed softly. "No. I had a bit of an argument with the chap I was with. I decided to walk home from the bottom of Oxford Road."

He felt a queer excitement, but he said nothing. When he saw she had her eyes closed, he turned off Oxford Road into a quieter side street. She moved, but made no comment.

He said, "Where do you live?"

"I've got a flat in Dorchester Mansions, in Eloff Street."

"Do you stay there alone?"

"No. I share with a friend."

He said, diffidently, "Must you go back there right away?"

"Of course. It's late. Much too late to start going anywhere else."

On impulse, he pulled the car up in a patch of shadow, caught her in his arms and kissed her. He felt her responsive lips on his, her warm body pressed against him; and as his consciousness slid into a narrow focus of passion, she pushed with both her hands, tore her lips loose, and said, "No. That's quite enough. Take me home. Please."

In a sudden spasm of rage he caught her hands, forced them behind her back, and held them there with his left hand. He felt with his lips in the hollow between her neck and shoulder, his weight forcing her down. His right hand moved, caressing at first and then, as she struggled, with more and more violence. She started to cry and scream.

In one flash of thought he knew he would have to frighten her into submission, or someone might hear. He let her hands go, grabbed the lapels of her coat, and fiercely jerked the collar tightly round her neck.

"If you don't shut up," he said, "I'll kill you."

She made a violent movement, trying to tear the constriction away; then all her muscles relaxed.

He said, "That's better, you little fool." He put his arms around her, drew her unresisting body to his. His lips sought hers.

Her mouth was half-open, flaccid. For another second he had a blind spasm of anger; then deep inside him he felt something cold.

In a flurry of panic he pushed her away, put the hot palm of his hand over her heart. Then slowly, he took his hand away.

He did not want to believe that she was dead.

He sat for a long time in the car, and he thought not so much about himself or his silent companion, as of his wife . . .

Out of his desperation, somewhere, somehow, an idea was born. The man she had been with . . . in the event of a police investigation would he not be the obvious suspect? The thing to do, then, was to put the body out somewhere near where he had found her, near the bottom of Oxford Road.

He remembered the plantation at Birdhaven . . .

When he had parked the car in the shadow of a tree, he lifted the body out carefully, and he also took with him the torch from the cubbyhole. He laid the corpse down gently. In the narrow beam of his torch he adjusted the clothing neatly, in accordance with his neat mind. And while he was doing this he saw her half-open mouth and, almost in the same second, the little pile of builder's lime lying next to the body.

And he thought, "If the police think that the lime caused her strangulation, and the lime is here, they would never dream that she was killed anywhere else." And with the thought his hand scooped a quantity of lime and forced it into the half-open mouth . . .

He went back to the car, mind numb, shoulders slumped from weariness. The light went on when he opened the door and his nerves grated in shock.

On the seat was the girl's coat and purse; on the floor were her shoes.

He couldn't go back. Not to the body again. Not now. But somehow he had to get rid of the evidence.

He drove, not knowing where he was going, but with an instinctive cunning that took him in a direction away from where he actually lived. He drove for a long time before he found the belt of trees, with the barbed-wire fence around.

He took a tyre-iron from the boot of the car, carried the girl's coat and purse and shoes with him. Right in the middle of the trees he pulled out a shrub, dug a hole with the tyre-iron, and buried the evidence. Before finally patting the soil down, he replaced the shrub.

Then home.

The eastern sky was beginning to brighten when he put his car in the garage. He had managed to approach without being seen; now he could creep into his room and pretend it was all a bad dream. There was nothing to connect him with the crime. Or could there possibly be something he had overlooked?

On impulse he went back to the car again, and he was glad he had done so. On the floor was a little button, obviously from a woman's blouse. He took it with him, went to the toilet, wrapped the button in paper, and flushed it down the drain.

In his room he quickly undressed, put on his pyjamas, and disturbed the bed to look as though it had been slept in. With a clothes-brush he carefully brushed the marks of his digging from his trousers and shoes onto a sheet of writing paper, and disposed of it in the same way as the button.

Only then did he relax enough to weep . . .

When Pieter Beukes first read this manuscript, he was inclined to be cynical about the confidence expressed in the opening paragraphs.

I said, "I won't guarantee every little detail is absolutely true, but I'm sure of the general facts. I know, for instance, that he lives in one of the northern suburbs, but the choice of Rivonia is probably no more than an educated guess. That's the area I felt such a man would most likely select as his home."

"A speculation," he said. "Like the film you say he saw?"

"Not quite. I can be much more certain about that. Look, from the clues, I can deduce reasonably that he was on his way home when he met Bubbles, that he was looking for female company. Therefore the early part of the night must have some relationship to his mood on the way back. He was obviously at a loose end: the likeliest explanation is that he was a married man, and that his wife was away. Bachelors practised in the art of she-hunting could easily satisfy their needs in Johannesburg. But the man I visualised would have killed time another way.

"Most likely he'd have gone to a cinema, and the film he saw must have heightened his mood of loneliness. I compiled a list of films showing in central Johannesburg that night—seventeen of them. I made it my business to see all of them. A Bette Davis film, *Winter Meeting,* was the only one that satisfied every criterion."

Beukes was obviously impressed, but one final point was niggling at him. "The lime in her throat—you know many papers came up with the theory that when some African tribesmen kill, they close the victim's mouth with earth to prevent the spirit talking about them. Why is there no hint of that in your story?"

"Two reasons, Pieter. First, Ben Bennett discusses the point in his section, and rightly dismisses it. No African would have left the body laid out so neatly. Nor could I believe a white man had tried to implicate an African. I'm fairly well up in tribal customs, but I'd never heard of that one. No, I'm convinced that the lime was used to indicate that the girl died at that spot, and nowhere else."

"Okay," said Beukes, "if you're so sure you know the killer, what's he going to do when he's read your story?"

For answer, I asked his typist to type out the following:

When Chummy reads the story he is going to panic. The closer the story is to the truth the more he will react. He will do anything to put me off the scent. He will write to me anonymously, and he will try to negative every positive point I have made.

I have said he is a man; his letter will be written as by a woman probably claiming she knows the truth about the murderer who has since died, or left the country, or is in some way out of reach of the police.

I claim the crime is one of impulse; the killer will say it was cold-blooded and premeditated. He will try to blacken Bubbles's reputation, but he will be very careful to stress the innocence of former suspects.

Finally, I claim Chummy lives in northern Johannesburg. The letter will probably be mailed to me care of *Spotlight* from somewhere to the south of the city.

This note was dated, signed by me, and countersigned by Beukes and his secretary. It was then sealed in a manilla envelope and locked in a safe.

This was about the end of November 1950. The edition of *Spotlight* dated January 1951 was on the streets shortly after Christmas, and had an unprecedented sale. The whole country was talking about the sensational crime feature.

On January 4 or 5 Pieter Beukes phoned me to tell me that he was holding several letters addressed to me care of his office. I said I would come round immediately.

Two or three letters came from old friends with whom I had lost touch. All the others, except one, were trying to sell me something. Before I even opened the final one, I felt my excitement rising. It was in a plain, cheap envelope. The name and address were in block capitals, written in pencil. Perhaps because of this, the postmark stood out in bold relief. It had been mailed in Primrose, a suburb of Germiston, a large town about nine miles south of Johannesburg.

The letter inside, on coarse, lined paper, had no address or salutation and was unsigned. Again, it was printed in block letters. It read:

MR CLEVER DICK GODFREY YOU WRITE NONSENS AND I WILL TELL YOU WHY. I HAVE BEEN LIVING AS WIFE WITH THE MURDRER FOR THREE YEARS AND NOT IN J'BURG. HE IS SAFE NOW AND CLEAN OUT OF THE COUNTRY AND NOW I CAN TALK. HE WAS A FORINER A PORTUGUESE AND HE HAD A FALSE PASSPORT. EVEN IF I TOLD YOU HIS NAME NOW IT WOULD MEAN NOTHING AND COULD DO NOTHING. HE KNEW BUBBLES EVER SINCE SHE WAS 12 OR 13 SHE WAS TRYING TO GET MONY FROM HIM. HE RODE A MOTORBIKE. HE ARRANGED TO MEET HER AT

BIRDHAVEN AT 1:30 AND DONE HER IN. THE TWO BOYS AT COURT KNEW NOTHING.

An animated Pieter Beukes compared this letter with my sealed forecast, and became even more excited. I must admit I savoured the moment, and added two more items of zest. First, I thought it was obvious that the illiteracy had been assumed. No illiterate, I claimed, would correctly spell "Portuguese," a word often misspelt even by educated people. Second, the idea of Bubbles setting up a rendezvous at Birdhaven on that particular night was obvious nonsense.

We drove to Caledon Square, the headquarters of the Cape Town police, made formal affidavits and lodged our exhibits. A few days later we received acknowledgment of the documents from Johannesburg.

The idea of using this letter as a follow-up to the original feature was shelved for the moment. The second story—for the February edition—had already been set in type, and the writing of the third feature was well advanced. Beukes decided we had an exclusive and could afford to wait until the right moment.

It never happened that way. In March I became editor of *Spotlight*. In July the series—an unprecedented success up to then—was unexpectedly stopped by the proprietors of the journal. Could it have had something to do with the next mystery for which the fictional solution had been advertised? I will always wonder.

After their unexpected move, my relationship with the management lacked confidence, to say the least. Then, in October, *Spotlight* was sold to a Johannesburg firm. They asked me to continue as editor in the Golden City, but at the same time I had received a screenwriting offer in London, which I accepted.

In 1954, back in South Africa, I was once again offered the editorship of *Spotlight,* with a brief to reconvert it from a monthly to a weekly.

Towards the end of that year, an Afrikaans-language magazine published a "confession" by someone calling himself "Rexie" that he was the murderer of Bubbles Schroeder. The "facts" given in this confession were so far removed from the truth that the hoax was obvious. The public, however, was not so critical. Once more, Bubbles was in the news, tongues wagged, letters were sent to me asking for my comments, and I felt that willy-nilly I was being dragged into an undignified controversy with an unmitigated fraud.

Fortunately, writing from Cape Town to the same magazine, Ben Bennett—who had every detail of the Bubbles mystery at his fingertips—tore "Rexie" to shreds. Since Ben's article appeared in Afrikaans only, I asked him to contribute a summary for my English-speaking readers. At the same time I urged him to enunciate his own theory of the killing. To explain the paradoxes of the case, he postulated two killers of different personalities. The idea was that he should criticise my theory and that I should reply in the same issue, so that the public would at least have two intelligent comments based on real clues for comparison.

Ben sent me his article, and with it the cópy of a letter received shortly after his original refutation of "Rexie." It was written, said Ben, on cheap, lined notepaper in Roman capitals. The writing instrument was a ball-point pen. As an address it carried only the word J'BURG. After preliminary references to the Bubbles mystery, it went on:

I WILL TELL YOU THAT SHE HAD ARRANGED TO MEET A MAN WHO KNEW HER WHEN SHE WAS 12 YEARS OF AGE AT 12:30 THAT NIGHT. HE WAS ON A MOTORBIKE NEAR THE PLANTATION WHERE SHE WAS FOUND AND HE DONE HER IN. HE IS A FOREIGNER AND MARRIED WITH A FAMILY OF CHILDREN. THE TWO BOYS WHO WERE ARRESTED DIDN'T DO IT. HE HAD A FAKED NAME AND HAD BEEN GOING UNDER A FAKED PASSPORT. HE HAS NOW LEFT THE COUNTRY. HE IS MILES AWAY FROM HERE GONE HOME TO HIS WIFE AND CHILDREN WHO HAVE GROWN UP IN HIS NAME.

This letter was signed: "ONE WHO KNOWS, JALK."

Ben, too, immediately handed this document to the police. To this day, it is probably nestling happily next to mine in the unsolved dossier labelled "Bubbles Schroeder."

The similarity to the first communication sparked the questions: "Why should Chummy write again? And why to Ben this time?"

I felt myself slipping back into the old groove of identification with the killer, and again I *knew* the answer. Here was Chummy, lulling himself into complacency because "Rexie" was drawing a thousand red herrings across the real trail, and then suddenly Ben

Bennett appears, revealing "Rexie" as a fake. A shock again, followed by panic—just like the last time. Only on this occasion it was Ben who must be diverted by a false trail.

The comparison of the two letters and what they implied was too good an angle to overlook in my projected friendly controversy with Ben, but before I added my comments to Ben's article, I went back to the original files, reports of the court proceedings and, in particular, to the medical evidence. And there I noticed a certain statement, the significance of which had been overlooked previously, which changed my whole conception of the case and to some degree my assessment of the character of Chummy.

The cause of Bubbles Schroeder's death was stated, quite unequivocally, to have been strangulation. But, as part of the physical description of Bubbles, it was said that she suffered from a condition of the thymus gland that could have induced death by strangulation *with only minor constriction round the throat.*

Such pressure could have been applied without any intention to kill or even to hurt. It could have been applied in anger, in lust, even in love . . .

When I wrote my article, I kept this point to the very end. My last eight paragraphs were addressed directly to Chummy. They read:

Perhaps you may have noticed that not once in this article have I referred to you as a murderer. I do not think you are. There is a grave doubt whether the death of Bubbles Schroeder was an act of murder.

The medical evidence at the preparatory examination shows that though Bubbles died from strangulation, the thymus-gland complaint from which she suffered had much to do with her demise.

The pressure applied to her throat was much less than would normally cause death in a healthy woman.

You best know your motives in applying pressure to Bubbles's throat. If you had no intent to kill, your chances of obtaining a lesser verdict than murder are good.

If you had no intent even to harm, but applied pressure to the neck in some form of rough play or passion, you will find the law merciful and understanding.

But you must meet the law halfway. You must not wait until some quirk of fate or brilliant detective work places you in the dock against your will. Then, obviously, any explanations you have to offer will be looked on with doubt, in view of your long silence.

There is only one secure way out for you—voluntarily to lift the

burden from your conscience, and pay whatever debt is due by you to
Society.

Give yourself up.

This article appeared in the issue dated November 11,
1955—Armistice Day. It was just before Christmas that a reply
was in my mail—the same type of cheap envelope and paper, the
capital letters written in ball point. But this time there was a
difference—there were paragraphs, and there was no illiteracy:

IT IS ONLY BECAUSE IT SEEMS TO ME THAT YOU ARE
REALLY BEGINNING TO UNDERSTAND THAT I WRITE THIS
LETTER AT ALL. OF COURSE I HAVE SUFFERED HELL
SINCE THAT GIRL DIED.

YOU ARE RIGHT IN YOUR DESCRIPTION OF WHAT HAP-
PENED. I PULLED HER COAT TIGHT ABOUT HER NECK
AND TRIED TO KISS HER. IT WAS A MADNESS OF THE MO-
MENT ONLY. IN FACT, BEFORE I REALISED SHE WAS DEAD
I HAD BEEN REPELLED BY THE SMELL OF BRANDY ON
HER LIPS.

I MEANT HER NO HARM. THERE WAS NO HATE, ONLY
LONELINESS. I DID NOT THREATEN HER, AS YOU FIRST
THOUGHT. I AGREE NO JURY WOULD EVER CONVICT ME
OF MURDER. BUT I CAN NEVER GIVE MYSELF UP. IF I
DID, THE SHOCK WOULD KILL SOMEONE WHO NEEDS ME
TO KEEP THEM ALIVE. I WOULD REALLY BE GUILTY OF
MURDER.

YOU APPEALED TO ME—I APPEAL TO YOU. DON'T
WRITE ANY MORE. YOU ARE ADDING NEW PAIN TO A
MAN ALREADY UNDER TORTURE.

I read the letter several times. Chummy had no obvious motive
to write; this time there was no attempt to put me off the scent.
And I thought of the only way I could tell him I knew he was sincere—by absolute silence.

Three years passed with no mention of the Bubbles case. I often
thought about Chummy and wondered who was the person—a
wife? a child?—for whose protection he was prepared to go
through a lifetime of suffering.

About this time a film made in Hollywood of one of my stories
was released in Johannesburg by United Artists—*The Girl in Black
Stockings*. They were anxious to capitalize on the publicity value
of a local author. A press showing was arranged, at which I was
due to harangue my fellow journalists.

Alas for the plans of mice and men! A week before the showing, I was taken to hospital with a coronary thrombosis. However, I was determined to have my day. A tape recorder was brought to my bedside, and with as much verbe as I could muster, I said my spiel. Since I knew everyone personally who would be present, my commentary became somewhat uninhibited, personal, and sometimes hilarious.

It was relayed to my colleagues over the cinema sound system. On the screen was a full-face, somewhat unflattering caricature of myself. The assembled newsmen loved it. One and all gave the incident sympathetic coverage.

At least two reports mentioned the name of the nursing home in which I was recovering. The day after they appeared, a young nurse brought me news that a friend of mine had phoned to wish me well.

I said, "A friend? Who was it?"

She was flustered. "He gave me the message, and when I asked for his name he said you would know who he was. I told him that I should have his name, and he laughed. He said to tell you it wasn't Rexie."

I put her at ease. "Yes, now I know who it was."

Later, I questioned her about the caller. Just a voice, she said. A young voice, a pleasant voice. He sounded happy to hear I was improving.

Four years later, as editor of the well-known Pan-African magazine *Drum* I left South Africa to establish more convenient headquarters in London. Since then I have pursued my journalistic career in England, but I still write a fair quantity of fiction.

About a year ago, and for the first time in many years, one of my stories under my own name was printed in a South African magazine. The title was "Except Clancy."

A few months thereafter, there was another letter from Chummy, still written in anonymous capital letters. He had sent it to the magazine in question, and one of the editors there who knew me and heard I was in London passed it on to a young journalist on his way to Britain.

The letter was very short. It said simply:

I ENJOYED READING "CLANCY." YOUR SILENCE HAS
BEEN MUCH APPRECIATED. GOD GO WITH YOU.

I have been doing some calculations. Bubbles died in August
1949. Your appeal for silence was in December 1955. Your message to me in hospital was three years after that. The "Clancy" letter came in 1977. If you read this article—and I hope you will—*a
full twenty-nine years will have gone by*.

I am writing this because it is my only possible way of contacting you. Pal, I hope you no longer feel threatened. I, too, wish you
well. And it seems to me I am a letter or two behind.

PETER GODFREY is the author of *Death Under the Table* and other
mysteries.

Report on a Dead Skip

Joe Gores

I SPENT twelve years as a private investigator before I began making enough with my typewriter to count myself a writer.

Typing thousands of field reports taught me always to get the who-what-where-when-why (so necessary to successful fiction) into my narratives, and to keep those narratives taut and my descriptions lean and crisp. No reader is more critical than a guy who will have to pay a whopping big fee on the basis of what he is reading in those reports.

During those dozen years I have never carried a gun, never investigated a murder, never window-peeped on an errant husband. Our clients were banks, financial institutions, automobile dealers, occasionally large corporations, on rare occasions massive insurance conglomerates. We specialized in skip-tracing (finding people who had skipped out—i.e., deliberately disappeared—for any of various reasons, usually financial), repossessing and chattel recovery, occasional embezzlement investigations, and, when times were tough, process serving. I worked, I would guess, some 15,000 cases.

I was also, given the average American's mystic attachment to his automobile, threatened or assaulted with just about every blunt instrument known to man (you haven't lived until you've been beaned with a three-pound can of coffee wielded by an irate housewife). Also with guns, knives, straight razors, fists, feet, and elbows, and of course the ultimate in lethal weapons, the automobiles themselves. I learned to carry extra handkerchiefs while process-serving, to wipe away the spittle of reluctant servees.

I had a great deal of what seemed like fun at the time, indulged my fascination with nighttime streets, and got to know the intimate workings of most large California cities. But I would not recommend the profession to anyone. The hours are long (seventy a week would be conservative), the pay indifferent, and the working conditions onerous—because your life must be geared to those of the subjects (the people you are investigating) rather than to your own convenience.

And you must be a practicing schizophrenic, because almost every investigation has two very different and distinct aspects.

First is the paper chase. Endless hours of pawing through records in federal and state offices, in musty county courthouses, in newspaper morgues and business records and credit company reports. Further countless hours are spent on the phone running down leads in other cities or states (or even countries), and in typing up reports of everything you are doing. In this phase of the investigation you have a lot in common with the scholar, the researcher, the genealogist.

But then you find your quarry. Now, because you must part him (sometimes forcibly, sometimes by guile) from something he values, comes the short hard burst of pure action.

Usually you are parting him from an automobile, but I have repossessed an airplane and a Chinese junk, house trailers and the instruments of a rock band, wedding rings and power saws and TV sets, the massive tires off a truck-trailer rig, and a $10,000 camera which involved bypassing the burglar alarms to dismantle half a business office at 3:00 A.M.

You trespass, you break-and-enter, you lie, you dissemble, you move through midnight streets on rubber-soled shoes which will not alert a sleepless quarry that you are near. From being spotted prematurely comes the ninety-miles-an-hour freeway auto chase so beloved to TV cop shows. Also the thrills. The danger. And the fear. During these times you face the brandished hammer, the opened straight razor, the shotgun as the shells are rammed into the chamber.

As a detective I never carried a gun, even though I own and use them on the firing range and in hunting, because I never knew when I might end up in a situation where I might use it. Or even worse, *not* use it when an antagonist with a gun of his own sees mine and uses his. Instead I cultivated for tight spots the "shining morning face" that Shakespeare credits to schoolchildren, and the ability to talk very fast while backing out a door.

In May 1966, while still a full-time private investigator, I gave a talk to the Northern California Chapter of Mystery Writers of America on my profession. This led, early in 1967 and at the urging of the late Anthony Boucher, to my writing a series of procedural private-eye tales for *Ellery Queen's Mystery Magazine* which I dubbed the "File" stories.

My first File Novel was published in 1972 as *Dead Skip*. I wanted to title each File Novel with a word or phrase regularly used by private detectives; a "skip" is a person who has skipped out—disappeared—and a "dead skip" is one on whom all current leads have been exhausted. The leads are "dead" and field work is suspended until new leads turn up.

I also wanted a central unity: I wanted the book to revolve around, ultimately, a single case rather than a constellation of cases being worked simultaneously. Finally, I wanted this case to be a fictionalization of a real case, and this is where the rub came in. Unlike fictional private eyes, real detectives usually carry between thirty-five and seventy-five open files at any given time. In an average work day I would report time spent on fifteen to twenty-five different cases.

But I had one investigation, carried out in April 1965, around which I was able to build *Dead Skip*. Our subject was a man I will call (as I did in *Dead Skip*) Charles M. Griffin, the car we were looking for was a 1965 Thunderbird convertible, and our client was a large branch bank in Oakland, California, which I will call California Citizens Bank. Charles M. Griffin, himself a dead skip, was one subject upon whom I lavished all my efforts exclusively during the time I had the case.

Why? Because it was a "deadline deal" for our client. The contract was about to go "over the wire." The bank was about to "eat the car."

Manufacturers insist on being paid beforehand for the vehicles the dealer wishes to put in his showroom. The mathematics become quickly apparent: if a dealer wants fifty new cars to display, and they have a wholesale price of $4,000 each, he must come up with $200,000 to get the cars.

He borrows the money from the bank—in the case of Charles M. Griffin, from California Citizens Bank—and puts up the cars as collateral. As each car is sold, the dealer "runs the paper through the bank." And since few customers can pay the full retail price of their cars in cash, the bank takes the conditional sales contract in lieu of a cash payoff. The dealer is off the hook to the bank, the customer has a new car, and the bank makes a handsome profit on its loan.

Unless the customer quits making his monthly payments to the bank.

The reasons for this usually are ill health, a work layoff, too much credit spending, a swinging life style, or—and this is what kept me employed all those years—the fact that the debtor is a deadbeat who purchased the car with full knowledge that he had no intention of paying for it. In the jargon of the trade, he "grabs the iron and runs." Over the years, for instance, our company repossessed nine different Cadillacs, purchased from nine different banks, from the same subject—a retired army colonel. But that's a different story.

In this story, Charles M. Griffin quit paying for his new 1965 Thunderbird.

If a single payment is overdue on an auto account at the end of the month, the bank calls it an "item" account. Notices are sent, phone calls are made. When it becomes a "two-month item" the bank's own field agents are sent out. Or, if the subject's credit and/or personal background are sufficiently shaky to warrant it, the bank may hire an outside agency, either to get the delinquent payments in cash or certified funds, plus costs, or to "drop a rock on"—repossess—the chattel in question.

Now if this outside agency cannot find the subject, he is a "skip" and the whole skip-tracing mechanism goes into operation. When the skip's third payment in a row is missed, his automobile has become a "deadline deal." Because after midnight of the day the *fourth* payment becomes delinquent, the bank has to "eat the car."

Up until that time, the dealer who sold the car has to take it back if it is repossessed, and pay the bank the balance of the contract, even if the car is nothing more than a heap of scrap iron with a motor number stamped into it somewhere. But after that fourth payment has become delinquent the car has, in the jargon of the trade, gone "over the wire." It has gone past the deadline. After that date, it is the bank and not the dealer who has to "eat the car."

If the bank does subsequently recover the vehicle, it has to dispose of the thing for what it can get (usually from a dealer at a wholesale auction). If it *never* recovers the car, it has to write off the entire loss. If this is, say, a $30,000 Lamborghini, such loss is felt very keenly indeed.

On April 28, 1965, when I was assigned the Charles M. Griffin case, the contract was three months delinquent. The fourth payment was due in two days, on Friday, April 30. The case had been worked for only two weeks by our Oakland office, because someone at the bank had been unable to believe a man of Griffin's steady life style and impeccable credit record (he had financed four previous autos through the Peninsula branch of Cal-Cit Bank with a perfect pay record) was indeed a dead skip.

He was. On review our Oakland manager had noted that no report had covered checking the garage at a former address of Griffin's to see whether he had stashed the car in there. So I went to Oakland.

Here is my first report (this, like all the reports which follow, has been altered only as necessary to keep me from being sued):

Followed to listed residence address of the subject, 1839 California Street. There is no garage. No one was home. Unit was not parked anywhere in the vicinity.

By the terms of my assignment, I could have gone home at this point. But it was a deadline deal. And one ends up in detective work essentially from an enjoyment of manhunting. I nosed around a bit:

In checking with neighbors, contacted the subject's ex-landlady, Mrs. Bergholz. She resides at 1830 California Street. She believes the subject is in jail; has no basis for this belief other than her appraisal of his character. Stated he owes her $200 rent, that he borrowed money from a loan company by putting up the furniture she had provided for his furnished apartment as collateral.

Stated he had been bonded by someone in connection with an auto wreck, and that he had jumped bail of $600. Further stated that when she had last heard, the subject was residing with his brother at 1545 Midfield Road, San Jose, no phone number known.

And none listed with Information, I found as soon as I left Mrs. Bergholz and called San Jose Information. It was now getting on toward midnight, and I had a full day's work the next day. And San Jose was forty miles from Concord, and another sixty miles from there to San Francisco. But what if—just what if—the subject had stashed that deadline-deal T-Bird at his brother's place in San Jose? So I drove down there. And found the house empty—no rugs, no drapes, no furniture. And no T-Bird in the garage.

At eight Thursday morning, I stopped at the San Francisco office to check the skip-tracing summary sheet on Griffin.

In the file I found only a thin crop for a car going over the wire the next day. There were just three additional leads to check out. First, his former employment:

Checked with Pacific Gas and Electric Company in San Francisco, listed work address for this subject. He began work on 20 November 1947, terminated on 22 January 1965. Per personnel office informant, "resigned to go into sales work." Subject terminated voluntarily.

So. He hadn't been fired. He had quit, after seventeen years. I could have tried to find and interview some of the people he had worked with, but Griffin already was looking like a man in flux for whom old associations would have small appeal. My next interview suggested a reason:

Checked at the office of Patrick J. Murphy, 514 North Delaware Street, San Mateo, attorney of record for the subject. Mr. Murphy stated that he is no longer the subject's representative, had been his attorney for a limited action (settling the subject's mother's estate in mid-1964).

Stated that the subject is unmarried, has "problems" but declined to state their nature.

Mr. Murphy, along with what I already knew, had given me a working hypothesis. That the subject, unmarried, had been close to his mother and that her death had led to psychological problems and perhaps heavy drinking. The reasoning goes this way: the mother dies and a few months later the subject becomes, in credit jargon, "flaky." He borrows money on his landlady's furniture; he buys the aging swinger's car, a T-Bird; he moves from address to address for no obvious reason; and finally, he leaves his employment of over seventeen years for one of the least stable professions, sales work. As to the possible boozing, he'd had a bad auto smash (possibly) the previous December. So I drove across the San Mateo bridge to Castro Valley to seek confirmation from his listed relative:

Followed to 3877 Castro Valley Boulevard, Castro Valley, listed previous residence address, and here spoke with listed reference Mrs. Harriet Western. This is subject's aunt, who has not heard from him in 6–7 months. He lived with her for a time following his mother's death and the subsequent sale of the mother's house. Before that subject lived with the mother. Informant stated subject had been "adversely affected" by the mother's death. Stated the subject has no brother in San Jose or elsewhere.

That took care of the file. From there on, all I had were the facts, suppositions, and conjectures supplied by the ex-landlady. She had given me five solid areas to investigate—one of which, the brother, apparently had been a lie made up for her by the subject (phone work by office skip-tracers the next day confirmed that no Griffin had ever lived at the San Jose address). The areas were explicit and evocative:

1. The T-Bird had been towed away after a smashup the previous December. Apparently it had been repaired.

2. The subject might be in jail (just a feeling, not a fact, but worth checking out).

3. He had been bonded in connection with the auto wreck to appear in court (suggesting possible criminal or civil charges stemming from it, supporting the possibility of heavy drinking).

4. He had jumped this bail of $600.

All, some, or none of this might be true. But it was what I had to work with. I drove north again to Concord where the subject's life had centered since moving out of his aunt's home:

Went to Concord Police Department at Willow Pass Road and Parkside Avenue. Sergeant on the desk stated that the subject had been involved on 6 December 1964 in a two-car smash with a Mary Wanda Moher, 3681 Willow Pass Road, Concord. Stated that the trial of the subject which grew out of this affair had been scheduled for 11 February 1965, but that it had been postponed.

More confirmation. The subject had been culpable in the eyes of the authorities. Could he have disappeared because he was ducking, not us, but a trial at which he might end up on probation, in jail, or without a driver's license? One way to find out:

Went around the corner to the Concord Court House, and here was informed that the subject's case had been redocketed for 16 June at 9:30 A.M., on a charge of drunk driving and violation of right-of-way. Informant here stated that the subject's bond was furnished by Gerald Coogan Bail Bonds, 913 Main Street, Martinez.

Before driving over to Martinez to talk with the subject's bail bondsman, who might or might not have been stuck for $600, and to see whether the subject might indeed be in the county slammer, I still had one address to check out in Concord: that of the woman with whom the subject had collided the previous December:

Followed to 3681 Willow Pass Road, Concord. Here met Mary Wanda Moher.
Informant stated that the subject struck her car at 11:30 A.M., and was inebriated at the time. Stated that this had occurred in front of the Drop-In Bar in Concord. Stated she thinks the subject works for PG&E in Concord. Stated this was the subject's third such offense in as many months, and that the police are determined to get him off the road this time around.
Informant further stated that the subject's lawyer had gotten a continuance in February because the subject had jumped bail or, she is sure, the subject would be in jail right now. Stated her insurance agent, Harvey E. Wyman, State Farm Insurance, Concord, might have further information. Finally, stated she had seen a unit similar to the subject's parked outside the Drop-In Bar about three weeks ago.

Mary Wanda Moher had given me three new leads to be checked out in Concord before I headed over for Martinez. The first stop, of course, was Pacific Gas and Electric. This sounded wrong, sounded like faulty transference of the fact that he formerly had been employed by PG&E across the Bay; but it had to be checked out. That T-Bird might be sitting in the employees' parking lot, in which case the bank would have its car back to the dealer's lot well before deadline.

But the T-Bird wasn't in the parking lot:

Went to the PG&E Concord Business Office, 2065 Concord Boulevard, and here spoke with a woman in the personnel department. They have no current or past record of the subject's employment with PG&E locally.

No joy. And none really expected. The subject was beginning to sound like a man who was making himself unemployable. If so, he was probably doing it at places like the Drop-In Bar:

Sipped a tall cool one so the bartender would keep his cool, and asked after the subject. Learned, from a bar-room lounger, that the subject is "so short he used to sit under the stools instead of on top of them." The bartender stated that to the best of his recollection, the subject had not been into the Drop-In since mid-February.

He might have been lying, of course: the subject might have at that moment been pickled in a butt of Malmsley in the back room. But it was more likely that Mary Wanda had been mistaken, because the mid-February date coincided with his no-show at the February 11 hearing on his drunk driving charge. So . . . en route once again:

Drove to 1820 Mount Diablo Boulevard, and here contacted Mary Moher's insurance agent, Harvey E. Wyman. He stated that in the December accident the subject's T-Bird (confirmed by license number that it was indeed our subject unit) sustained $400 estimated damage, and the Moher car sustained $750 confirmed damage. Stated that the man to contact for information is Mr. Lowell Lawton, agent in charge of the insurer's office in Santa Rosa.

Immediately upon leaving informant's office, placed a call to Mr. Lowell Lawton. He was out of the office and would not return until tomorrow at 9:00 A.M. The girl stated that no one else was authorized to furnish me information from the claim file against the subject.

By now it was midafternoon, and I still had to get over to Martinez to check out my two remaining leads. This was an oil-company town on the edge of the Carquinez Straits where oceangoing tankers could come to off-load their belliesful of crude for the vast refinery complex headquartered there. The Contra Costa County Jail was on Pine Street just across from the county admin building, and checking there gave me no record of the subject.

Last stop, the bailbondsman who had put up the $600 which the subject apparently had jumped. If the subject had indeed stuck him for the bond, I could count on cooperation in return for my promise to let him know where the subject was if I ran him down:

Mrs. Coogan stated they are looking for the subject to have him brought back into the jurisdiction so they can recover their $600. He did indeed jump bail on them last February. They have only the old Concord address on him. Stated that the subject's attorney is Wayne E. Hawkley of Concord.

It was late in the work day, but I figured that by hustling I could reach Hawkley's office before it closed. I did so:

Was informed that Hawkley had gone for the day. His office refused to give out his home phone or residence address. His office also stated that Mr. Hawkley is in court all this week and next week, and will not be available. His secretary volunteered, however, that they have no current address on the subject. She stated that he occasionally calls them, but that he never gives them an address or phone number.

On the way back across Bay Bridge to the City, at about eight o'clock that night, I reviewed what I had going for me the next day, deadline day, Friday, April 30.

I could recheck everything I had done that day. The only things with obvious life in them were (1) Lawton, up in Santa Rosa, who had an insurance file on the subject; (2) old friends and associates at PG&E in the City (very doubtful); (3) the aunt (even more doubtful).

But there was one thing in the file to recheck. I had noted that our DMV—Department of Motor Vehicles in Sacramento—check on the subject's driver's license and auto registration was two weeks old. If he had picked up any moving violations in the interim—not unheard of for someone who was drinking heavily and driving—he might have slipped and given the Highway Patrol a new residence address. If he had, it would be in the files.

The next morning, deadline day, I called the insurance man in Santa Rosa at 9:03 A.M. I had planned to phone our Sacramento contact after that for an urgent search (quite expensive) of the DMV file on the subject. My call to Lawton made it unnecessary:

Lowell Lawton had the file in front of him, expecting my call. He stated that on 23 April he had gotten a new address for the subject of

1377 Mount Diablo Street, Concord, from a DMV records-check reply. He further stated that he had mailed the subject a letter concerning his liability in the auto accident to that address on the same day. To date, the letter has not been answered but has not been returned by the Post Office as undeliverable.

Man, this was it! An address on the subject that was only a week old!

It should have been easy, but somehow I had the feeling it wasn't going to be.

My feeling was right:

Drove to 1377 Mount Diablo Street, Concord. Subject unit was nowhere in sight and the address, in poor repair, is occupied by a man and wife and several children.

Woman who answered the door declined to state her name. Stated the subject is unknown to her, but when I asked about subject unit she stated, "Wait a minute, that rings a bell. Howie Odum was driving a car like that last week. I had a ride in it." Informant stated she remembered Odum telling her that mail might come occasionally for the subject, and that if it did, she should hold it. She stated that Odum would pick it up if any came. Stated she believes Odum, not the subject, is driving this unit regularly, and stated that Odum lives in the Pittsburg area up around Suisun Bay and the Delta.

Informant requested that I not let her husband know that Odum had been around, as they had formerly been friends but now "are enemies." Stated, under further questioning, that Odum is just out of the jug on parole from a two-year federal charge.

I was running out of time. Less than twelve hours to the midnight deadline our client had to get the unit back on the dealer's lot. I spent part of my time driving down to Oakland:

Went to Oakland and there contacted Mr. Saul Savidge, parole officer for Howard Odum. He stated Odum has just gotten a new job in Brentwood, but Mr. Savidge does not yet know the nature or location of this job. Informant stated that Odum has been living at 1644 Galindo Street, Room 6, Concord. I am to contact informant on Monday if subject unit is recovered from Odum over the weekend, since Odum has no permission to drive an automobile and to do so is a violation of the terms of his parole.

Back to Concord, in a hurry. The noose of time was tightening around my neck, and I was in trouble. My female informant who had remained nameless had stated Odum lived around Pittsburg up near Suisun Bay. His parole officer said he lived in Concord. The two towns were far enough apart—ten miles or so—that the discrepancy bothered me:

Followed to address for Howard Odum received from the State Parole Office: 1684 Galindo Street, Concord, which is an extension of Monument Boulevard. There is a parking area here—it is a huge rambling private dwelling converted to a rooming house—but subject unit was not around. Checked at the door for the manager. Not there. Checked with several tenants. Odum is known there, living in Room 6 at the head of the stairs. Neither subject nor subject unit is known here. Under the metal numeral on the door of Room 6 was a note: HOWIE: I'M OVER AT MARY'S. CHARLIE. There was no answer at the door.

I went away for a belated cheeseburger, feeling desperate. Odum was my last lead, it was nearly four in the afternoon, and I had just a bit over eight hours to get the car and get it back on the dealer's lot. I was gambling everything on Odum now. If he *wasn't* driving the T-Bird, even if I found him . . .

Returned to the rooming house at 1684 Galindo Street, Concord. Subject unit not around. No answer at Odum's door, and the note from Charlie was still there. Charlie apparently was still over at Mary's.
Was successful in contacting the landlady, Mrs. Fredericks. She stated that Howard Odum plans to move over to Antioch over the weekend, because he has a girlfriend over there. He plans to move in with her. Informant did not know the girlfriend's name, but stated that the address is 1902 Gavallo Road in Antioch. Stated she had seen a red/white T-Bird, but that the unnamed girlfriend was always the one who was driving it on these occasions.

That tied in. Antioch was out by Pittsburg, a few miles further along toward Stockton on California 4, called the Industrial Highway (hence the name Pittsburg) during the great days of ship traffic between San Francisco Bay and Stockton on the old Stockton Ship Canal. The T-Bird not being seen around the rooming house except when the girlfriend was driving it was probably an attempt to keep the Parole Officer from finding out that Odum was breaking parole by driving a car. Which is just what I did to Antioch, fast as the rush-hour traffic would let me. Six o'clock. Six hours left:

Drove to where Howard Odum's girlfriend is reportedly living at

1902 Gavallo Road. This is a twelve-unit apartment building, new. Subject vehicle was not in the apartment house lot or in any adjacent street parking. There is no resident manager, so was unable to confirm that Odum is moving here. Names are on the mailboxes, but since we do not have the girlfriend's name this does us no good.

Checked all the apartments. People home in nine of them. At one, a teen-age girl stated that she had seen a 1965 red/white T-Bird convertible parked in the lot several times during the past couple of weeks. She noticed it because "my boyfriend's a car freak and he digs gross cars." Informant further stated that either "an ugly blonde girl" or a "tall sandy-haired man" was driving the unit, but she did not know in which apartment the girl lived or the man visited.

There I was, fingernail-chewing time. Our T-Bird? Or another? Odum driving it (obviously not our subject who would fit "under the barstool") or someone else? Stay here and wait? Or check downtown Antioch in case Odum and his ugly girlfriend were out on the town and I could grab the car off the street before the deadline?

I compromised. Cruising the Antioch streets, while checking back at the apartment house every half hour. Six-thirty. Seven. Seven-thirty. Eight. Eight-thirty. Oh, damn, damn, they weren't coming up to Antioch tonight until after the deadline . . .

At 9:24 P.M. returned to 1902 Gavallo Road. At this time spotted red/white Thunderbird convertible in the apartment house parking area. Checked license number. It was subject unit. Was opening and starting unit with lockpick and hot wire when a man who identified himself as Howard Odum appeared. He was carrying a monkey wrench and challenged my possession of the vehicle with a threat to use the wrench on my head, stating he would "tighten your nut for you with this wrench." I stated he was breaking parole by driving the unit and also by moving without informing his parole officer. Stated that if he uttered one more threat, spoke one more word, I would leave subject vehicle with him but would report the entire exchange to his parole officer.

At this point, Odum surrendered keys to subject vehicle. Stated sadly that he had paid $200 for subject's equity in the unit. He had a receipt from the subject to this effect. He stated he has no idea of the subject's whereabouts, but that he believes "the cat has split the state, man" because the subject has never picked up the mail Odum has collected for him.

Odum further stated that he would like to pay off the total contract price in cash on this vehicle. He seems sincere in this desire, and it would take everyone off the hook on this contract, so I suggested that he contact client's office in this regard.

Returned unit to dealer's lot prior to deadline. Condition report with receipt signature from dealer appended. Close and Bill.

Banks do not like us to report events that could later be questioned by an opposition attorney in some possible future civil suit. So I did not cover the 75-mile-an-hour drive to Oakland, ducking across highway dividers and going the wrong way down a one-way street to lose a pursuing Highway Patrol vehicle trying to nab me for speeding. I did not cover somehow breaking an office window on the used-car lot of Berkman Ford in Oakland at 11:41 P.M. to trip the silent alarm and bring police who held me until Berkman could arrive at 11:56 P.M.

Berkman was a gentleman. He signed the car in at one minute before midnight, laughing, did not press charges against me, and did not even bill the agency for the broken window. He'd been in the car business for a lot of years and liked a good repo story as well as the next man.

As it turned out, I never got to use the return of the car in fictionalized form in *Dead Skip,* because in the novel finding the car was not the end of it. There had been deadly assault, there had been murder, in the novel the time element had been preserved but the deadline had been a life-and-death one. . . .

All this had to be neatly tied up. Because, while in real-life detection you only get bits and pieces of it (Nora Charles remarks in *The Thin Man* after Nick has told her what they have on the murderer, "There seems to be enough of it, but it's not very neat"), in fiction you make it neat. You get it all. In *Dead Skip* the disappearance of the fictional Charles M. Griffin is unraveled with all its whys and wherefores.

In real life I never found the real Charles M. Griffin, nor did I try. I got his car, which is what I was hired for. I never found out if he showed up for his trial in June, or if he made his peace with his mother's death, or if he got off the sauce. I never even found out if Howard Odum paid off the T-Bird. We closed our case and the bank paid our bill, and I went on to several hundred other assignments during the eighteen months between the closing of the file on Charles M. Griffin, the dead skip, and the end of my full-time detective career as I turned to the typewriter as a full-time writer.

JOE GORES's novels include *Dead Skip*, *A Time of Predators*, and *Hammett*.

The Invisible Man

Julian Symons

THE PUZZLE

THE CAR was standing at Elishaw Bridge crossroads, on the road
from Jedburgh and the Scottish border, as Evelyn Foster drove up.
She helped to run her father's taxi service at the village of Otterburn, a mile or two down the road, and was on her way home
after taking a party to Rochester.

Now as she drove up, the stranger got out of the car and spoke
to her. He said in an accent that she recognized as North Country,
although it was not exactly Tyneside, that he wanted to get a bus
to Newcastle. The people in the car had brought him this far from
Jedburgh, but now they were taking the road south, to Hexham.
Could she give him a lift?

He was a pleasantly spoken, dapper little man, neatly dressed in
dark blue overcoat, dark tweed suit, and bowler hat. Evelyn Foster
considered, told him that her Hudson car was for hire, and said
that she would take him into Otterburn, where she wanted to
refuel, and then see where he could catch a bus. The occupants of
the other car, a man and a woman, did not get out. The stranger
thanked them for their hospitality, and the car drove off down the

road to Hexham. The stranger got into the Hudson and sat beside her. The time was nearing seven o'clock on a cold, hard January night.

Within a few minutes they were at the Foster garage, in Otterburn's single street. She had told him that the fare to Ponteland, a journey of twenty-odd miles over the Northumbrian moors, would be about £2, and he agreed to this. From Ponteland he could easily get a bus into Newcastle. In the meantime, he said, he would go along to the Percy Arms, just along the road, and have a drink. She could pick him up either there or just beyond, at Otterburn Bridge.

Evelyn left him, and went into the house. There she saw her mother.

"What does he look like?" Mrs. Foster asked.

"Oh, very respectable. Gentleman-like—he looks a bit of a knut."

"Where is the man now?"

"He's gone down to the Percy Arms for a drink."

Her mother thought that £2 was rather too much to charge, and her father said that the fare should be £1 16s. Her sister Dorothy suggested that it was unwise to travel alone with a stranger over the lonely moor, and said she should take as companion George Phillipson, a joiner in the village with whom Evelyn was friendly.

"I'll call for him," she agreed.

She borrowed her mother's torch, and she drove away. The time was twenty minutes past seven.

She did not see George Phillipson in the village (although in fact he was there), and did not call for him. The stranger hailed her at the Bridge, got into the car, and they began the drive across the moors. While they drove the man in the bowler hat talked to her, and what he said took on some importance in view of what happened afterwards. He did not know much about Newcastle, he told her, but lived in the Midlands. He had a car of his own, he said, and he appeared to know a lot about cars.

So the time passed, pleasantly enough, until they reached Belsay, only six miles from Ponteland. Now he suddenly told her to turn back.

"Why do you want to go back, when we have come so far?"

"That's nothing to do with you," he said, and now his manner had changed.

She turned the car. He crept along the seat towards her, and took hold of the steering wheel. "Oh no," she said. "I will do the driving."

He lifted his hand and struck her over the eye, so that she could hardly see out of it. He took the wheel, pushed her over to the side of the car so that she could not move, nipped her arms. Then he drove back most of the way to Otterburn and stopped on the hill at Wolf's Nick, beside the snow-covered Ottercaps. Now, surprisingly, he offered her a cigarette. She refused it.

"Well, you are an independent young woman," the stranger said.

Her impressions after this were confused, but terrible. He struck her, kicked her, knocked her into the back of the car. Then he assaulted her, despite her resistance. She became unconscious. Vaguely she was aware that he had taken a bottle or tin from his pocket, that he was pouring something over her, that the something had gone up in a blaze, that she was burning.

There was a bump, as though the car were passing over rough ground. The bump roused her, burning as she was, and she managed to open the car door and push her way out of it. She found herself on the frosty moor. She thought she heard a car draw up, she thought she heard a whistle, but she could not be sure. With agonizing slowness she began to crawl back across the moor towards the road, and help. . . .

At about ten o'clock that night Cecil Johnson, driver of one of Foster's buses, was passing Wolf's Nick, on the journey from Newcastle to Otterburn. He saw something smouldering on the moors and, with the conductor, got out to investigate.

"Why, it's the firm's new Hudson," Johnson cried as they approached the car. The back of it was almost burned out. The roof was a sheet of glowing embers, fanned by the dry, frosty air. One

back tyre was still burning, otherwise there were no flames. There
was nobody inside the car. Then they heard groans.

A few yards away they found Evelyn Foster. She was lying face
downwards, trying desperately to suck the ice on the moor. The
flames had burnt her so that she was practically naked from the
waist down.

"It was that awful man," she said, as they knelt down by her
side. "Oh, that awful man. He has gone in a motor-car."

Johnson wrapped her in his overcoat, and they took her home.
The doctor was summoned and came to Otterburn from Bel-
lingham, nine hilly miles away, but time was of little importance,
for there was nothing to be done. Evelyn Foster died early the
next morning, but before she died she was able to tell her story to
her mother while the Otterburn constable, Andy Ferguson, sat
near by taking it down. The account of it that has been written
so far is the story that she told to Andy Ferguson in the hours before death. Although in great pain, Evelyn Foster was perfectly
lucid while making her statement, and even apologized to the doctor for bringing him out on such a night. What she said about the
assault was, in view of what happened afterwards, particularly interesting.

"Did he interfere with you?" her mother asked.

"Yes."

Now Mrs. Foster broke down and wept, and Evelyn cried: "Oh,
mother, I couldn't help it. I was fighting for my life."

Evelyn did not know, as everyone present agreed, that there was
no hope for her, but a little while before she died at seven o'clock
in the morning, she must have realized it.

"I have been murdered," she cried. "I have been murdered."
They were her last words.

It was a horrifying crime, but not, the Northumberland County
Police must have thought, one which was likely to resist solution
for long. There were a good many clues—the occupants of the car
from Jedburgh, who would certainly be able to identify and fully
describe the stranger; the barman in the Percy Arms, where he
had been going for a drink; possibly the people in the car that had
picked him up after the crime. Or if this car did not exist (for she

had been vague about the car and the whistle), and the man had tried to escape on foot, he certainly would not get far without being noticed, on the frostbound and lonely moors.

And there were other, material clues, found on the scene of the crime. Near to the car a man's glove was found, and so also was Evelyn's scarf. There was a footprint near by, and a mould of this was taken. Her purse had come out of her pocket and lay on the moor, with the money in it untouched. Altogether, there seemed quite sufficient evidence to discover and identify the murderer, and Captain Fullarton James, the Chief Constable, expressed himself as confident that the case could be handled locally. Neither now, nor at any later time, was Scotland Yard called on for assistance.

But the clues that had seemed so substantial all led nowhere, and to no person. The stranger seemed to have been an invisible man—invisible, at least, to everyone but Evelyn Foster. Several motorists were traced who had been in the vicinity of Jedburgh that Tuesday afternoon and evening, and had taken the road to Hexham, but none had admitted meeting a man like the stranger. The man had told Evelyn that the people in the car had given him tea in Jedburgh, but no hotel or café in the town or near it remembered such a party coming in. Every farmhouse, public house, hotel and café for miles round was visited, and the most dramatic manhunt ever known in Northumberland was carried out on the moors. This search was without result.

There was, of course, the usual crop of false clues. There was a man who had behaved suspiciously and had asked for a lift to Darlington, a local shepherd had seen a stranger on the moors, there was a man in Newcastle who talked like an American and had spoken strangely of the crime, and another man who entered a house in Newcastle and told the occupants that there was a body in the back of his car. All these men were between twenty-five and thirty years of age, all were clean shaven, all wore bowler hats and dark overcoats. They served to confirm the vagueness of a description which applied to hundreds of men in the district.

In Otterburn village, too, the man had been invisible. He had said that he was going to the Percy Arms, but the barman there told the police that no stranger had come in on that Tuesday night. Nor, he added, had Evelyn Foster herself come in to ask for him.

This was perhaps the first fact that caused the police to feel doubt about the truth of Evelyn Foster's whole story.

And once doubt was felt, there was plenty of confirmation for it. In one detail at least, Evelyn Foster's story was inaccurate. There were no marks of burning on the heather between the road and the point at which the car stopped. The car was found in gear, and a local motor engineer told the police that it had been driven slowly off the road, and set on fire after it had stopped. The fire had not originated in the front of the car, and there was every indication that petrol from a tin carried in a luggage box at the rear had been used. An empty petrol tin was found on the carrier platform at the back of the car, and the neck and cap were discovered near by.

There was the further point that her story of the man pushing her over in the seat and then driving back from Belsay to Wolf's Nick was very improbable. It is very difficult to drive in such a position, and the handbrake on this Hudson car was on the right. Surely she could have pulled it, or got her foot on to the foot brake, to stop the car?

The evidence which must have finally determined the police view of the case, however, was that of Professor Stuart MacDonald, professor of pathology at Durham University, who examined the body after death. Professor MacDonald found extensive burning, most severe on the middle part of the body and in the front. The distribution and severity of the burns suggested that some portions of her clothing had contained an inflammable substance. The burning had started in front, and was most severe on the upper and inner thighs. Its intensity diminished, both upwards and downwards. The distribution of the burns suggested that the girl had been sitting down during some period of the burning.

But the vital points brought out by Professor MacDonald were two. First, there was no sign whatever that Evelyn Foster had been raped. Second, there was no sign of any blow on the face or head sufficiently violent to have stunned her.

It was four weeks after Evelyn Foster died that the inquest, formally opened within three days of her death, was resumed. It was held in the little War Memorial Hall at Otterburn, next door to the

Percy Arms. The Coroner's table was draped with a black cloth, and the jurors sat at a trestle table. They were all local men who had known Evelyn well, the vicar, the sub-postmaster, the proprietor of the Percy Arms, a farmer, mill workers. The hall was lighted by acetylene gas, and the light was needed, for the surrounding moors were now in the grip of winter. Some of the roads to Otterburn were impassable, and Captain Fullarton James ran into a snowdrift while on the way to the inquest, and had to be dug out.

This jury of local men heard some thirty witnesses out of the two hundred from whom the police had taken statements. There is no doubt that they were expecting to have some account of strangers rumoured to be in the district, and of police investigations into their behaviour. One of the jurymen, indeed, had himself seen a stranger—although not one he could positively identify—near the Post Office at about seven o'clock.

Instead of this, they listened to a step-by-step account designed to show that Evelyn Foster had set fire to the car herself. They heard the engineer, they heard Professor MacDonald. They were warned by the Coroner that Evelyn Foster's statement was not to be taken as evidence of fact.

The Coroner showed clearly enough his own agreement with the police viewpoint, in the questions he asked Professor MacDonald:

Coroner: Assuming that the car was standing where you saw it, Professor, and the door was open, and she threw some petrol into the back of the car, and then set fire to it—her left leg probably on the running board, her right on the edge of the step into the back of the car—could flames have come back and blinded her?

MacDonald: I think it is possible.

Coroner: Assuming she herself had upset some petrol over a portion of her clothing and then ignited the car, then that would have been a possible cause?

MacDonald: Yes.

Coroner: If she had taken the petrol tin and poured petrol over herself in that way, is it possible that she might have got two extra splashes on the top above the breast?

MacDonald: It is possible.

Why should Evelyn Foster, a quiet, rather timid, unimpeachably respectable girl of twenty-eight, run her car on to the moors and attempt to burn it? The car had been bought by Evelyn herself out of her savings—she had some £500 in the Post Office when she died—and, to obtain a cheaper rate, had been insured in her father's name. It was suggested by the Coroner that she would have benefited financially by burning the car—he apparently did not realize that the insurance company would not pay more than the car's current market value.

"On the other hand," the Coroner added, generously providing another motive, "you have cases where, for some inexplicable reason, either for notoriety or for the sake of doing something abnormal, a person would do a thing like this."

The summing up was practically a direction to the jury to say that Evelyn Foster fired the car herself. They were out for just over two hours. When they returned the foreman, McDougal, who was head gardener at Otterburn Towers near by, stood up and read the piece of paper in his hand.

"The jury find a verdict of wilful murder against some person unknown."

There was silence. Then the Coroner said: "I suppose you mean that somebody deliberately poured petrol over her and then set her on fire."

"Yes."

The Coroner wrote it down. Then he rose. "That concludes the hearing. Thank you, gentlemen."

It was not, however, the last comment made on the case. On the day after the verdict Captain Fullarton James made a statement which aroused great indignation in Otterburn. He said:

"We are satisfied that the motor-car in which Miss Foster's supposed murderer is said to have travelled from Jedburgh does not exist.

"We are also satisfied that the man she described does not exist."

INVESTIGATION AND ANALYSIS

Did the man exist? This was the question that I set myself to answer on a visit to Otterburn in a fine week of September 1956, more than twenty years after Evelyn's death. Foster's Garage is still in the main street, but the family's original anger at the attitude of Coroner and police had faded with the years. They could add nothing new to what had appeared in the newspapers, and had no hope of a solution to the crime. I talked, however, to a large num-

ber of people in Otterburn, Newcastle and around about, who
were more or less directly connected with the case. I also talked to
senior officers of the Northumberland County Police at Morpeth.

These gentlemen received me with courtesy and friendliness,
but the friendliness was blended with some reserve. There was
more reason for this than the rash statement of Captain Fullarton
James. At the outset of the case the police had committed a serious blunder. The burnt out car was discovered soon after ten
o'clock on Tuesday night, and the police knew of it very shortly
afterwards. They put no guard over it, however, until Wednesday
morning.

In the meantime (as I learned from a newspaperman in
Newcastle) an enterprising journalist had gone out to Wolf's Nick,
examined the car thoroughly, lifted the bonnet, found Evelyn
Foster's scarf on the ground and put it over the car headlamp, and
—it was strongly suggested to me—made the footprint of which the
police took a mould. No evidence about this footprint was offered
at the inquest. No fingerprint evidence was offered. Nothing was
said about the glove found on the scene—was this also perhaps
dropped by the reporter?

I should add that this blunder is not officially admitted by the
police. A local policeman, now retired, strongly denied that the car
had been left unguarded; the police at Morpeth refused to comment on the point. That it is a fact, however, is proved by one
small detail of the evidence at the inquest. The police constable
who first found Evelyn Foster's scarf, late on Tuesday night, saw it
lying on the ground and left it there. When Inspector Russell
visited the scene, on Wednesday morning, the scarf was hanging
over the car headlamp. If the car was guarded continuously, how
had it got there?

This initial error does not, of course, invalidate the theory of
arson, but it does suggest that acceptance of this theory would
have been welcome to the police. In Otterburn village I found
great bitterness about the case, and much criticism of the police.
There were roadmenders, I was told, who had seen a car at Elishaw Bridge at the time Evelyn's car drew up; there was a local
schoolmistress who had been stopped by a stranger at Otterburn
Bridge, a man so unpleasant and strange in his manner that she
quickly left him; there was another roadmender who had heard a

car turn round outside his house near Belsay (it was suggested by
the police that Evelyn Foster had never driven further than Wolf's
Nick). None of them was called.

Everybody, police and locals, agreed that the Otterburn police
constable, now long retired, was the man who could tell me more
about the case and the people involved, than anybody else. When I
found Andy Ferguson, living now at Seaton Burn near Newcastle,
he refused quite positively to say anything at all. The glove, the
scarf, Evelyn Foster's character? His lips were tightly closed.

My own conclusion from those days spent in Otterburn is a firm
one: Evelyn Foster was murdered. And there are several points
which tell us something positive about her murderer. But before
coming to them, let me analyze what may be called the negative
side—the case against Evelyn Foster, which was based on her
dying statement.

There are four main points to be answered:

(i) Her failure to enter the Percy Arms and ask for the
stranger.

(ii) Her unlikely account of the way in which he drove back
from Belsay.

(iii) Her story of being attacked and raped.

(iv) Her story of the car that approached afterwards, and the
whistle.

Let us go through the points in order. She said that the man
"hailed her" at the Bridge, which is no more than a few yards beyond the Percy Arms. If she really meant that he hailed her—
called to her—then she might have heard him and not stopped at
the hotel. It must also be remembered that her story was told in a
low voice and spasmodically, so that the constable taking notes
could not always hear what she said.

The second point, like much else in the story, is really in her
favour. If she had wished to do so, she could easily have invented
so many much more probable incidents which would have involved
a change of seats, and his taking the steering wheel.

She said that the man hit her, and this possibility was not denied
by Professor MacDonald, who agreed that a light blow in the eye,
or even a blow on the head, might well leave no trace. She did not

say that the blows stunned her, but that she "became unconscious," possibly from shock or fright. The questions put by the Coroner were almost throughout phrased so that her story appeared in the most unfavourable possible light.

The point about the rape is the most interesting of all. When her mother first asked Evelyn what had happened, she replied: "Oh, it's been that man. He hit me and burned me." There was nothing here about rape. Later she agreed when her mother asked if the man had "interfered with her," but at first Mrs. Foster did not necessarily put a sexual interpretation upon this reply. In fact she did so only at the suggestion of the police solicitor.

I should add that the possibility, which was at one time in my own mind, that Evelyn Foster might have been carrying on an affair with a local man, unknown to her family or other Otterburn inhabitants, was decisively disposed of. The police never found anything to support such a theory; and I was assured by more than one person in the village that the community was so closely knit that it would have been absolutely impossible for such a relationship to have existed without being known to people in the district. Professor MacDonald's opinion was that she had died a virgin, although the nature of the burns made it impossible for him to be quite sure.

And finally, a car did stop at Wolf's Nick, at about half past nine. The driver saw smoke and flames from the car on the moor, could see nobody moving out there, and drove on without stopping to investigate. His later movements were checked, and his story authenticated. This could have been the car that Evelyn Foster heard.

There is also what may be called the problem of the missing matches. Evelyn did not smoke, or carry matches. No matches were found in or near the car. She had no lighter. How, then, did she set fire to the car?

And there is another point. If, as was suggested, she meant to set fire to the car and claim that it had been an accident, what would she have said about the missing passenger? Certainly no insurance company would have paid up without verification from him.

Summing up, one may admit that Evelyn Foster's dying statement is not tidy, nor wholly satisfactory. Yet the contradictions involved in denying it are quite staggering. Accept it as a statement basically true (although inaccurate in some details) and we have a picture of the murderer.

He was a man with a criminal record, he probably lived or had lived in the North East, and he was a skillful car driver. It is quite likely that, just before the Otterburn murder, he had committed another crime.

Here is the reasoning behind these conclusions.

His criminal record. Once we accept Evelyn's story, and accept as a fact that there *was* a car at Elishaw Bridge, we must ask: why did not its occupants come forward? There can be only one good reason—that they were afraid of revealing themselves to the police. This would be natural enough if they were criminals, who had recently done a job up in Scotland, and had decided to split up temporarily. It would be interesting to know how far the police pushed this line of enquiry.

He probably lived in the North East. Or at least he knew it very well. The road from Otterburn to Belsay has not greatly changed since 1931, although at Wolf's Nick the embankment has been built up. At that time, however, there was *practically no other spot along this road* where a car could have been driven on to the moor. The bank here was steep, the drop between 4 feet and 4 feet 6 inches, but it was not precipitous. The person who, on this dark night, knew exactly where he should stop to drive the car off the road, obviously had very considerable local knowledge.

He was a skillful driver. To drive the car down the bank was a tricky, and even dangerous, operation. There was no reason why Evelyn Foster should have risked it—or, incidentally, have tried to fire the car from the back rather than from the engine. On the other hand, there was every reason why her murderer should want to get the car off the road and on to the moor. It meant that he ran much less risk of immediate detection by a passing car, and thus helped to facilitate his escape.

There remain two questions. Why did he do it and how did he escape? We are in the region of what is no more than logical conjecture in suggesting that the man had a record not merely of crime, but of violent crime. There can be little doubt that when he first asked for a lift, he genuinely wanted to be driven to Ponteland. Something on the way changed his mind. Perhaps Evelyn

Foster asked indiscreet questions, perhaps he suddenly felt himself in danger of discovery through her, perhaps his presence alone with her on the moors roused the urge to sadistic violence that is felt by many criminals. We do not know the reasons, only what happened.

Nor do we know how he escaped—whether he had an accomplice who picked him up, whether he managed somehow to get to Newcastle, or made his way to Hexham and there rejoined his companions, or found a hiding place on the moors. He walks out of the story, after killing Evelyn Foster, as abruptly as he had walked into it; but the memory of the invisible man, neat, gentlemanly, bowler-hatted, the man who was seen by nobody but Evelyn Foster but who surely existed, still haunts the people of Otterburn and the moors.

JULIAN SYMONS' crime novels include *The Players and the Game* and *A Reasonable Doubt*.

Crime Against the Body Politic

James Grady

IN 1976 a mysterious group of Texas oilmen, bound by blood and the corporate tie, carefully planned and executed a crime.

No one was murdered, nothing was stolen. The Texans, according to government experts, are not lawbreakers. Nevertheless they committed a crime—not against the body corporeal or the body of the law, but against the body politic.

My office partner, Gary Cohn, and I were unaware of the Texans' existence when our boss, Jack Anderson, strolled back from his large corner office to our disorderly cubbyhole. "Hey," Anderson said softly, "one of you guys got a minute?"

Jack Anderson's "Washington Merry-Go-Round," the nationally syndicated daily newspaper column and its offshoots (sometimes dubbed "Muckraking, Inc."), is housed in a three-story townhouse on 16th Street in Washington, D.C. At one time the house was the home of Vice-President (1912) James S. Sherman, whose untimely end came one year after he moved into the house which, with its turrets and drawing rooms and fireplaces, almost qualifies for southern-mansion status. In the 1920s it became an

57 CRIME AGAINST THE BODY POLITIC

opulent bordello, complete with oak panels, red draperies, and a bidet.

Since he took over the Drew Pearson column in 1969 and moved into the townhouse in 1975, Jack Anderson has continued the Pearson policy of exclusivity and political muckraking. (There is a fine but definite line between gossip and muckraking: the first is titillation without substance; the second, while it may titillate, has meat.) Raking muck, and raking it exclusively, is not easy—especially in the post-Watergate era when every aspiring journalist yearns to be not just a reporter but an *investigative* reporter. Anderson has been a prototype for the breed ever since he joined Drew Pearson's staff at the end of World War II.

Today time has combined with circumstances to cut down on Jack's reporting. He still handles a few stories but he is hampered by his fame: knowledge of an Anderson investigation alerts wrongdoers to their peril, and catching them becomes that much harder. Anderson's gray hair, his handsome blockish face, and his slightly paunched form are too familiar for him to drift anonymously through Washington, one of the political world's smallest towns.

Thus, like Nero Wolfe, Jack is forced to depend on others to be his eyes and ears. Archie Goodwin is played by two people: Opal Ginn, secretary and administrative aide who serves as guardian of his gate; and Les Whitten, a lanky energetic Renaissance man who translates Baudelaire when he's not nailing crooks and mountebanks. Les now shares Jack's byline, and Anderson correctly describes his chief colleague as the best investigative reporter in the country.

Anderson and Whitten are backed by eight full time associates (of whom Gary Cohn and I are two) and a rotating cast of interns and free-lance reporters, all of whom churn out copy that Anderson double-checks, then reworks into his own scathing style for his column or TV/radio spots.

Gary Cohn and I were the newest members of the professional staff that muggy September afternoon in 1976. Although we'd been intern-apprentices nearly a year and we'd made our bones at the recent Republican Presidential convention, we were still scrambling, still eager. When Anderson made his rare trip back to our cubicle and stood in shirtsleeves, tie slightly askew, eyeglasses in one hand, a piece of green copy-paper in the other, there was no question that we "had a minute."

Gary hung up the phone; I turned from my typewriter; and we waited.

"One of my old sources tells me there's something funny going on with Texas election campaign money," Anderson said. "Does either of you two want to work on it?"

Gary looked at me. Each of us wanted it, but neither wanted to cut the other out.

"We'll work on it together," Gary said.

Jack Anderson slipped his glasses part way up his nose and peered down at the scrap of green paper. Only Jack can decipher the black scribbles of his private shorthand. "I don't know much about it, but my source gave me the name of a contact who does."

Gary and I wrote down the contact's name and phone number.

"We'll take care of it," I said.

"Many thanks." He strolled away.

Gary asked me, "How do you want to handle it?"

My typewriter held an uncompleted story that I wanted to turn in that evening. "Either we wait and go see the guy in the morning," I said, "or you can take him now."

"I'll take him now." Five "quick phone calls" and he was gone.

Gary and I had worked together regularly since we'd joined the staff. He's a New Yorker with so much pent-up energy that as a boy he had to drink milk shakes to keep from losing weight. When he joined the Anderson organization he was so high-strung his hands would shake and he found it impossible to stand still more than one or two seconds, but few people are so aptly made for their jobs with Anderson as is Mad Dog Cohn, who joined us after one year of law school. By all the logical rules his scruffy blond hair, blue-jean and work-shirt appearance should have rendered him a sad joke in stodgy Washington—one cannot picture him being able to convince nervous bureaucrats, harried Congressional staffers or pompous Senators to give him the time of day, let alone leak or confess to him; he's loud, aggressive, infuriatingly stubborn —and yet he is extremely successful.

Gary has the special charm of a street urchin and a very conscious knowledge of just how far a situation can be pushed. His youthful brashness beguiles the bureaucrats and solons.

Gary loves the battle; I love the victory. My reporting technique is broader, more systemic than his. I prefer to get all the pieces of a man's transgressions carefully detailed so that in confrontation he has little choice but to confess or refuse comment. Gary, by contrast, would rather charge into the man's office, confront him with rumors of his guilt, and battle him into a confession.

I had joined Anderson's staff after finishing my second novel* and a fellowship stint on a Senator's staff. One of my friends from journalism school in Montana was a professional associate of Jack's; he recommended the office to me—Anderson needed free help, as he was short two college interns at the moment.

I showed up intending to acquire a bit of experience and ended by staying in the unpaid job until Jack had a paying vacancy.

Gary Cohn and I make a strange reporting pair—a ball-of-fire New Yorker and an easygoing Montanan—but the combination clicked and we still share the suspicion that Jack's putting us in the same cubicle was more than accidental.

Two hours later Gary burst back into the office. "These guys are funneling secret money into campaigns." He was excited. "They're not reporting the sources of the money. Jack's guy knows of three campaigns they've put bucks into, and there are probably more, especially on the Ways and Means Committee."

"Who are 'they'?"

"Oilmen," he replied smugly. "The contact thinks they're with some firm called Quintana."

Oil companies have greased Washington with money for years. It's an old story in which new chapters are told endlessly. But while the presence of a special-interest group and its money in a political campaign may be a story worth exposing, it may not necessarily be a good story or a significant story of crime against the body politic. Countless special-interest groups organize under the law and pass out thousands of dollars each election year.

Still, the muckraker does his best to uncover as much of the

---

* *Shadow of the Condor.—Ed.*

truth as possible, as much of the behind-the-scenes activity as he can; each exposé makes the next crime a fraction harder for the next would-be transgressor.

When we began our probe of the Quintana case we assumed it was a shady political operation (rather than an above-board one) because it had the earmarks. At the outset we found three Congressional campaigns with patterns of suspicious contributions. Not much—but enough of a spoor for trained noses. We had a paper trail we could start chasing.

The election laws require each candidate to keep detailed lists of all contributors who donate more than $100 to his campaign. The candidate files periodic reports with various federal and state authorities. These reports are available for public inspection.

Each contributor must be identified by name, address, occupation, and principal place of business. The date and amount of his contribution must be stated. The standard Federal Elections Commission (FEC) form has space for eight filings per page. Most Congressmen's campaigns fill up several hundred such forms, while Presidential races can generate thousands of pages of contributors.

The man Gary visited—Jack Anderson's source—provided us with copies of pages from two different campaigns. There were suspicious filings on each page. For example, we found on one page four contributors—all from Houston; all in the same building at the same address; three of them on the same floor; each of the four gave $300 on the same date; each listed as his occupation "investor."

We knew there was chicanery here but we weren't yet sure what the pattern meant. The contributors might have been victims of a corporate or union shakedown to contribute their own money to candidates supported by the employers. Or they might have conspired among themselves to pass out the bucks. Their real intentions were hidden. Before we could find a story we needed to link the contributors to a common entity, probably (according to our source) a firm called Quintana; only then could we reasonably speculate on what kind of story we had, if any. But the clues were intriguing. Instinctively Gary and I believed they would lead us to an alarming case of campaign-fund manipulation.

The FEC had opened its public offices in 1975 in a downtown

government building; we made our way there, prepared for an eye-watering session with microfilm readers.

It would have been hopeless to grope our way blindly through FEC files in search of our Texans. It can take as long as three hours to examine *one* candidate's filings. With nearly 1,000 races on file, such a chore was impossible for us. But we had a key. Our source had told Gary that tax legislation was rumored to be a major concern of the Texans. We narrowed our concentration to the Congressional tax-writing committee, Ways and Means.

For several days Gary, an intern, and I pored over the records. We sought out any references to Quintana, Houston, oil or energy-related occupations; any recurring pattern of contributions or contributors that seemed at all suspicious.

By the end of the second day we knew we were onto something hot.

Time and time again, Texans had showered money into campaigns, often on the same day, often from the same approximate address. At times we found the same listings of contributors, in sequence, in different campaigns.

We developed a list of approximately twenty names—systematic contributors. Some of them seemed unquestionably linked to one another; other links were less clear. Most of them gave their occupations as "investors" or "energy producers" but failed to list their companies by name.

"What we've got to do," I told Gary, "is identify them. Link them together. So far, none of them's listed Quintana. We've got most of them in the same building but we can't prove they're all from the same group."

"Some of these other funny filings from places outside Texas could be Quintana too, for all we know," he said. "Let's call the bastards."

"Not yet. Let's try and link them closer together."

"How?"

"Let's just wait a little, okay? I've got an idea."

I called a sometime source, all-time friend in a Texas Congressional office that we knew had not received Quintana-related funds that year. He gave me the names of several Texas oil and gas associations.

I struck oil on the third long-distance call. By then my cover-story—I was checking on the addresses and company affiliations of a number of oilmen "so my firm can contact them"—was sounding plausible even to me. (The cover-story was true as far as it went; but it left a great deal unsaid.)

The oil associations became our unintentional and unlikely allies in our probe of wrongdoing within the oil business. When a polite woman on the other end of the phone line finally told me that her group kept membership lists and that she would be glad to help me, I barely kept from yelling. She laid the phone on the desk. I heard happy chatter, typewriters clicking, and the sound of her footsteps as she walked across the room to fetch the record book.

"Hi there," she said cheerfully. "Back again. Sorry it took so long. Now who do you want to know about?"

Slowly I read her the list of twenty-some names.

She identified several of them as officers, directors, or associates of a Houston oil firm. Its name: Quintana.

"What kind of firm is that?" I asked innocently.

"Well, I don't know much about it. I do know it's a family business."

"Thank you very, very much."

"Not at all. Y'all call back if we can he'p you again."

Next morning Gary started to shout at me as soon as he came past the Xerox machine. "Grady! I called those bastards last night and I got 'em, I got 'em!"

"What do you mean you called them?"

"Quintana. Their receptionist confirmed a lot of those names. It's a family-owned firm. Then she turned me over to some flack who said we'd better talk to their lawyer if we had any questions."

He leaned back to get his breath. "And you know who their lawyer is? You know who he works for?" He stabbed his finger toward me to punctuate the name: "John Connally. He's from Connally's firm. His office is there, in the Quintana headquarters, right in the goddamned firm!"

Few Texans or Washingtonians have reputations that glisten with more muckraking magic than that of John Connally—former Governor, would-be President, Democrat turned Republican, Nixon crony, acquitted milk-scandal figure; the man who was shot with John F. Kennedy. The scandals of Watergate, whirling about

John Connally, had buffeted him but he had emerged unscathed.

Connally's monster law firm in Texas employs more than 200 lawyers, we learned. This dampened our enthusiasm a bit. But still, when we mixed Quintana's way of doing political business with Connally's political past, at the very least we found it an intriguing juxtaposition.

We had a confirmed list of Quintana associates, a list of several Congressmen who had been showered systematically with their money, and a connection to one of the country's key power-brokers, John Connally. It was a story.

We still needed to try to reach the Quintana executives, officially to give them a chance to explain themselves and actually to solicit additional information from them. We also needed to call the Congressmen for comment: we intended to name them in the story and we make it a rule to try and get comments from everyone we name.

Of reporting's five "W's," we had enough of the who, what, when, and where to write our story. But we didn't have proof of the *why* and that troubled us.

We felt we knew, of course. Special-interest groups pass out dollars to candidates for tediously obvious reasons. But we lacked hard evidence in the Quintana case.

"If there was only some way we could show those Congressmen whoring for Quintana." Gary paced the cubicle. "Is there a key vote or something?"

"In the first place," I told him, " 'whoring' is pretty strong. Probably you can't apply it to all the Congressmen who got money from Quintana. If they do what they do because of . . . hell, because of philosophy, and just happen to get oil's support, that doesn't make them whores. If they do it directly and merely for money, then. . . . But you know we can't prove that with *any* of them. I doubt we'd ever find one key vote—I don't think there is such a thing. It would have to be on the Floor of the House, since these guys aren't all on the same committee. And then we'd find they'd voted with other Congressmen who didn't get oil money, so we'd never be able to use a vote as a link."

"There's got to be something," Gary insisted. "Somewhere. Something they did together, some group they belong to, some . . ."

"Wait a minute, that's it!" I interrupted him. "An association. There's got to be an oilmen's association in town that rates Congressmen by their voting records. We'll find the association, get our hands on their ratings, and see how these guys stand."

Every important industrial, social or special-interest group with any national membership maintains a representative or lobbyist, branch office or headquarters in the nation's capital. The Washington Yellow Pages list more than six pages of associations. Quite a few of these groups rate Congressmen on their voting records, assigning points, on a scale of 100, for the Congressman's record of "good" votes (that is, votes that agree with the group's stand).

What we went to seek was such a poll from an oil-industry group, rating the Congressmen who'd received the suspect money. We hoped it would back up our working hypothesis that Quintana was rewarding friends of the oil industry with money.

I phoned a man in the energy business. Helpfully, he referred me to the Independent Petroleum Association of America (IPAA), the only oil-industry group that made comprehensive voting analyses of Congressmen's records.

A woman with a pleasant voice answered the phone at IPAA and graciously offered to send me a copy of IPAA's ratings for the 94th Congress. The IPAA office was only a few blocks from our building; I told her I would walk down and get it—I was far too impatient to wait for the mails.

Gary accompanied me. Throughout the five-minute walk he was damning "oil barons" and "whores." He didn't button his lip inside; while we waited in IPAA's plush outer office he hassled the secretaries with obnoxious pressure: "Who runs your lobbying? What are you people doing? Don't you think the public has the right to know how you operate on Capitol Hill?"

As soon as I was handed the precious document I hurried him into the nearest elevator, loudly proclaiming my thanks to the IPAA woman as the doors slid shut on us.

In the elevator we scanned the list. It was dynamite. Every Congressman who'd received Quintana money weighed in with a high rating—75 or better.

The IPAA charts strengthened our case: the industry itself had labeled Quintana's beneficiaries as good friends of oil.

The IPAA ratings also gave us additional potential candidates for our investigation. Any Congressman with a high rating was a suspect: had they *all* received generous cash donations from Quintana?

By now we felt we might be running out of time. Quintana had an increasing number of clues that we were on their trail. Besides, other stories were backing up, the election wasn't far away, and perhaps other reporters had heard by now of the Quintana morass and might have decided to try for a story. All these pressures augured for cutting off our legwork: go with what we had.

But as eager and nervous as we were, Gary and I decided to try and nail down more evidence. We returned to the FEC, armed with IPAA's list of high-rated legislators, and at the same time we began to make phone calls in which we asked the Congressmen on Quintana's list of benefactors to comment on Quintana.

Our probe for Congressmen's comments was more than courtesy. We hoped it would establish specific links between Quintana and the lawmakers. We weren't too optimistic, however, and the responses bore out our expectations: we found a few Congressmen who admitted they knew the Quintana crowd but we obtained no proof of shady deals. No one was likely to confess that easily.

Then we tried to break through the Quintana barrier itself, seeking comment from the corporation's executives. As soon as we told the telephone receptionists our names, the executives disappeared. Either they couldn't come to the phone or they were out. They returned none of our messages. When we finally broke through to one company official and plied him with repeated and varied arguments, he would only say that the lawyer from John Connally's office had passed the word to all Quintana personnel that they were "not to confirm or deny any information to either Mr. Cohn or Mr. Grady."

The Connally attorney himself did not return any of our numerous calls.

But our examination of FEC filings paid off and we knew we couldn't hold the story any longer. We wrote the column together.

We'd found nine Congressional candidates, eight of them incumbents, who had shared $26,100 of Quintana's cash when we went to press. The column appeared on September 28, 1976.

After that date we found an additional eight Congressmen who had been showered with $11,500 of Quintana's cash in exactly the same shady fashion.

One of the Congressmen in that second group was Rep. Jim Wright (Texas Democrat), an 80-percenter on the IPAA rating scale. In 1977 Wright was elected majority leader of the House of Representatives.

On March 8, 1977, Wright led four oilmen into a White House meeting with President Jimmy Carter and the new President's chief energy adviser, James Schlesinger. It was a short but profitable meeting for the oilmen: they convinced the President to support a tax-break for independent oilmen known as "intangible drilling costs," a $30 to $50 million bonanza that Congress had taken away from the oilmen in earlier legislation. As this article goes to press, the tax-writing House Ways and Means Committee has accepted the President's proposals for the oilmen's tax credit.

One of the four oilmen whom Majority Leader Wright took to see the President was a man whom we had identified as an executive of Quintana. But when confronted with the facts, a spokesman for Representative Wright bristled at any implication that the Quintana cash, the White House meeting and the sudden reversal in government tax policy are anything other than purely innocent honest politics. "Wright doesn't personally know" the Quintana official, insisted the spokesman. The Quintana executive and the other three oilmen were "suggested to Congressman Wright by someone in Dallas" (the spokesman didn't know who) as independent oilmen who would express representative views on the issue.

"You know," the spokesman said, "there are some guys up here who try to do their job, and then you get something like this. . . . I don't know what you're reaching for, but it just isn't there. We'll leave it at that."

Leave it at that? Hardly. The Quintana shenanigans are a classic example of crime against the body politic: cash quietly passed to friendly politicians, behind-the-scenes lobbying, a change in public policy. Legal? Yes—but.

The Quintana contributions unfortunately are not rarities in American political life. Similar cases occur every day, and the Jack Andersons and Les Whittens have a new story to pursue every day. But every day we keep at it because the best preventive and cure for the disease of corruption is the disinfectant of sunshine that is administered by raking the muck out from under the rug.

JAMES GRADY is the author of *Six Days of the Condor* and *Shadow of the Condor*.

The Man Who Killed Himself Six Times

Donald Hamilton

"MURDER?" said Sheriff Howard Stegall, of Robertson County, Texas. "Who says it was murder? Henry Marshall killed himself. If it hadn't been for the way he went about it, nobody'd have given it a second thought."

We were talking late at night in the air-conditioned sheriff's office in Franklin, the county seat. Few people outside Texas had ever heard of Franklin, population 1,065, or of Henry Harvey Marshall, before Billie Sol Estes's cotton deals hit the front pages in 1961 and a Department of Agriculture spokesman in Washington, never identified, suggested to the press that the "suicide" of Marshall, former head of the cotton-allotment-transfer program in Texas might be something other than it seemed. At this, people began looking into the ten-month-old case, and the feeling got around that there might, indeed, be something just a little odd about the death of a man who committed suicide by shooting himself five times in the stomach with a .22 bolt-action rifle.

Sheriff Stegall is a heavy, powerful man of fifty-three, with a craggy, weathered face. His eyes, with little creases around them, are the wary eyes of a man accustomed to grinning, who hasn't had much to grin about lately.

"They gave us a rough time," he says wryly. "Reporters, FBI men, investigators. And the Texas Rangers, those publicity hounds. They couldn't track a bull elephant across a snowbank! And all they really had in the way of evidence was the way he shot himself. That doesn't mean anything. Look here." He pulled out a newspaper. "Here's a story of a woman who committed suicide by shooting herself five times with a .45 automatic—and she lived for ten minutes afterwards! I still say it was suicide. That was our coroner's verdict when it happened, and the grand jury backed him up. . . . No, sir, I won't let you take my picture. I'm not going to have any more writers and reporters making a monkey of me if I can help it. It wouldn't have been so bad if they'd stuck to the facts."

Facts in the case of Henry Marshall are easy to come by. The only trouble is they don't always agree with each other, and they don't always make sense. There is, for instance, the fact that five shots were fired but only four empty shells were found. Well, finding ejected empties in a grassy meadow isn't always an easy job, and a .22 rimfire case isn't very big. But then there is the fact that while five bullets went into the body, only four came out—and the fifth bullet was *not* found inside the body. To date, no bullets have been found.

There is the fact that Marshall had received a blow over the left eye heavy enough to cause the eye to protrude noticeably. There is the fact that, lying in an open field, he had in his lungs at the time of death a concentration of carbon monoxide that may have been as high as thirty percent, which is getting up toward the lethal dose. If Henry Marshall committed suicide, he apparently did it six times, once with gas and five times with the gun.

On Saturday morning, June 3, 1961, Marshall was, according to most witnesses, a rather overworked man who, however, was not exhibiting any spectacular signs of suicidal abnormality. He weighed around two hundred pounds, was almost six feet tall, and wore glasses. Fifty-one years old, he had had a heart attack in 1958, but had made a very good recovery.

He lived in Bryan, Texas, the home of the Agricultural and Mechanical College of Texas—commonly known as Texas A and M—which is also the Department of Agriculture's headquarters in the state. Marshall had been an agent and supervisor with this department and its predecessors for twenty-five years; only a few years previously he had earned an award for superior service. The certificate, framed, still hangs on the wall of his home in Bryan.

Mrs. Marshall, an attractive, dark-haired woman, seems to have had no qualms or premonitions on that Saturday morning.

"He always went up to the ranch in Franklin on Saturday," she said. "I made a lunch for him to take along like I always did. He was acting just as usual. . . . The gun? Why, he often carried that in the pickup. He said he was taking it along to shoot armadillos."

The armadillo, a scaly beast that looks rather like an opossum in full armor, is prevalent enough in that part of Texas to qualify as a pest. Her husband didn't hunt much, Mrs. Marshall said, but he did make a practice, out on the ranch, of knocking over armadillos whenever he could, using the .22 rifle.

On this particular morning he started for Franklin, thirty miles away, a little earlier than usual because he was to leave his young son, Donald, with his brother-in-law, L. M. Owens.

After dropping off Donald, Marshall paid two bills in town. His behavior seems to have caused no concern to anyone. He drove away in his pickup truck toward his 1500-acre ranch, upon which he had some forty-odd head of cattle—not a big spread, by Texas standards, but then, Marshall was not primarily a cattleman. However, according to a colleague in the Department of Agriculture, I. H. Lloyd, the man who was later to take his place, Marshall took his cattle raising seriously.

This is not the wide-open flat plains area of Texas; the country is rolling, with small creeks and patches of dense woods surrounding open meadows or pastures. There are doves and quail in the pastures; there are deer in the woods; and Marshall, like the other ranchers in the neighborhood, customarily leased the place to hunters in the fall.

Marshall, having known the country since childhood, did not bother to take the easy way. He drove in by a back road, opened a final gate, closed it behind him, and proceeded to drive past some deserted shacks, across a meadow—and into a fog of mystery that may never be dispelled. The time, according to the best estimates, was about 10:30 A.M.

He was not expected home until late in the afternoon. In the meantime, Mrs. Marshall, in Bryan, was making preparations for a coffee party she was to hold at a friend's house soon; and her son Donald was having an enjoyable outing with his uncle. These two got back to Franklin shortly before five o'clock.

At five, Mrs. Marshall called from Bryan to learn how soon her husband and son would be home. L. M. Owens said the boy was right there; Henry had not been by to pick him up yet.

Some fifteen minutes later, Mrs. Marshall, worried now, called her brother again and asked him to drive out to the ranch and look around.

"We all kind of looked after Henry since his attack," says L. M. Owens, a wiry man with brown hair. "I always used to tell him, if he had a flat tire or got stuck out there, just to sit down and wait; I'd be along looking for him."

Owens made a quick trip out to the ranch, searched the most likely spots, and returned to see if Marshall had showed up. He hadn't. Owens picked up a neighbor named Bennett and headed back out. Presently, cruising along a narrow lane, they spotted tire tracks at the gate where Marshall had turned in, and trailed them. This was about six-thirty in the evening.

"The first thing we saw was the pickup," says Owens. "Then we saw him lying there. I thought of course it was his heart."

But Henry Marshall had not died of a heart attack. He lay in the grass beside his pickup truck with bruises on face and hands, five wounds in front, four in back, and no holes in the front of his shirt, which was unbuttoned and disarranged. There was blood on both sides and on the rear of the truck, which had acquired a dent since last seen. There were spent .22 cartridge shells on the ground. L. M. Owens recognized the box from which the cartridges came; it was a box that had been found at a deserted house not far away when he and Henry Marshall and their respective sons had been walking around the place about a month earlier.

"Henry offered them to me," Owens said, "but I didn't have a gun to fit them; I told him to keep them."

Owens left his companion to stand by the body, and hurried back to town. He notified Sheriff Stegall, who got hold of the local justice of the peace who also serves as coroner, and an undertaker; they also picked up Robert Marshall, the dead man's brother, who had heard Henry was missing and had been out looking for him.

At this point I found discrepancies. Sheriff Stegall claims that L. M. Owens, Robert Marshall, and Mrs. Marshall all reacted to Henry Marshall's death as if they had been expecting him to kill himself. The family denies this, pointing out that his heart condition was reason enough for them to worry, and brace themselves for the worst, when he did not show up.

"When L. M. told me he was gone, I asked if it was his heart," Mrs. Marshall says. "L. M. said no, it was the gun. It was only late that night I learned it wasn't an accident."

This came later, after the sheriff, coroner, and undertaker had viewed the body out at the ranch.

"It was getting kind of dark by this time, of course," says L. M. Owens. "They had to shine the light."

Perhaps for this reason, no pictures were taken; nor were the gun or pickup truck tested for fingerprints. The sheriff and coroner seem to have come to the immediate conclusion that Marshall had killed himself, despite the awkward method used. They justify their decision by pointing to the nature of the wounds, obviously contact wounds, with powder burns, and to the fact that things had been taken out of Marshall's pockets and placed on the seat of the truck—by Marshall himself, they feel, in preparation for suicide. A razor blade found on the seat, they consider, represents a final instrument of death to be used if everything else should fail.

The body was sent to Bryan where, says Robert Marshall, the Bryan undertaker refused to accept it, refusing to bury a suicide.

Robert Marshall is a cowman of fifty* with a rugged, tanned face and the pale forehead of a man who always wears a hat in the sun. He firmly believes his brother was murdered and, with the widow, he has posted a reward of two thousand dollars for proof leading to conviction of the murderer. He also thinks the investigation was bungled by Sheriff Stegall.

"If it hadn't been for Manley Jones in Bryan," he said, "we wouldn't have any pictures at all."

* Substantially revised for this book, Hamilton's article was first written in 1962—his only foray into real crime investigation—and it is to that year that the present tense refers, in this essay.—*Ed.*

Mr. Jones, the Bryan undertaker, sent for the authorities, who not only made photographs of the body, but took X-rays as well, trying to locate the bullet for which there was no exit wound. The body was embalmed. The funeral was held on Monday. On Wednesday, thirty miles away in Franklin, the death was officially pronounced suicide by justice of the peace Lee Farmer, acting in his capacity as coroner.

The gun, having been checked ballistically to make sure it matched the cartridge cases found—which it did—was returned.

In the meantime, at Texas A and M, Mr. I. H. Lloyd, who had often discussed cattle breeding with Marshall in the past, had taken his place in the Agricultural Stabilization and Conservation Service, known familiarly as the ASCS or just ASC. Lloyd, a plump, bald man of forty-eight who wears bifocal glasses, has nothing but praise for Henry Marshall, whom he'd known for twenty-one years.

"I never worked with a more genial, dedicated man with less foolishness about him," says Lloyd. "I found things in very good shape here when I took over."

Nevertheless, good shape or not, on July 5, 1961, only a month and two days after Henry Marshall's death, Lloyd requested an official investigation of the Texas cotton-allotment-transfer program that had been under the supervision of his dead predecessor and was now his baby.

The program has come in for a lot of newspaper discussion. As explained by Lewis David, Marshall's former superior, the program grew out of the fact that the amount of acreage a farmer can plant in cotton is strictly limited by the ASCS. Each cotton farm has an allotment which is not transferable—*unless* that farm should be taken over by the state under its power of eminent domain, say for the building of a dam. Then, to prevent hardship, if the dispossessed farmer buys a new farm within three years, he can apply to have his old cotton allotment transferred to his new place. At least this was the situation at the time of Henry Marshall's death.

All was well until certain speculators in West Texas—Billie Sol Estes's part of the state—found themselves with newly irrigated land on their hands, suitable for raising cotton very profitably. Unfortunately, since cotton had never been raised there in the past, there were no allotments. Without allotments, there could be no cotton.

Some bright character remembered the legal loophole made for the poor cotton farmer who'd been put off his land to make way for progress, and the hunt was on—for dispossessed farmers with allotments that could be transferred but had not been.

The mechanics of the deal were simple enough. The farmer was sold a piece of the speculator's land, no money down, so much a month. He had his orphaned cotton allotment transferred to this land. He then leased the land back to the speculator, pocketed the lease money as payment for his allotment and trouble, and forgot the whole thing. When he failed to make the first payment on the place, the land reverted to the speculator who could now raise cotton on it—or sell it to someone who could, at a whacking profit.

Naturally, there had to be a few side agreements to make this operation safe for both parties. The farmer had to be sure he wouldn't be stuck with any penalties if he neglected to make his payments. The speculator had to be sure the allotment would actually be transferred. If it wasn't—if the ASCS refused to approve the transfer, for instance—the whole deal was off. But not to worry. Billie Sol Estes had political contacts.

While the format arrangements were not strictly illegal, the secret side agreements were. The program had been instituted to prevent hardship to farmers, not to make money for speculators. According to Lloyd, Henry Marshall had been heard to comment that these deals were subterfuges. There have been suggestions that he was doing more than comment at the time of his death. However, technically at least, it was Lloyd, his successor, who really blew the whistle on Billie Sol Estes.

The report based on Lloyd's investigation came out around the first of October, and that, as they say in Texas, was when the egg really hit the fan.

That winter saw a great deal of trouble coming Mr. Estes's way, and in the spring of 1962 the name of Henry Marshall hit the news again. On April 18, Bryan Russ, county attorney of Robertson County, read the news release mentioned earlier, in which an unnamed Agriculture Department spokesman in Washington suggested that Marshall had been murdered. (The nature of the evidence on which this suggestion was based has never been made public.)

Bryan Russ was a good-looking, well-brushed young man with a law degree from the University of Texas, who had been prosecutor of his county since 1953. He had never met Henry Marshall. During the winter, however, the name had come to his attention when Mrs. Marshall had made a futile effort, through her lawyer, to have the suicide verdict changed. Now it seemed to Russ that the time had come for him to take action in the case.

"If anybody's really been murdered in my county," he says, "I want to know about it."

Russ consulted with District Judge John M. Barron, whose 85th Judicial District included both Brazos and Robertson counties. Judge Barron agreed that a grand-jury investigation was indicated. A grand jury of twelve was impaneled to hear testimony and weigh evidence in the Robertson County Courthouse annex.

Upon this complex of old buildings, and the quiet, shady, shabby square around it, in May of 1962 descended all the personnel and paraphernalia of modern law enforcement and communication. Texas Rangers and FBI men mingled with newspapermen and TV cameramen, all sweating in the Texas heat. They swatted flies. One harassed reporter complained in front of Sheriff Stegall, who retorted that there hadn't been any flies in Franklin until the newsmen came.

The grand jury sat for nearly five weeks. It was actually in session eleven days, or about a hundred hours. It heard testimony from more than seventy-five witnesses, including Billie Sol Estes himself.

The first sensation was the exhumation of Henry Marshall's embalmed body, and the autopsy performed by Houston Medical Examiner Joseph A. Jachimczyk, a well-known forensic pathologist, assisted by Dr. Ray Cruse, of Hearne, Texas. Dr. Jachimczyk's report contains the first mention of carbon monoxide in the case: a concentration of 15 percent was found in the lungs. Making allowances for the losses due to embalming, this indicates that as much as 30 percent could have been present at the time of death.

The autopsy report is twelve pages long and goes into minute detail. It states, for instance, that peas, beans, and raisins were found in the stomach. Mrs. Marshall says the raisins were part of the lunch she had packed for her husband—the only part that had been eaten when the lunch was found. The peas and beans, she thinks, must have been from his dinner of the evening before.

Dr. Jachimczyk takes up the matter of the missing bullet. He suggests that it could have dropped out through one of the incisions made in the course of embalming. However, the evidence seems to indicate that the body was X-rayed before being embalmed. Less likely, Dr. Jachimczyk thinks, is the possibility that two bullets found their way through the same exit hole.

He discusses the bullet wounds at length. Three of them, he says, were incapacitating. His conclusion, taking into account gas, bruises, and wounds, was: *possible suicide, probable homicide.* It strengthened the suspicions of those who had felt that there was something very fishy about Henry Marshall's death.

Testimony before the grand jury is not made public. It is not known, therefore, what contribution Billie Sol Estes made to the case. Rumor indicates, however, that he had recourse to the Fifth Amendment, or its Texas equivalent, several times.

A minor commotion was caused by the discovery that the hat Marshall had been wearing had a hole in it. Examined by the FBI, the hole turned out to be nothing but a hole.

A filling-station attendant named Griffin, who worked in the nearby town of Hearne, created another furor by calling up County Attorney Russ and saying that the sight of Marshall's name in the papers had reminded him of a man who'd been asking directions to Franklin, and particularly to the Marshall place, around the time Marshall was found dead the previous spring. Griffin said the man had been dark, with scars on his face—pockmarks or acne scars. He had been driving a white station wagon. Griffin had sold him gas and answered his questions. The following day the man had returned and said, as nearly as Griffin could remember, "You sent me to the wrong Marshall, but I got my deer lease anyway." He drove away. Griffin never saw him again.

Nobody else had seen him, either, and no deer leases had been issued to pockmarked strangers at that time. A picture of the man was drawn by the Texas Rangers from Griffin's description and widely circulated, without result.

The final sensation of the trial was the statement of the grand-jury foreman on Monday evening, June 18:

The Robertson County grand jury after considering all the known evidence has determined the evidence is inconclusive to substantiate a definite decision at this time or to override any decision heretofore made.

In other words, the death of Henry Marshall was still suicide. How the jurors reached their conclusion is not known, since grand-jury transactions are shrouded in legal secrecy. Some time later, however, a juror named Pryse Metcalfe, a local grain dealer who also happens to be Sheriff Stegall's son-in-law, wrote a letter defending the decision that throws some light on the reasoning behind it.

The jury felt, Metcalfe said, that the testimony showed Marshall to have been in a depressed state. It was felt he could have committed suicide in a way that explained the evidence. Specifically, it was suggested (a) that he first tried to kill himself by breathing the fumes of the truck exhaust, using his unbuttoned shirt as a kind of tent, (b) that failing in this attempt, he had got up and shot himself the required number of times, and (c) that he then either fell hard enough, or thrashed around violently enough in dying, to cause the bruises on his face and hands.

A good many people, in Texas and elsewhere, found the grand-jury's decision, to say the least, disconcerting. A month after the jury's dismissal, Colonel Homer Garrison, Jr., Director of the Texas Department of Public Safety, made public a letter he'd written to Judge Barron in which he stated that a preliminary investigation conducted by Captain Clint Peoples of the Texas Rangers showed that Mr. Marshall's death could not have been the result of suicide; the Department would therefore continue its investigation on the assumption that Marshall had been murdered.

Colonel Garrison's letter points out that it would have been necessary for Marshall to have had sufficient control of his equilibrium to have fired five bullets into the front of his left abdomen with a .22-caliber bolt-action rifle, taking it down each time and ejecting the fired shell. The five bullets passing through his body traveled at substantially the same angle, giving further indication that he would have had to have good control of his faculties. This grim feat of stoicism and endurance, Colonel Garrison points out, would have had to be performed by a man who had previously inhaled a near-lethal dose of carbon monoxide; a man who, it had been determined, had trouble straightening his right arm due to a childhood injury.

The man to whom the letter was addressed, Judge Barron, at whose orders the grand jury had been convened and dismissed, agrees with Colonel Garrison's conclusions. The judge is a distinguished-looking man of forty-eight whose family has lived in that part of Texas since 1869.

"I did not preside at the investigation, that is the function of the county attorney," Judge Barron told me. "I guess that leaves me free to say, unofficially, that I believe Henry was murdered. No, I won't speculate about the motive. He was a brilliant, methodical man, probably the best man the Department of Agriculture had in this state, but very quiet. He never talked much about what he was doing."

Marshall's reluctance to talk about his work becomes important in a consideration of his exact position with respect to the shady cotton-allotment transfers. This question has been the subject of much heated discussion. There have even been suggestions that Marshall was playing ball with Billie Sol Estes: Will Wilson, Attorney General of Texas, was quoted in the press to this effect. On the other hand, it has been suggested that Marshall was secretly preparing a trap for the speculators.

According to Pryse Metcalfe, the letter-writing juror, the grand jury was convinced by the testimony that "an extreme amount of pressure was applied to Mr. Marshall concerning the legality of these transfers." Metcalfe presented this as a motive for suicide. Whether or not his reasoning is valid, it certainly indicates that Marshall was deeply concerned with these matters at the time of his death. And it cannot be overlooked that immediately after taking over Marshall's job, I. H. Lloyd called for an investigation.

Lloyd did not say, publicly, what prompted his action. There seemed to be no more than two logical possibilities. Either he found signs of guilty complicity on his predecessor's part, and moved quickly to protect himself; or he found some hot evidence Marshall had been collecting against the speculators, and put it to instant use.

Actually, it does not matter greatly, except to Marshall's family and his memory, which supposition is true. If Marshall was getting ready to spring a trap, there was good reason for killing him. But if he was guiltily involved, there was also a motive for murder. People have been killed because they got nosy and learned too much about profitable illegal operations; but they have also been killed because, involved, they were about to crack and spill the beans. (In fairness, it must be pointed out that no evidence has yet been produced to indicate that Henry Marshall profited in any way from his position as head of the cotton-allotment-transfer program.)

Well, was it in fact murder, or did Henry Marshall kill himself, as Sheriff Stegall and Justice of the Peace Lee Farmer still stubbornly insist? Farmer, a big, strong-looking, elderly man with white hair says, "When I come to the Pearly Gates, if St. Peter asks me about Henry Marshall, I'll still say it was suicide. Death from gunshot wounds, self-inflicted, is the way my report reads. Nobody told me to write it that way, and nobody bribed me to, either."

The possibility that he is right in his stubborn judgment can't be completely dismissed. As Dr. Jachimczyk, the pathologist who examined the body after exhumation, writes in his report: ". . . one cannot say, however, on a purely scientific basis, that a verdict of suicide is absolutely impossible in this case; most improbable, but not impossible."

It's a bizarre way of committing suicide, however, and it conflicts with the known character of Henry Marshall, a quiet, careful, systematic, methodical man. No preparations were made for suicide. The gun was one he often had with him; the cartridges were old ones he had found by a deserted shack. And according to the grand jury, his first idea was not to shoot himself, anyway; it was to poison himself with exhaust fumes. But he had apparently made no provision for this whatever. No equipment has been found that could have been used to pipe the gas into the truck cab, which would have been the logical way of going about it. No, if the grand-jury's theory is correct, Marshall simply lay down at the rear of his truck with his shirt over his head and tried clumsily to trap enough monoxide to kill himself. The assumption must be that he either cracked up very suddenly after leaving town that morning apparently normal, and went into a crazy, inefficient, frenzied form of self-destruction . . . or that he didn't do it.

Of course, it's also a bizarre way of committing murder. It has a kind of wild, haphazard, inexpert look that hints at a spur-of-the-moment crime performed by a panic-stricken amateur. Along these lines, it has been suggested that Marshall might have run into a poacher or trespasser. However, that possibility has been explored by the authorities and dismissed. This leaves the proba- bility that Henry Marshall met his death at the hands of an out- sider who simply loused up the job in a crazy way—or did he? After all, it was officially dismissed as suicide and still is. If it was actually murder, that can hardly be called bungling. The murderer almost got away unsuspected; he certainly gained almost a year's start on the police; a start that may prove decisive in the end.

Perhaps it's best to leave the last word on the case to the Texas Rangers, who have been accustomed to the last word in Texas criminal matters for over a hundred years. Company F of the Rangers is stationed in Waco, sixty-five miles north of Franklin, and has its headquarters, unromantically enough, in a one-story shopping center at the edge of town.

Captain Clint Peoples, in charge of the Waco company of Rangers, is a compact man of fifty-one, not tall for Texas, who has been in law enforcement since 1930.

"I've been on this case since May eleventh, nineteen sixty-two," he said. "It puts us under a real handicap, coming in eleven months late like that." There was no doubt in Captain Peoples's mind that Henry Marshall was murdered. Peoples was the investi- gating officer who supplied the information upon which his supe- rior, Colonel Garrison, based his announcement that the Depart- ment of Public Safety still considered the case one of murder. Peoples dismissed the possibility that it could have been, so to speak, a local case; a crime committed by somebody close to Mar- shall. "We've checked them all out thoroughly," he said to me. "No, we haven't eliminated the pockmarked man who was asking for Marshall in Hearne. We're still hunting for him."

He declined to disclose his theory about the mechanics of the crime while the investigation was still in progress.

"Well, the shooting came last," he said reluctantly. "Yes, I guess you can say he was hit on the head first. It knocked him out. There was serious brain damage. No, I'd rather not talk about how he got monoxide in his lungs at this time. We're convinced the shooting came last, though. The motive? Well, there's no doubt that Marshall was opposing some cotton-allotment transfers, checking into them, and came into opposition with"—at this point he grinned briefly—"with various people. That's all I can say right now."

Captain Peoples still had the death weapon in his car. He consented to pose with it, but reacted unfavorably when I made some comment about the possible value of publicity to him and the Rangers.

"Publicity?" he said. "We're not working for publicity. We just want to catch this fellow."

But they never did.

DONALD HAMILTON is the creator of the Matt Helm spy series, as well as novels like *The Big Country*.

A Good Address

Aaron Marc Stein

IF YOU LIVE in the city, you quickly learn to ignore the ululating sirens of passing police cars. All too often I had heard the cars race up Park Avenue with the sound swelling only to fade off to the north. The cars always rolled on past. They would be heading for Spanish Harlem. That one afternoon, however, there was a difference.

It was August 28, 1963. New Yorkers in the tens of thousands had boarded early-morning buses bound for Washington and the great Civil Rights March, but apart from that it seemed an ordinary late summer's day in New York. Just returned from abroad and with a publisher's deadline harassing me, I was putting in long hours at the typewriter. It was the end of the afternoon. The lowering sun was pouring a golden wash over the full length of East Eighty-eighth Street from Central Park to Gracie Mansion. The stockbrokers were coming home from Wall Street and the stockbrokers' wives were returning from their afternoons of shopping or of bridge or of Junior League-organized good works.

I was within a few minutes of knocking off for the day when the police-car sirens pulled me away from the typewriter because this

time they came to full crescendo and their scream bit off directly
below my windows. I went to look out. From Madison Avenue
down to Park the street was filling with police cars. The two en-
trances to the apartment house opposite, 57 East Eighty-eighth
Street, were blue with policemen. A stream of heavy-shouldered
men, easily recognizable as plainclothes detectives, was flowing into
the building. Within a few minutes newspaper reporters and television news crews appeared at the Park Avenue Corner. The police
for a time were holding them there.

An ambulance rolled in. The attendants unloaded their stretcher
and hurried into the building. Then they were quickly out again
and reloading the still empty stretcher. The reporters were shouting questions. Through the sealed windows of my air-conditioned
room I couldn't hear them. For me it was a scene in mime. One of
the ambulance men, just before he climbed into the ambulance to
drive away, held up two fingers—two people and both beyond anything a hospital could do for them.

I left the windows long enough to phone down to the lobby and
ask the doorman what he knew.

"Two girls murdered over there," Pat Farley told me.

Back at the windows I saw something that touched me more
closely than had the merely geographical proximity. A couple
came out of the building. They were middle-aged. Well dressed,
they walked with painfully sustained dignity. Hovering about them
solicitously, detectives escorted them to a police car and drove
them away. Though I couldn't place the recognition, the man was
someone I knew. There was something about him that was familiar and it was more than the familiarity that might have come from
seeing him around the neighborhood.

Soon afterward the news reports started coming over. Two
young women, who with a third shared apartment 3C at 57 East
Eighty-eighth Street, had been murdered. The two victims were
Janice Wylie, twenty-one, and Emily Hoffert, twenty-three. The
bodies, horribly mutilated and lying in a pool of blood, had been
found by Max Wylie, father of one of the victims. Max Wylie was
identified as an advertising man, editor, and author and as the
brother of the best-selling novelist, Philip Wylie.

The report pinned down my recognition. I had known Max
Wylie some twenty-five years before when we had met for several

discussions of radio dramatic scripts. He was a gentleman, a man of taste and sensitivity. Before I had ever known him, I had met Philip Wylie at a few parties. I had enjoyed the company of both brothers.

For big-city newspapers homicides are not invariably news stories. When a report of one comes to a New York newspaper City Desk, it is tested for newsworthiness. The tests are three. Are the circumstances sufficiently lurid to make a good story? Is any prominent name involved? Is it a good address? Unless the murder meets at least one of these tests, it rates only a brief paragraph on an inner page if it is carried at all. The Wylie-Hoffert murders drew banner Page One headlines in all the papers.

Lurid circumstances? The room where the bodies were found had two beds in it. The bed nearer the door was piled with luggage but looked otherwise undisturbed. The bedclothes of the second bed were soaked with blood. The bodies of the two victims were on the floor between the blood-soaked bed and the window. Janice Wylie's body was nude. Emily Hoffert's was fully clothed. There was a stab wound in Janice Wylie's chest. Her thighs were covered with blood and there was much blood on her chest, neck, and face. Her abdomen had been slashed open and her intestines revealed. There was blood on Emily Hoffert's green skirt and the upper part of her body was soaked with blood. There were several gaping wounds in her neck.

Both girls were tied at wrists and ankles with strips of material from a white sheet. Then the bodies had been bound together at the forearms and waist with strips of material from a chenille bedspread. Janice Wylie's body showed evidence of having been sodomized. Emily Hoffert's body showed no evidence of sexual assault. The circumstances were lurid enough.

Prominent names? Janice Wylie's father was well known in writing circles and in the worlds of broadcasting and advertising. Her uncle Philip's fame was wider spread. Emily Hoffert was the daughter of a prominent Minneapolis surgeon. After Smith College Emily had done a year of graduate work at Tufts University in preparation for teaching. The third occupant of the apartment was Patricia Tolles, daughter of the Dean of Hamilton College. Janice and Patricia had known each other through their fathers, who had been classmates at Hamilton. Patricia and Emily had been room-mates at Smith. The girls passed the prominent-name test.

A good address? East Eighty-eighth Street is in that part of town the newspapers call "the fashionable upper East Side." In an earlier day the phrase had been "the silk-stocking district," but by 1963 the women of the neighborhood had long since been going stemmed in nylon. In actuality not all of the area was fashionable. From Central Park to Park Avenue the two blocks of Eighty-eighth were lined with a few splendid town houses, survivors of an earlier era, and with luxury apartment buildings.

East of Park Avenue the street was mixed. There many of the old tenements, built to house Irish and German immigrant la-borers, still survived with some of their old tenants still in resi-dence. These patches of older housing, however, had been shrink-ing as here and there clumps of tenements were torn down and replaced by luxury apartment towers. At the eastern end of the street, where it approached Gracie Mansion, official residence of New York's mayors, conspicuous affluence again was solid.

Fifty-seven East, however, lay west of Park Avenue. In an area of apartment buildings cooperatively owned by their tenants, it was an exception. It was a rental building and rent-controlled. It had a doorman, but otherwise it was less heavily staffed than its neighbors. Just on its location between Madison and Park ave-nues, however, the City Desks identified it as a good address.

Since the story generated drama and developed peculiar twists, there was not the customary fade-out after the first sensation. It held the headlines at least until November, when the assassination of President John Kennedy provided a story of murder that had even more prominent names and an even better address. For a time the assassination pushed Wylie-Hoffert off Page One, but the Wylie-Hoffert story not only did not die. It made its Page One comeback.

The apartment had two bedrooms. The room in which the bod-ies were found had been Emily Hoffert's. The other bedroom had been shared by Janice Wylie and Patricia Tolles. Patricia worked as a researcher in the Time-Life book division and she had to be at work—twenty minutes away by subway—at ten.

Patricia and Janice had moved into the apartment at the begin-ning of the month. Emily had joined them there, but finding life in the apartment too lively for her taste, Emily had been in the process of moving to other quarters. On that August 28 morning Patricia had risen early to ready herself for going to work. She had been careful not to wake Janice.

She was in the bathroom when the phone rang. Janice picked it up. It was someone at *Newsweek,* where Janice worked. Her normal hours at the office were from ten to six. She was asked if she would mind working from eleven to seven that day. She didn't mind. She was glad of the extra sleeping time.

Janice had been planning to go to Washington for the Civil Rights March and for that she would have been early up and out, but the night before her father had persuaded her not to go. Max Wylie distrusted crowds.

Patricia and Emily had breakfast together in the kitchen. After breakfast Patricia opened the service door of the apartment and set the garbage out on the service landing for collection. Afterward she was certain that she had let the door slam shut to lock it automatically and then double-locked it by turning the bolt.

Patricia Tolles went off to work. Emily Hoffert had errands to do. Needing for her moving a car larger than her small Fiat, she had borrowed a Dodge from a friend in Riverdale. That morning she drove up to Riverdale to return the Dodge and pick up her own car. She arrived in Riverdale shortly before ten, having taken about a half hour for the drive. As her friend remembered it, she started back downtown in her own car between ten forty-five and eleven. It could be assumed that she would have reached Eighty-eighth Street by eleven-thirty.

Eleven o'clock came and went and Janice Wylie hadn't appeared for work. At two-thirty the *Newsweek* office began calling the apartment. When there was no answer to repeated calls, they called Mrs. Wylie. Janice's mother had no ideas, but Janice's sister Pamela suggested that Janice had probably changed her mind again and had gone on the march in Washington.

Mrs. Wylie called Patricia at Time-Life. She thought that if Janice had gone to Washington, she would probably have left a note in the apartment. She asked Patricia to look for a note when she got home from work and to call her. Patricia, however, knew that Janice had promised to be at *Newsweek* at eleven. She made several calls, trying to locate Janice, but nobody knew anything. It seemed peculiar but Patricia set it down to confusion bred of some undelivered message. She stayed on her job till her six o'clock quitting time.

She let herself into the apartment by the foyer door. The door of the foyer closet stood open and a man's tan raincoat she didn't recognize lay on the floor, half in the closet and half out. The mail, usually pushed under the front door, was off the floor and stacked on the foyer table. As she moved on into the apartment, she glanced through the glass door of the dinette into the kitchen. She saw the back service door she had bolted that morning. It was open about two feet. At the end of the hall that led to the bedrooms she saw light. The lights were on in the bedroom she and Janice shared.

She went into the bedroom and found wild disorder. Her things and Janice's things were strewn all over the room. The mattress of Janice's bed was bare. The sheets had been stripped off it. Frightened and enraged, she noticed that the light was on in the bathroom opposite her bedroom. In the bathroom she saw a crumpled bedsheet on the floor, a bloodstained strip of white sheeting near the washstand, and on the washstand a carving knife out of the kitchen. The knife had blood on it.

She called the police. She reported to them that she had found her apartment in a disordered mess and that her roommate was not to be found. Next she called Janice's parents. They lived nearby on Eighty-sixth Street. Max Wylie told her not to touch anything. He rushed over to the apartment with Mrs. Wylie trailing after him. When the police arrived, Janice Wylie's father had already found the bodies.

Police investigation turned up other details. Two carving knives were found in the bedroom with the tips of both blades broken off. On the floor was one blade tip under Emily Hoffert's legs. Near the bodies was an open jar containing Noxzema. The jar cover was a few feet away as were the neck of a broken soft-drink bottle and a Gillette blue blade. In an open bureau drawer there was a metal razor-blade container for blades like the one found on the floor. On a bedside table was a clock radio. Its cord had been pulled from the socket. The clock had stopped at 10:37 and twenty seconds. On Emily's blood-soaked bed they found the tip of the second broken knife and slivers of soda-bottle glass.

The detectives checked through the building. There was a door from the service stairway to the building lobby. It could not be opened from the lobby side. One of the detectives experimented with the door. He found that it invariably locked on swinging shut. No matter how gently he eased the door closed, the lock clicked to. He was convinced that there could have been no access to the service stairs through the lobby.

The building superintendent insisted that no one could have come in from the street by the building's service entrance and gone upstairs without being challenged. A detective slipped out of the apartment, left the building, reentered by the service entrance, crossed the basement to the push-button service elevator, rode up to the third floor, and reentered apartment 3C. He'd gone all the way unseen.

It was assumed that Janice Wylie had been the first victim and that Emily Hoffert, returning from Riverdale, had stopped at the apartment to pick up the few remaining things still to be moved to her new apartment. She had walked in on the killer and he had silenced her.

The police checked out the "good address." They rounded up known sexual deviates and people in the neighborhood who had criminal records. They followed as a lead every name they found in Janice Wylie's address book.

The building porter had collected garbage in midmorning and midafternoon. In the afternoon there had been no garbage outside the door of 3C but, while picking up outside the door to 3B, he heard noises in the kitchen of 3C, shuffling feet, and running water. He remembered that the door had been slightly ajar but not enough so that he could see in. He placed the time between three and three-thirty, but he also admitted that he'd had a few beers in the afternoon. He said a few beers wouldn't make him drunk.

A Greek exchange student living in 3D said she had seen an "angel-faced" stranger in the elevator that morning. For months afterward the police paraded suspects before her. None was the man she had seen.

The police talked with a couple that had been employed on the service staff of the building for a three-year period that had ended two years before the killings. The woman spoke of a man who had been a porter there and said that he had tried to molest her young daughter. The police located the man. He retaliated with the charge that the woman was a drug pusher and he named a man who had been buying drugs from her.

The detectives located the buyer. Willing to talk, he said that the woman was his connection and that she had run a "shooting gallery" in the basement of the "good address." The files furnished verification. The woman had been arrested with three others in 1958 in a narcotics raid in the basement of 57 East Eighty-eighth Street. In 1961, while she and her husband were still employed there, two men had been arrested in the basement on a charge of possession of heroin. The police checked all these people out and all were cleared.

In the blocks to the east and the north of the "good address" there was no paucity of men with criminal records. Among others the police picked up Ricky Robles. He had a record. He lived on East Ninety-third Street. He was a handsome twenty-year-old. He could have been called "angel-faced." He had once had a thirty-dollar-a-day drug habit, but when the police picked him up less than two weeks after the killings he looked well and healthy. He rolled up his sleeves and showed his arms. There were no needle marks. He said he was off narcotics.

At seventeen he had been arrested on a charge of receiving stolen goods and he was said to have admitted to about one hundred burglaries and robberies, some of them with violence. In one case he was accused of striking a woman robbery victim with the butt of his pistol. Faced with a charge of assault and robbery he had pleaded guilty to the lesser charge of assault second degree. Sentenced to Elmira Penitentiary, he had been there for more than three years before he was released on parole June 3, 1963. He had been a model prisoner and while at Elmira he had earned a high-school diploma. On parole he had a job as a lathe operator and he was given good marks by his enthusiastic employer and fellow workers. He was living with his family.

The last week in August he had been on vacation. He remembered wryly that his mother, who was superintendent of the tenement in which they lived, had taken advantage of his vacation to enlist him for a heavy cleaning of the building. The morning of the twenty-eighth he had been scrubbing the stairs. In the afternoon he had helped a friend of his mother's paint her apartment. His mother backed his alibi and a flock of neighborhood women offered corroboration. Two sets of unidentified fingerprints had been found in the apartment. His did not match. There was no reason to hold him.

There was a professional burglar who lived in the neighborhood. A few months after the girls were killed he entered an apartment on East Eightieth Street. He ransacked it, but he took nothing. The apartment belonged to two young women and they found that he had left his picture for them and attached to it a note inviting them to a swinging party he was giving that night. Since he left his telephone number, the police were able to go to the swinging party. When they questioned the swinging burglar, he said, "Two single girls. What's the harm in trying?"

They could find no reason to hold him for the Wylie-Hoffert murders.

Janice Wylie had been a party girl with a taste for people she considered interesting. In many cases what she had found interesting the detectives found peculiar. *Newsweek* offered a $10,000 reward for information leading to the apprehension of the killer. If cranks all over the country had been belaboring the police with tips before that, the reward offer did nothing to diminish the flood.

Max Wylie and Janice's sister Pamela pointed out a few names in the address book they thought might be suspect. The police checked them out and came up with nothing. The detectives, however, were hooked on the address book.

A check on one youth revealed that from age sixteen to twenty-two he'd had a career of robbing and assaulting women and of attempted rape. When he was twenty-one and on parole from Elmira, he had dated Janice Wylie, then fifteen. Ignorant of his record, the Wylies had considered him a fine young man from a distinguished family.

It seemed a most promising lead, but the man was employed and records showed that he had been at work throughout the day on August 28. His fingerprints didn't match.

There were other men with histories of violence. There were also women. The police explored the possibility of a lesbian killer. Detectives watched one woman who paraded the streets of Greenwich Village with two little ones in a baby carriage, one in pink baby clothes and one in blue. When one of the detectives made a close approach and one of the little ones reached out for him, he was startled by a brown and hairy paw. The lady amused herself by parading with two tiny monkeys, enjoying the consternation of the motherly types who would lean into the carriage and coo.

There was even a touch of the supernatural. It was introduced not by the detectives but by the City Editor of the *New York Journal-American*. The editor found a dying mystic called Florence Psyche. Accompanied by one of his reporters, he took Max Wylie to see her on her deathbed.

Not without some prompting, she visualized the murder scene and said the killer changed his clothes in the basement, bundled up the bloodstained clothes, took them to a nearby church, and hid them in the belfry. She said they would find the bloodstained clothes in the belfry and that she saw a connection between the killer and a forest—big trees.

The reporter went to the Church of St. Thomas More at 65 East Eighty-ninth Street. He was permitted to go up to the belfry. He found only a small room thick with undisturbed dust.

In the early hours of April 14, 1964, Minnie Edmonds, a black day-worker was knifed to death in a Brownsville street. Her body was found with her dress pulled up. Her panties were found under the body. Minnie Edmonds was not a prominent name. The killing was savage but for Brownsville it was hardly extraordinary. Brownsville has never been a good address. At its best it had been a Brooklyn ghetto and it had become a hopelessly deteriorated ghetto. By every index used to measure such things it was in the forefront of the competition for the distinction of being Greater New York's worst neighborhood.

The Edmonds murder, therefore, received scant attention. Nine days later, again in the early hours of the morning and only a block from where the Edmonds body had been found, Mrs. Elba Borrero, a nurse on her way home from night duty, was attacked by a young black who forced her into an alley and threatened to rape and kill her. She screamed. A patrolman came running and her attacker fled, leaving Mrs. Borrero unnerved but uninjured. The officer chased the fugitive two blocks before he lost him. During the chase the policeman fired four shots. The shots brought more police. The neighborhood was searched with no success. Mrs. Borrero furnished a description of the man, a pencil he had

held against her throat in pretense that it was a knife, and a button
she had torn from his coat.

At the beginning of daylight the officer returned to the area to
look for a possible trail of blood. He thought he might have hit the
fugitive with one of his shots. He found no blood but he did come
on a loitering black youth. Under questioning, the young man,
who was soft-spoken and given to mumbling, gave his name and
said he was waiting for his brother. They were going to go to work
in a neighboring plant.

The patrolman was satisfied, but then the young man volunteered a mention of the police chase earlier in the night, asking
what that was all about. He said he had seen the chase and had
seen the man take cover in a house on Amboy Street. At his own
suggestion he guided the policeman to the tenement. Shortly thereafter three young men came by and the youth joined them. He said
he had to go to work.

When the word reached the precinct, the detectives assigned to
the Edmonds case were interested. The patrolman gave them the
name, George Whitman. The detectives went to the plant where
George Whitman was supposed to be working. There was no
George Whitman on the payroll. Why had he lied?

The next morning the patrolman and one of the detectives were
on the street corner where the young man had been loitering the
day before. He came by and they picked him up. Asked if he was
the man who had spoken to the police officer the day before, he
said he was. Asked for his name, he gave it and this time he produced his driver's license. The name was George Whitmore, Jr.

He had lied about his name and he had lied about the place he
worked. The detective told him to come along and he went eagerly. Later he was to say that he had given his right name to the
patrolman. It was not impossible. A mumbled Whitmore might
easily have been heard as Whitman. The other lie he was also able
to explain away. He had been on his way to the plant to take a job
but he had neglected to bring along his Social Security card and
without it he hadn't been taken on.

Turned away from the plant, he had gone to his girl's house.
Since he had been ashamed to admit that he had been so footling
and had missed his chance at employment, he had, both with his
girl and with his family, built a fantasy on his encounter with the

policeman. He'd been telling them that he had spent the time at the police station going through the mugshot files, trying to identify the man he had seen.

When he was taken to the police station, he went in the expectation that his dream of importance was coming true. He was going to be asked to identify the man he had seen in flight from the police. At the station house, however, he was just kept waiting. There were no books of pictures for him to look at.

Mrs. Borrero was brought to the station house. She was not shown a lineup. Instead she was given a view of Whitmore through a peephole in a door. She was trembling and in her agitation she pushed the door slightly ajar. She identified Whitmore and then asked to hear his voice. The detective gave Whitmore the words the attacker had used.

"Lady, I'm going to rape you. Lady, I'm going to kill you."

Mrs. Borrero went into hysterics. It took time to calm her, but then there was a confrontation. Through the slightly open door Whitmore had heard her identify him and he tried to convince her that she was making a mistake. She held her ground.

George Whitmore, Jr., was placed under arrest. His pockets were emptied and their contents spread on a table. The detective who made the arrest called a second detective with whom he had been working on the Edmonds case and there was a half-hour's wait until the second man arrived. Whitmore claimed that during this half hour the detective and the patrolman beat him. The police officers denied it. Since his body was unmarked and since immediately after this alleged beating he ate a meal which he could have been in no condition to keep down after such a pummeling as he described, his claim was not believed.

The detective who made the arrest was a formidable-looking man. He had at one time been a semiprofessional football player. The partner he called in was a man of kindly and gentle manner. The kindly one began by asking Whitmore if he was hungry. He ordered rolls and coffee and the two detectives and the patrolman ate with Whitmore. The kindly one questioned Whitmore about his family and his life. He was easy and friendly as though he were taking a fatherly interest in the boy. Whitmore told him that no one had ever spoken to him so nicely in his life. His father had never spoken to him like that.

The detective told the boy that he didn't have to talk to him if he didn't want to. He didn't tell him that the alternative would be to talk to his formidable and unsympathetic partner, but it is the accepted technique of this sort of two-man questioning to set up the implication.

Mrs. Borrero had identified him. He was in trouble. They wouldn't be able to help him unless he told them the truth. Gently the detective drew from George an admission that he had been Mrs. Borrero's attacker.

Armed with that admission, the two detectives went to work on the Edmonds killing. With much patient leading they obtained from him a confession to the Edmonds homicide. By that time it was well into the afternoon. He had been in custody for more than seven hours and under questioning for most of that time.

Then the major event began. Other detectives had arrived at the station house and among them Detective Edward Bulger. During the time when running down all the Wylie-Hoffert leads had required the services of detectives pulled in from all parts of the city Detective Bulger for a time had been assigned to Wylie-Hoffert. In the Eighty-eighth Street apartment he had found something everyone else had overlooked, a paper wrapper from a razor blade on the bathroom floor. Nobody but Bulger had been impressed with his find, since the razor blade discovered near the bodies was of a type that came out of a metal container and not out of a paper wrapper. Bulger's interrogation methods, furthermore, had impressed his superiors over in Manhattan as being too crude. He had been sent back to Brooklyn.

Now, looking idly at the stuff that had been taken from Whitmore's pockets, he fastened on a snapshot picture. It was a picture of a white girl with blonde hair. She was sitting on the back of a convertible in what appeared to be a rural setting. To Detective Bulger's eye it was a picture of Janice Wylie. Bulger came into the questioning and Bulger considered himself to be possessed of special knowledge in the process of questioning blacks. He told other detectives that by watching a black's stomach he knew when a black was lying. When a black lied, his stomach went in and out.

They began by questioning Whitmore about where he'd gotten the picture. He said he picked it up off a garbage dump. That seemed too absurd. Trying for an answer that would satisfy them,

he said his girl gave it to him. After all, they couldn't help him unless he told them what they wanted to hear. When that didn't go
down well and they appeared to want him to say he had stolen it,
he obliged them by saying he had stolen it from the house of his
girl down in Wildwood, New Jersey. Wildwood is a shore-resort
town where Whitmore had lived most of his life. Written on the
back of the picture there was a phone number and "To George
from Louise."

Asked about the phone number, he said it was his girl's number.
A detective dialed it and a woman came on and said, "Cape May
Court House." The detective hung up and told Whitmore he had
been caught in another lie. The number was the number of a public building. Actually it was the number of Louise's private home
in the town of Cape May Court House.

Up to this point nothing had been said about the girls on East
Eighty-eighth Street. The questioning was directed toward drawing
from him an admission that he had stolen the picture from Apartment 3C at 57 East Eighty-eighth Street, Manhattan. Working at
satisfying the gentle type who spoke to him so nicely, Whitmore
was groping for what they wanted to hear and he said he had
stolen it from the apartment. At that point they brought the girls
into the questioning and Whitmore tried to back off.

He was urged to tell the truth. The detectives weren't mad at
him. Nobody was mad at him. All he had to do was tell them the
truth. Nobody told him the girls were dead. One of the detectives
told him that he had just spoken to the girls on the telephone. The
girls were all right and they weren't mad at him. That calmed him.

The detectives had him in the apartment. It was now a matter
of filling in the details. How did he get to Eighty-eighth Street?
Whitmore knew only one place in Manhattan, the bus terminal on
West Forty-first Street. He had come and gone between Wildwood
and New York by bus and between Brownsville and the bus terminal by subway.

He said he had gone by subway to Forty-second Street. The op-
tometrist who fitted him to eyeglasses said that without such cor-
rection he was myopic to an extent the eye man characterized as
"economic blindness." Whitmore had broken his glasses in a pickup basketball game before August 28 and people who knew him

were convinced that he couldn't have managed the subway without them. He couldn't read the signs.

From Forty-second Street the confession had him just walking along aimlessly and looking in store windows. He walked across to Park Avenue and up Park to Eighty-eighth Street. The route posed problems. It is impossible to turn directly into upper Park Avenue from Forty-second Street. Grand Central Station lies athwart the avenue and it is necessary to skirt the terminal, the Pan Am Building, and the Grand Central Building to come around into upper Park Avenue.

It took prompting to straighten that out. Then there was a problem of getting him into the building. He said he went into the building to go to the roof to look around from up there. Since 57 East was not as tall as any of the surrounding buildings, its roof would have been a peculiar choice but then, without his glasses, a distant view would have been no good to him. The detectives refrained from going into any of that. With patient guidance they succeeded in having him put himself in apartment 3C. On his way to the roof he had seen the kitchen door open and had gone in. When they asked him about picking up empty soft-drink bottles in the kitchen, he jumped at that. If all he was to be accused of there was the theft of a few empty bottles, why not go along with them on that?

It went on and on. With Detective Bulger's assistance, Whitmore, who liked to draw, even drew a floor plan of the apartment.

By six-thirty, when the jubilant Brooklyn detectives finally summoned the Manhattan detectives who had been working on the Wylie-Hoffert case, they were armed with a complete statement. The Manhattan detectives, nevertheless, were skeptical. The *Journal-American* was not. Someone in the precinct station house phoned the news of the confession to the *Journal-American,* giving the paper a scoop. While the rest of the press employed the customary safeguards—"alleged," "the police say"—the *Journal-American* offered no such qualifications. They handled the story as a drama in which Detective Bulger was given the status of the most brilliant of fictional detectives.

The Manhattan detectives drew up a long list of points where the confession was at odds with the hard evidence. For example, the confession had Whitmore leaving Brownsville at ten, riding the subway to Forty-second Street, finding his way to Park Avenue, window shopping up Park (where shop windows are few and for the greater part of the route totally nonexistent), strolling into Eighty-eighth Street, going into the lobby of 57 East in the momentary absence of the doorman, finding his way to the service stairs (through the door that couldn't be opened from the lobby side?), starting up to the roof, but going into 3C instead when he saw its service door ajar. The clock in the murder room, however, had been stopped at 10:37 and twenty seconds. The subway ride from Brownsville to Forty-second Street would alone have taken virtually all of that time.

While the Manhattan detectives went off to show the Wylies the snapshot which to the Manhattan men didn't seem a likeness of Janice Wylie, the Brooklyn detectives worked with Whitmore at bringing his confession into better alignment with the known facts. What with all this police questioning and the hours during which the Assistant DA was taking down Whitmore's formal statement, it was after four in the morning before George Whitmore's confessional marathon came to an end.

When the picture was shown to Max Wylie, he was uncertain but he thought it was not a picture of Janice. Mrs. Wylie was more definite. Without hesitation she said the girl in the photograph was not her daughter.

The detectives took the snapshot down to Wildwood where they located the girl in the picture. She had never seen the snapshot but she remembered the occasion. She had been out on a picnic double date and the other girl had been snapping pictures. The detectives located the other girl. She recognized the photograph. She had moved since and the picture had gone out with the trash at the time of her moving. Neither girl had ever known George Whitmore.

No announcement was made of this discovery. Only later when Whitmore's lawyer went to Wildwood and duplicated the search did the facts about the picture come out. At that time the girl in the picture became another victim of the case. Rumor had it that she had known George and had been his girl. Once when she was out marketing, a woman spat at her.

Meanwhile George Whitmore, under indictment in the Borrero attack, the Edmonds killing, and the Wylie-Hoffert murders, was in detention. He was six months in the Bellevue Hospital prison ward undergoing psychiatric examination. When his lawyer confronted him with what he had learned about the picture, Whitmore explained that he had found it on the garbage dump, had written "To George from Louise" on the back of it, and had carried it around in an effort to convince the other boys that he had a beautiful girl.

When he had been questioned about where he had been on August 28, his first answer had been "dancing at the Savoy," a reply that had seemed too patently absurd for any consideration. His lawyer in the course of his Wildwood researches found a hotel where Whitmore had been in the habit of hanging out because it was frequented by black entertainers who came to the resort town to perform. Adjacent to the hotel was a bar called The Savoy and witnesses remembered being there with Whitmore watching the Civil Rights March on TV. Blacks remembered where they had been and what they had been doing on that great day.

The Wylie-Hoffert indictment, nevertheless, held. There was the confession. In the press Whitmore had been tried and found guilty, but then there was a complication. On October 3, 1964, Nathan Delaney, a narcotics addict with a record of two felony convictions, was arrested in the Spanish-Harlem killing of a drug pusher. He volunteered to the detectives who arrested him that they had the wrong man in the Wylie-Hoffert killings. If convicted, Delaney, as a third-time felon, would be faced with a life sentence. He said that Richard Robles, a friend of his, had come to his apartment about noon on August 28, 1963. He said his friend's clothes had been spattered with blood and that Robles told him that he had "just iced two girls."

With the Whitmore confession grown wobbly, Robles looked the likelier suspect. He lived in the neighborhood of the murder apartment. Unlike most addicts, he had a record of robbery with violence and, since he was a neighborhood addict, there was a good likelihood that he had known 57 East Eighty-eighth Street from the days when its basement had been a narcotics source and a shooting gallery. That was enough for a beginning. There was no need to include the peculiar thought that Florence Psyche might have been divining bilingually when she talked about a forest and big trees. Robles is Spanish for oak.

Delaney's wife was brought in and she corroborated her husband's story. Delaney was not prosecuted for the Spanish-Harlem killing. Although on his story he had concealed his knowledge of the crime for more than a year, he was not charged as an accessory in the Wylie-Hoffert murders, and he later received suspended sentences on two narcotics charges.

Robles was picked up and confronted with Delaney in the District Attorney's office. He cried frame and called Delaney a liar. The police didn't have enough to hold him.

Although there were rumors of a new suspect in the Wylie-Hoffert case, Whitmore remained under the Wylie-Hoffert indictment and on November 11, 1964, was brought to trial in Brooklyn on the Borrero assault charges. Mrs. Borrero stoutly insisted on her identification of George Whitmore. She had put in for the $10,000 *Newsweek* award. No mention of Wylie-Hoffert was permitted at the trial and the button she had torn from her attacker's coat was not offered in evidence, although it had been to the FBI laboratory for examination along with Whitmore's coat. The coat alone was offered.

Whitmore's claim that he had been beaten by the arresting detective and the patrolman did come up. In cross-examination the prosecutor asked him how many times the 200-pound ex-football-player detective had punched him in the stomach. When Whitmore said he didn't know, the prosecutor suggested a figure. Fifty times? Whitmore accepted the figure. Although the obvious impossibility of that damaged his credibility in the eyes of the jury, it was a public exhibition of Whitmore's incurable delusion that, by giving his tormentors the answers they obviously wanted from him, he could win them over to helping him.

The FBI report on the button and the coat had indicated that there was no evidence that the button had come off the coat. It didn't match the other buttons on the coat and the threads attached to the button didn't match the threads from a torn-off button still attached to the coat. This FBI report had not been given to the defense and the prosecuting attorney in his summation told the jury that the button matched the coat.

"Haven't we nailed George Whitmore right on the button?" he said.

Whitmore was convicted. The conviction was subsequently

thrown out when a juror revealed that during the jury deliberations there had been reference made to the Wylie-Hoffert indictment and that there had also been comments that indicated racial prejudice. Subsequently, still standing under the shadow of the Wylie-Hoffert indictment, Whitmore stood trial for the Edmonds murder. The jury couldn't reach an agreement. The judge was forced to declare a mistrial.

Four days after that, when the New York District Attorney had been accused by the Civil Liberties Union of keeping the Wylie-Hoffert indictment in force after the police had cleared Whitmore and of doing it as a political favor for his fellow prosecutor in Brooklyn, the Wylie-Hoffert indictment against Whitmore was finally dismissed. He stood two further trials on the Borrero charges and both times was found guilty because Mrs. Borrero stood firm on her identification.

On the Edmonds murder he could not be brought to trial again because the Supreme Court's *Miranda* decision had intervened. Since there was no Edmonds evidence apart from Whitmore's confession and under *Miranda* the confession could not be used against him, there was no ground left for prosecution there. On Borrero a higher court brought into question the validity of the peephole identification, and in January 1968 Whitmore came out on bail, having by that time served thirty-eight months, only a couple months short of the time that would make him eligible for parole. Interest in prosecuting him further on the Borrero charges was by then less keen than it had been.

Meanwhile in Manhattan, after the confrontation with Delaney, Robles had been watched and followed. Late in October of 1964 he attended a party where he got high on goofballs. Overdosed, he collapsed and was nine days in the hospital. During those nine days the police bugged the Delaney apartment. The Delaneys were enlisted in an attempt to draw from their old friend, Ricky, damaging admissions to be picked up on tape. Delaney himself was wired for sound. A portable tape recorder was fastened to his chest. The Delaneys had a plentiful supply of cheap heroin. Robles believed that the police were supplying the Delaneys. There's never been any proof of that, but it does remain that the Delaneys were well supplied and at a cost well below the street price.

Even though Robles knew that his old friends had accused him of the Wylie-Hoffert murders, he sought out the Delaneys as soon as he was out of the hospital. It may have been that he hoped to learn from them exactly what they were telling the police. What is certain, however, is that he was back on heroin and they were his generous suppliers.

Through December and January Robles was a frequent visitor in the Delaneys' bugged apartment. The tapes recorded drugged conversations in which the three seemed to be cooperating in a scheme under which the Delaneys would feed the police enough information against Robles to insure Delaney's immunity from prosecution for the Spanish-Harlem murder but which in some way would not be enough to convict Robles in the Wylie-Hoffert killings.

Delaney brought up details of the murders which he said the police had fed him and among them they fitted the details into the story. The three of them giggled over the way they would make a farce of the trial.

On January 26, 1965, Richard Robles was placed under arrest. Although he asked for his lawyer, the request was ignored while he was taken to the Delaney apartment and shown the microphones and then questioned for four hours. This whole procedure was taped. Since his requests for his lawyer were on the tape, any admissions the police and the prosecutors might have had from him would not have been admissible as evidence. It can only be conjectured that the police, having been burned on Whitmore, this time wanted to make absolutely certain that they had the right man.

The first his lawyer learned that his client had been arrested was when he had the word from a newspaper reporter. He hurried to Robles and had a half hour with him. The police contend that after that Robles made a full confession to them. Robles and his lawyer deny it.

He went to trial in the fall of the year. As the trial progressed, he kept assuring his lawyer that his friend, Nathan Delaney, would take the stand and say the magic words that would turn the trial into a farce. Nathan Delaney took the stand but he didn't say the magic words. Ricky Robles was convicted and sentenced to life imprisonment.

It was life imprisonment and not the electric chair, because in May of 1965, the New York State Legislature abolished the death penalty except in cases of the murder of a police officer or a prison guard. Bills to this effect had been introduced every year for seventeen years and for seventeen years they had not carried. In May 1965 the State Senate voted 47 to 9 for abolition. The composition of the Senate hadn't changed that much. The Senators made no secret of the fact that Whitmore had changed them.

In the *Miranda* decision the Supreme Court had taken into consideration cases where confessions had been obtained by beating and torture, but there, too, the history of the Whitmore confession weighed in the decision.

People have remarked to me again and again on how extraordinary it was that, even as I was writing a detective story, a great detective story was simultaneously happening all but on my window ledge. The Wylie-Hoffert case, however, could not have been more unlike a detective story. No satisfactory work of detective fiction can depend on the confession of the accused or on damaging admissions made by the accused. Detective fiction requires the assembling of hard evidence into a logical proof. In the case against George Whitmore, Jr., every piece of hard evidence went only to destroy Whitmore's confession and the case against Whitmore would have collapsed almost immediately if, when hard evidence was uncovered, the police and the prosecutors had not concealed it.

If in the case built against Richard Robles hard evidence was presented, it was only because it appeared on the tapes as fed to Robles in those drugged plottings of the "farce."

Furthermore there are the loose ends. If Robles arrived at the Delaney apartment at noon fresh from icing the two girls, who was shuffling around the kitchen and running water when the porter picked up 3B's garbage between three and three-thirty?

Also in the story presented to the jury Robles entered the apartment by climbing out of the window from the service-stairs landing and stretching across to the open kitchen window of apartment 3C, a long and hazardous reach to a window he couldn't see. He would have been doing it with no way of knowing whether he was going to find the kitchen window open or shut. This might well have been thought up as a feat so incredible that it might be one of the items calculated to turn the trial into a farce. Evidently it didn't worry the jury. In a detective story it would worry any alert reader.

Dozens of suspects had been turned loose because their finger-prints didn't match either of the unidentified sets in the apartment. In the case of the Whitmore confession all thought of the finger-prints was dropped. In the case against Robles it was argued that the experienced burglar had obliterated his prints or had been careful to wear gloves.

The prosecution was so far satisfied to rely wholly on the drugged maunderings of the tapes that they never attempted to confront Robles with a witness who might have placed him in the building on that August-28 morning. The exchange student who had seen an "angel-faced" stranger in the elevator had by the time of the Robles arrest left the country. She was not flown back to New York to look at this prime suspect even though he was young and handsome and might have seemed "angel-faced" to her. She was not even shown a picture of Robles.

There was also the question of the broken carving-knife blades. The huskiest detectives worked on such carving knives trying to break them as the knives at the murder scene had been broken. None of them succeeded. How did Ricky Robles, who was far less strong, break the blades?

Any detective story worthy of the name creates a closed causal nexus. The Wylie-Hoffert case is a fragment torn out of the chaos of the actual world.

AARON MARC STEIN is better known, both as author and as detective, under the alias "George Bagby."

The Real Detectives

Hillary Waugh

SOME YEARS AGO, an arrangement was made for Patrick Murphy, then Police Commissioner of New York City, and officers of the Mystery Writers of America to meet together at a press conference for the purpose of making a startling announcement: mystery writers were going to lend their brains, plotting skill and deductive ability to the police to help them solve crimes!! The press conference was held, the Police Commissioner made remarks thanking MWA for the help, MWA officers made general statements about crime, and the impression left hanging in the air was that mystery writers would soon be meeting with police officials on a regular basis to help them with their problems.

Whose idea was this? It was purportedly spawned by a movie star whose mystery film was at that moment opening in New York theaters. The movie star, however, did not appear in person to promote his great new weapon in the war on crime. He did not want, so his press agent explained, his own presence to intrude upon the merit of the idea.

It did not take great detective ability on the part of the mystery writers present to deduce that this had all been concocted by the

press agent to promote the movie. It can be assumed that the same
conclusion was reached by the Police Commissioner. It was certainly reached by the attending members of the press who asked
pointed questions as to who had rented the suite and made the arrangements—answers to which no one seemed to know.

There is no denying that the idea was at least novel. To the
public at large, it might even seem like a not-implausible suggestion—if the police could be made to hold still for it. Has not the
public been conditioned by stories headlining every uncovered instance of police corruption, scandal, brutality, and false arrest?
Then there was the vicious "Police are pigs" campaign by the
rioters of the sixties. Nor let us forget the story lines of the old B
movies, to wit: "All cops are dumb; only Boston Blackie, Bulldog
Drummond, the Saint, the Falcon, and Philo Vance can solve
crimes." Add to that the soaring crime rate and it would not be
surprising if the conclusion were reached that the police needed
help.

What about mystery writers as Galahads to the rescue? Would
this not be a natural? Mystery writers are the inventors of those
great detectives whose genius is to the police mentality what the elephant is to the flea, whose intellectual prowess unsnarls the most
tangled web and unearths the darkest secret. And are not these
writers even smarter than the detectives they create? They not only
solve their detectives' puzzles, they design them as well, a feat
even more ingenious. Surely, mystery writers are among the clev-
erest of people. They must be far smarter than the average criminal—who has already proven himself more than a match for the
police. If we want to improve crime-solving, would this not be a
good route to take?

That, I am afraid, is as far as I can make myself pursue this
flimflam. I was a participant in the aforementioned press conference as one of the invited mystery writers. I had also spent a lot of
time with the New York Police Department, riding with the Homicide Squad, Manhattan North, and meeting the squad detectives of
Harlem. I, therefore, well knew the other side of the coin and I
had to wonder, as we went through the farce that had been foisted
upon us, "Why does the Commissioner put up with all this nonsense?" His presence gave an import to the proceedings that they

did not warrant, yet he remained pleasant, gracious, and sincere. Part of it might, of course, be argued as public relations: once there, he could hardly walk out in a fit of temper. However, I suspect that another motive was the operative factor, a tactic that professional policemen develop which would best be illustrated by the following.

After I had been with the Homicide Squad long enough to establish rapport with its members, one detective took the trouble to tell me in great detail about an unsolved case he had. It went like this:

A group of models came to New York for a fashion show and were bunked in a clutch of rooms in a hotel. Two girls in one of the rooms heard sounds of a struggle and muted cries from the room adjoining. They went to see if the girl was in trouble. As they knocked on her door, it was opened by a gray-haired man who was breathless and somewhat distraught. He said, "Excuse me, ladies," stepped past them, and went to the elevator. The women went inside and found their fellow-model strangled, her arms and legs taped.

Things went well for the police at first. Investigation showed that the tape could only have been purchased at a certain drugstore in Miami. A description of the gray-haired man fitted an executive in the Organization. More than that, he had just returned from Miami. One of the models, being given a look at this man, definitely identified him as the one leaving the hotel room. The other model wasn't sure.

It looked like an open-and-shut case and the police were about to move in when another piece of evidence showed up. It was a dinner check from a Miami restaurant that the suspect had signed and which bore not only the date, but a time-stamp. And the hour stamped was such that it would have been impossible for the suspect to have caught a plane to New York in time to kill the model at the moment she had been killed.

The only suspect in the case had been cleared; the police had never found anyone else to connect with the crime, and the case lay open on the books, a total mystery.

The detective who told me this story did not do so to give me material for a book. He did not tell it to me because I might mention his name. Nor, certainly, did he tell it because he thought a mystery writer would be more likely than a police detective to fit all the puzzle pieces together in their proper place.

He was telling it to me, instead, because its solution had defied the best thinking of everyone enlisted in its cause. There was no place to go, except to present the evidence to everyone new who came along on the off-chance that somebody, sometime, might come up with an idea, an angle, an answer that hadn't been thought of before. There wasn't any real expectation of this, of course. The attitude wasn't one of hope but, rather, "What is there to lose?"

Which is why, I think, Commissioner Murphy held still for that foolish press conference.

Though I pondered the matter of the murdered model, I did not come up with worthwhile new contributions. I was struck, however, by the difference in approach between the novice (myself) and the pro (the detective). Given that story, my and most people's reaction would be a great reluctance to let go of the gray-haired suspect who fitted the requirements of murderer so perfectly, except for that one pesky restaurant bill. Isn't there some way to get around that tiny, but devastating, stumbling block?

And it is at that precise point that the mystery writer and the professional detective part company. The mystery writer's mind starts clicking in high gear along the lines of how the time-stamp could be discredited: error, deception, anything—and then we have our murderer! The mystery writer focuses on how this could be managed—wherein lies the key to his next book. His fictional detective will retire to quarters for three days and emerge with the explanation of how the time-stamp alibi had been faked. "Take the gray-haired man away, Inspector."

The real detective operates from a different philosophy. Falsified time-stamps which are to serve (if restaurant slips just happen to be checked) as an alibi for a murder fifteen hundred miles away are the stuff of which dreams are made. It's a million-to-one shot and if real detectives expended their energies pursuing such odds, what-ho the crime rate!

Real detectives are too pragmatic to be tempted by such lines of endeavor. The moment that restaurant chit was uncovered, the police kissed off their suspect. How could they combat that piece of evidence in court, even if they wanted to?

What is impressive is that their kiss-off is total. Though I, an outsider, was reluctant to let go of the only suspect, the detective, stuck with an unsolved case, could dismiss him completely. "Think," he said, "how lucky he [the gray-haired man] was that we found that slip. Otherwise he might have been arrested, and even if he were later exonerated, his career could have been ruined." That restaurant check not only convinced the detective that the only suspect was innocent, it concerned him that such a fragile shield separated him from disaster.

We have been discussing, thus far, two traits of real detectives: (1) They will invite ideas and listen to anything, no matter how fanciful. (2) They will dismiss, without a backward glance, their best or only suspect once evidence is found that clears him.

How else do real detectives differ from those of fiction? The ways are many, so let us limit ourselves to a few of the more obvious.

The first and foremost, the most striking distinction between real and make-believe detectives is one that Commissioner Murphy strongly stressed in an article about TV's depiction of policemen and what is wrong with the picture. He pointed out something all policemen do as a matter of course that is completely outside the orientation of the actors, directors, and writers of TV shows, movies, and novels. What real detectives do as the Commissioner put it, is "eyeball" everything.

If one has not been in close association with detectives, it is hard to grasp what this means. It is not as simple as Sherlock Holmes's admonition to Watson, "You see but you do not observe." This was, you will recall, in reference to the good doctor's inability to quote the number of stairs to their lodgings, though he had climbed them a thousand times. Dr. Watson had not noticed the most elementary aspects of his environment, which is true of most of us.

The "eyeballing" problem would not be solved, however, by actors keeping their eyes roving, or by writers having their detectives make periodic comments about their surroundings. The habits that have become ingrained in competent, experienced detectives are lessons in observation that Sherlock Holmes would be hard-pressed to match. A few personal experiences are worth reporting to give a picture:

You get into the back of an unmarked police car. A detective is on either side, another is behind the wheel, and the sergeant is riding beside the driver. It's a friendly, relaxed group, going to get a sandwich perhaps, or to the two-five squad to pick up some files or, in the early days, just to show the visitor around the stamping ground. There is general conversation, there is kidding. It could be any carful of people going someplace with no sense of urgency. Except that, if the visitor in the back seat is paying attention, he will note something unusual about the other occupants in this particular car. Unlike ordinary people, they do not look at each other when they talk. Each is, instead, looking out his window, studying the street. And they don't just look at *things,* they look at *certain* things. And they all see the same things—which are not, generally, the things the rest of us will see if we look out our car windows (which we usually don't).

A couple of illustrations are in order. This first one took place during my early outings with the Homicide Squad, when I was still looking inside the car instead of out. We pulled up in front of a fireplug on Seventy-second Street one evening so that one of the detectives, who hadn't had any supper, could grab a sandwich.

There was general conversation and then, out of the blue, one detective said, "He doesn't know who we are." Another added, "He doesn't know whether to come over or not."

I said, "What? Where?"

"That apprentice cop across the street."

I finally managed to make out the dim, gray-shirted figure on the far side of the heavily traveled thoroughfare. The detectives, however, had instantly spotted him, dutifully tagging cars, and they had detected his uncertainty as to what he should do about the strange black sedan that had stopped in front of the hydrant across the street. He chose to ignore us, but the incident produced dry remarks from the detectives on the inability of foot patrolmen to identify the department's unmarked cars. "Any four-year-old kid in Harlem," one detective said, "—when you turn the corner, it's 'Police car! Police car!' Then you park for a minute and some cop puts a ticket on it."

Then there was a later time, when I was trying to be adept at looking out windows and "eyeballing" everything. I was riding with two detectives up a deserted Madison Avenue late at night and, peer as I might, there was nothing to see. We halted at a stoplight and as I looked around at the nothing, one detective said, "They're sure going at it hot and heavy," and the other said, "Necking up a storm." I said, "Who? Where?" and they replied, "That parked car across the street."

Sure enough, there was a standing car at the other curb. I had seen and ignored it, assuming it to be empty. Now, discovering it to be otherwise, I still couldn't make out what, if anything, was going on inside. But they had. Both of them. They were conversing freely in a language I hadn't even begun to learn.

This is the real difference between the detectives writers create and the police as they actually are. Because a writer has not had a policeman's training and conditioning, the police of his creation do not think, feel, and respond as an actual policeman does. The police of his creation are not tuned in on the wavelength of the actual policeman. They do not speak the language. For the most part, they do not even know the language exists. Thus, while the ersatz policeman of the fiction writer may gain the allegiance of his audience, swallowed if not totally digested, he will not claim the attention of real policemen—who are purported to be notorious nonreaders of mystery stories.

There is an obverse side to the coin. If civilians have trouble making like policemen, the police have equal difficulty making like civilians, which it is sometimes their need to do. One detective summed it up, commenting on the difficulty of infiltrating an area to get information: "You dress up in a white uniform and pedal an ice-cream cart up the street and six blocks ahead of you the word is out, 'Cop coming! Cop coming!' "

I've seen professional detectives mystified by these "makes." They don't know what they're doing wrong, the same way the writers don't know what they're doing wrong, and the fly in the ointment is conditioning. The detective is conditioned one way and the civilian another. The detective looks out of car windows instead of at the person he's talking to. The detective can't help "eyeballing" everything as he pedals his ice-cream cart, and the savvy, streetwise civilians know ice-cream vendors don't do it that way.

What else do detectives do that the average citizen doesn't?

What else sets them apart from the rest of us—including the writers who try to depict them?

Fictional detectives on TV and in novels, even when the utmost realism is being sought, treat the public with a certain deferential consideration, a "Sorry to bother you, ma'am, but would you mind answering a few questions?" attitude. This may be done less in ignorance than in an effort to make policemen sympathetic, to show them as friendly, next-door neighbor types, good to their mothers and kind to animals.

Real policemen may be as good to their mothers and kind to animals as anybody else. At home they may even be friendly, next-door neighbor types. On the job, however, they have a totally different orientation and their behavior is going to follow a markedly different pattern.

Consider a homicide in New York City. The squad detective whose turn it is, "catches" it. Likewise, the homicide detective whose turn it is, shares the responsibility with him and the two work on it together. Of course, where necessary, many other detectives will be engaged in the matter as well, but those two are the ones whose case it is. Needless to say, the goal of all these detectives is the swift apprehension and conviction of the perpetrator. To this end, everything else is secondary.

Thus, if a murder victim is found in an apartment in the middle of the night, or a body is lying at the bottom of a stairwell, the investigating detectives are not going to tap on neighboring doors with a "Sorry to bother you" air, or wait until morning so as not to disturb the slumbers of the other residents. It's, "All right, everybody out!" and they go around banging on apartment doors in turn saying, "Open up. Police!"

There's also a preparatory action taken—at least in New York—which writers should note. Before the detectives bang on any doors, they fasten their gold detective's shields (real gold, as I recall) to their shirt pockets in plain sight to assure frightened apartment dwellers, peering through their peepholes, that they are who they say they are. It is an unwise Gothamite who unlocks his door and lets in whatever fate lies outside just because that fate calls, in authoritative tones, "Open up. Police!" That shield is a necessary assurance that all the noise and commotion are legitimate.

Nor will the detectives, once the neighbors have opened their doors, pussyfoot around with gentle requests for assistance. For one thing, it's bad psychology to invite the *questionee* to gain control over the *questioner*. For another, the detectives cannot waste time on amenities or expend effort fencing. They have quarry to catch and seconds count. Also, who knows but that one of the neighbors has guilty knowledge?

The above arguments are purely academic, however. Pussyfooting, by its nature, can't happen. Detectives, by dint of training, discipline, and experience, are figures of authority. They have been conditioned to move forward where others hold back. They head toward trouble rather than away. They are the ones who have been there before and know what to do. Add to that the "big stick" they all carry in the form of their shield and their gun and it is axiomatic that when the detective appears on the scene, he will take charge and civilians, like it or not, will instinctively defer to him.

Therefore, when a detective fastens his shield to his shirt, knocks on a door, and says "Open up. Police!" he expects to be obeyed, and the expectation will show in the sound of his knock and the tone of his voice. On the other side of the door, the citizen expects to obey. To disobey is to invite suspicion, which is to invite scrutiny, which is worse than obeying. Most people, even those with nothing to hide, like to remain as anonymous as possible vis-à-vis authority.

These are some of the psychological factors at work when detectives investigate a crime and they speed the investigative process by inhibiting needless impediments. Writers of fiction, intent on the detectives' public image, would produce more realistic figures if they realized that the detectives' motivation is capturing the culprit, not winning popularity contests. This does not mean detectives are deliberately rude or hostile (not if they're smart) for then they are creating their own obstructions. A proper understanding of a detective's psychology involves an understanding of his goals.

This brings us next to the matter of interviews and interrogations. There is a difference between the terms. Interrogation is what a detective does to a suspect, trying to elicit information that will damn him. Interview is what he does with a nonsuspect, to elicit information that will damn someone else.

There may be a difference in the terms but, in my experience, there is very little difference in technique. This is because a detective has become so skilled in asking questions, his techniques for compelling true answers and exposing the false are so honed, his methods so ingrained, that he does not differentiate. He knows only one way to ask questions. Therefore, even the most insignificant figure in a case, questioned about the most insignificant item, is going to suffer the full power of the detective's interrogatory technique.

Consider the following: A Harlem woman hasn't been seen by her neighbors for several days. They appeal to the building superintendent, an elderly black man who can't enter her one-room apartment because of the locks on her door. He therefore gains access through the lone window, this being at some personal risk since he must climb over balconies four floors up. Inside, he finds the woman in her nightgown, face down on the floor, dead. Her face is smeared from a bloody nose but, since nothing's been touched, a plausible explanation is that she suffered a heart attack while preparing for bed and pitched forward, dead. In any event, no suspicion was being directed against this thin, elderly superintendent who found her body. Yet it was an education to hear one of the homicide detectives question him on the stairs outside the apartment.

In books and movies, detectives query people in a neat, logical sequence, each question suggesting the succeeding question. This is a rational, scientific approach which would bespeak a rational, scientific detective. It has the added advantage of enabling the reader or viewer to follow the detective's train of thought and sense his goals. At the same time, however, it also enables the interviewee to follow the detective's train of thought and sense his goals, thus enlarging the interviewee's opportunity to misdirect the detective, which is hardly the course the detective wants to chart.

The questioning of the super on the stairs was not like that at all. Every question the detective asked came from a different angle and related to a different subject, thus forcing the super to undergo a continuous change of orientation. The pattern was patternless and questions jumped erratically: "How long has the woman lived in that room?" "Where do you live?" "What's the name of the people next door to her?" "Do you know any of her friends?"

"Who told you you ought to climb in her window?" "How long have you been working here?"

A guilty person, or one trying to propagate a lie, would be under the constant demand to rethink his lie in terms of each new question so that he didn't trip himself up. And this is going to take time—more time than it will take a person telling the truth—which tells the detective who's lying about what.

Even a person telling the truth has to hesitate and think. And the fact he has to hesitate makes him feel he's showing guilt, even though the detective knows better. In this instance, the poor superintendent, innocent of any wrongdoing and trying desperately to answer the detective's questions honestly, nevertheless felt himself sounding guiltier and guiltier. He began to falter so badly that the detective, who couldn't ask questions any other way, had to put a steadying hand on the old man's arm and say, "It's all right, Pop. Don't get upset."

This is, of course, not the only questioning technique by which detectives gain information and spot liars. There are others. The hardened criminal, however, persists in his lies no matter how contradictory he may sound. He knows, barring other evidence, if he does not admit anything he will go free, for the detective's conclusions on a man's integrity are not admissible in court. Nevertheless, such information is useful for the detectives to have in the general war against crime.

The preceding may indicate some of the inherent ridiculousness in that press agent's dream of having mystery writers help the police. There is more.

For one thing, police detectives are not as dumb as the tastemakers and media manipulators make them out to be. The police force in New York, for instance, numbers some 26,000 members, of whom 2,600, or 10 percent, carry the gold shield of detective rather than the white metal (silver-colored) shields (they aren't called badges in New York) of the uniformed force. This 10 percent represents the cream of the crop of a 26,000-man organization which does, after all, have minimum standards of acceptance, so you're going to find a lot of first-class brains at work.

Add to that the kind of training these detectives have been subject to, the years of experience under their belts (the youngest member of the Homicide Squad was thirty-six years old) and

throw in on top of that one overwhelming advantage they enjoy—
they know their environment. With all that going for them, can
anyone seriously believe some greenhorn, even if he boasts an IQ
of 200, can come in and give them lessons? I was, myself, what
the press agent was proposing: A mystery writer working with the
detectives. The only difference was, I wasn't helping them, they
were helping me. This was because they knew what they were
doing and I did not. Nor would any outsider venturing into any
unknown field.

Some excerpts from my own indoctrination might best illustrate
the matter. My first night with the Homicide Squad, since nothing
was pressing (members of the Homicide Squad sit around waiting
for murders to happen; no murders, no work), they took me for a
ride around their bailiwick, the north half of Manhattan. It was
11:00 P.M. and as we cruised, the sergeant, riding beside the
driver, indicated the flitting, ghostlike figures on the streets. "You
see those people?" the sergeant said. "They're all junkies.* Every
one is a junkie."

I thought to myself, "Interesting, if true, but I suspect the sergeant is laying it on a little thick. Quite probably a few of those
people actually are junkies, but my guess is that most are ordinary
citizens going about their business."

That was the mind of a tyro at work evaluating a strange, new
neighborhood in terms of the neighborhoods he had known. Needless to say, I wasn't with the Homicide Squad long before I came
to know the sergeant hadn't been exaggerating one iota. Every
person on the streets at that hour was a junkie. Harlem evenings
were not ateem with returning moviegoers, dog-walkers, gabbing
neighbors, or romantic couples. No one but junkies dared venture
after dark from their barricaded apartments. But this was something I had to learn.

Another thing I learned was that the production of children in
Harlem was not necessarily accompanied by a marriage license.
Childbirth out of wedlock may be a commonplace today but a decade ago it was reasonably expected that where there was a child,
there was a husband.

Not so in Harlem, and I quickly noted that when we went to the

* Heroin addicts.

scene of a child death (usually a crib death, not an infanticide) the detective, in interviewing the young mother, never asked about her husband. He would, instead, say, "When did you last see the father?" or "Where's the father?" and the girl would answer, "Yesterday," or "Last week," or "He's in jail," or some such.

Then there was the case of an abortive holdup. At least one person was killed but the object of the holdup, a young, flashy, swarthy, fast-talking type, was unharmed. When questioned, he knew nothing about anything. People had tried to hold him up, he didn't know them, he didn't know why.

A visiting mystery writer might guess the dark-haired, glib near-victim knew more than he would reveal, but what the more might be was the stuff of which mystery novels were made.

"Where do you live?" the young man was asked, and it turned out he was from New Jersey, quite a distance from upper Manhattan.

What was he doing here?

He said he had friends in the area and thought he'd drop over.

The mystery writer would smell a rat in that one too, but he would need further clues before he could deduce what was really going on.

Not so the detectives. "How much money are you carrying?" was the unexpected (by the mystery writer) next question they asked him.

The man started to dismiss the amount as trivial but changed his mind. He told the police he wouldn't try to kid them, he had $1500 on him, and produced his loaded wallet to prove it.

Why on earth, the writer wondered, would the man gratuitously reveal this information? And why, for that matter, was he carrying such a large amount?

The writer comes to realize, with more experience in the environment, what the detectives knew from the first. The man had arrived in town to make a buy (heroin)—thus the question about the money he carried—and some junkie or double-crosser was laying for him.

As for the interview between the sharp young man and the detectives, it was a charade. The detectives knew his story was a lie, and they knew what the real story was. And he knew that they knew—which was why he didn't bother lying about the money he was carrying. All of them also knew he would not reveal who had nearly killed him, that there was no evidence against him, and that he would be turned loose. There was nothing to do but play out the game. The ritual of the questioning was conducted and the young man was released.

The young man will, of course, be fully aware that he narrowly escaped with his life that night and that certain protective measures should be taken in the future. No matter how fearful he may be, however, he would never turn to the police for help. Nor will he stop coming to Manhattan to make further buys. As one detective said, "You can never wipe out the drug traffic. There's too much money involved."

The sum and substance of all this is that it's the mystery writer who learns from the police, not the police from the mystery writer. In fact, it is disconcerting to discover that the brilliant deduction with which the mystery writer plans to have his genius detective solve the crime turns out, in real life, to be about the first thing a good detective thinks of. In fact, it is a challenge to create a fictional crime that will keep real detectives guessing for long. In my own case, I gave the homicide detectives the clues of the plot I was concocting to see how they would handle them and it was eerie the way they, without knowing it, were homing in on my villain. I had to keep inventing additional complications for, as I said to them, "I want this case to take a week and you'd crack it in twenty-four hours."

Part of the real detective's skill at crime solution comes from the fact that he takes nothing for granted. Consider the case of a man whose body was found hanging above the bathtub. It looked like murder by his worst enemy. The homicide detective, however, collected the water in the tub's drain trap for analysis and, lo and behold, it was ice water, not tap water (there's a difference). The victim had committed suicide using a block of ice, in the expectation that his enemy would be charged with his murder.

That's a prime example of not taking anything for granted, but there are lesser ones. A detective's report never uses the word "gold" in describing jewelry, rings, etc. It uses "yellow metal" instead. "Gold" means the 14-karat stuff and a detective could be in trouble if he described a stolen brooch as "gold" and the recovered brooch turned out to be brass. And if it is your intention, as a writer, to complicate your plot by having the scheming widow omit a couple of items when she lists the jewelry that was stolen, forget it. The detectives will dutifully record the baubles she finds are missing, but they will then match that list against the insurance-company records and if there's a discrepancy, they'll be back, knocking on the widow's door to find out why.

Nor do real detectives go out of their way looking for work. If a bloody body is found in a stairwell, the Homicide Squad will start investigating "just in case" but it's not accepted that the body is a murder victim unless or until the Medical Examiner's Office says it is. People do, after all, drop dead of heart attacks at the top of stairs and end up bloodied and battered at the bottom. Detectives, like other people, don't make their life any harder than necessary, and nothing is much harder than hunting for murderers when no murder has been committed.

One final significant difference between real detectives and the TV, movie, and novel variety. This is the matter of empathy and concern. Fictional detectives are very often portrayed as caring and sympathetic, as getting personally involved with each new case. This may be how the writers themselves feel, or it may be an effort to make their detective heroes appealing.

In real life, however, this degree of emotional involvement could not possibly be maintained. The human system cannot stand it. The number of cases a homicide detective works on in the course of a year, the number of dead bodies he looks at—in all stages of mutilation and/or decay—requires that he grow a protective shell around his feelings. Constant pounding on a sensitive spot develops a callus and no detective will respond to the hundredth corpse the way he responded to his first, in the same way that no doctor will respond to his hundredth appendectomy as he did to his first, nor the social worker to the hundredth tale of woe as to the first. They may recognize that the hundredth is as important as the first and treat it that way, but the emotional response won't be the same. Detectives, exposed to more of the vagaries of the human condition than the rest of us, become inured to more. They become shockproof. They have witnessed what the rest of us cannot even dream of. I felt the need to acknowledge this in one of my books by saying, "Homicide detectives see, first-hand, such aberrations of human nature as psychiatrists only read about."

One is not to deduce from this that detectives don't ever care. They have to keep their personal involvement at a minimum if they are to survive, but sometimes their deep-hidden concerns do break through. I am reminded of the case of a little nine-year-old Harlem girl whose assaulted and mutilated body had been found in an abandoned refrigerator in a vacant lot. The police knew who had committed the crime. They even knew where the man was—in Puerto Rico. For that or some other reason, they could not touch him. The case, open and unsolved because no arrest had been made, was three to four years old. But the detective telling me about it suddenly went to the file, pulled from it the picture of the perpetrator, and pinned it to the bulletin board. His action was speaking for them all and it was saying, "Let us not forget this man! If we cannot ever get him for what he did to that little girl, perhaps we can get him *hard* for something else."

This article has obviously been written by one who has not only had close contact with the police but has been much impressed by the police. The article sounds, in fact, like a panegyric and readers with a less charitable view of our law enforcement agents may tend to dismiss it with the conclusion that the author has: (1) Been brainwashed. (2) Been bought. (3) Been sold.

It is only proper, therefore, to show the dark side of the glass. One member of the Homicide Squad, a fascinating raconteur of entertaining tidbits, was summarily suspended from duty pending a hearing. I did not ask what the charges were, nor did anyone volunteer the information, but the matter must have been serious indeed.

Another detective was kicked downstairs—shunted to a detective squad in the far hinterlands. Hints were given me as to the cause, but they remain only hearsay.

I report these facts by way of indicating that homicide detectives aren't supermen or angels. They have the same foibles and failings in the same proportion as the rest of mankind.

Perhaps this is the biggest difference of all between the detectives of fiction and those in real life. The real detectives are very fallible and very human.

HILLARY WAUGH's police-procedural mystery novels include *Pure Poison* and *Death and Circumstances*.

Death in Transit

Justin Scott

I LIKE RESEARCHING a novel by talking to people, asking them questions. It's much more engaging than reading for research because, as you carom through people's lives gleaning detail for your fiction, you occasionally slam full-tilt into reality.

Of course, there are problems with engagement. When the reality is more than you bargained for, you still have to keep on taking notes—despite confusion, fear or horror—or it all slips away like a moment lost. And, trying to isolate your own story in a blizzard of information, you may miss a bigger, better story swirling around you. I encountered both difficulties one sunny afternoon in a cool, gray county morgue.

I was researching a police procedural. Hosted by an articulate undercover detective, I was given the grand tour of the county's modern police headquarters. He took me through the detectives' offices, the communications center, the identification unit, the crime laboratory, and a station house. The officers in charge explained what they did and answered my questions. Though polite, many were distant, as if they knew that the next time they met a civilian, it might be their turn to ask the questions.

On the way to the morgue we stopped at Homicide. The Homicide squad was the pride of the Police Commissioner and the detectives knew it. New men joined their unit by invitation only. They swaggered about with the pride and self-assurance you'd expect from an elite force that had solved twenty-three out of twenty-four mystery deaths the year before, and I saw in their attitude an opportunity to give my fictional character—a lowly precinct detective—something both to resent and aspire to.

A brisk chat with the beefy captain of the squad—a quick, jolly man with tough little eyes—was interrupted by a report from his lieutenants. I was allowed to stay and listen. They had spent the morning investigating the death of a middle-age man whose mother had discovered him lying face down on his living-room floor in a pool of blood which had oozed from his mouth and nose. Though certain details seemed suspicious, particularly the victim's enormous collection of stereo equipment—about a store full—and the word from Robbery that he was suspected of fencing for teenage thieves, there was no sign of forced entry or struggle. The detectives at the scene were becoming convinced that the man, whom neighbors characterized as strange, had died of a fall, possibly following a brain hemorrhage.

The body had been sent to the morgue and there was a sense of letdown in the Captain's office. His men had thought they had a mystery. Now it appeared that unless new evidence was uncovered in the autopsy, such as an indication that a blunt instrument had helped him to the floor, all they had was an unsavory citizen checking out with death by natural causes.

They joked about the man's filthy house. He had owned several dogs that, by the evidence, did their walking indoors. "You step here, squish. You step there, squish," said one detective, pantomiming the morning's investigation. And they chuckled about the dead man's mother. She had pestered them all morning, insisting that her son had been murdered, until they suggested that she save his dogs from the pound by taking them home to her house.

Her dog hated his dogs, she said.

Then she left, as if afraid they would force her to take his animals.

I was learning that cops typically brush shoulders with sad and weird folk most of us cross the street to avoid.

I finished my notes of the Homicide Captain's explanation of investigatory procedures for mystery deaths, and my host took me to the county morgue to meet the Medical Examiner. The ME was a novelist's dream. He was witty, handsome in a tweedy way, utterly charming, and served by a young assistant who was one of the most beautiful women I had ever seen.

Oddly enough, I had already written a preliminary draft of the section of the book which dealt with the ME, and here were my characters, exactly as I had created them, right down to the easy rapport the man and woman shared. I looked around his plush office and made a note. I had failed to imagine the clutter of books and manuscripts on his desk and windowsills.

We discussed the elements of fresh- and salt-water drowning, and the tests for each, on which the plot of my book hinged. Contrary to popular misconception, the evidence is found in the chambers of the heart, not in the lungs. They liked my plot and suggested some aspects of murder I hadn't considered. Then my host asked the results of the post mortem (called a "post" in the business) on the mystery death we had heard about at Homicide. I listened with relief. Anything to stall going down to the morgue.

Assisted by his lovely lady, the ME had done the post personally. Everybody, it seemed, loved a mystery. They too had been disappointed. He was quite sure that the man had died of a brain hemorrhage. He had cut open the victim's elbow to check for a particular type of bone break, which, he explained, commonly occurred in a hard, face-down fall. There was no break, indicating that the man had probably been dead by the time he hit the floor. Unless the chemical tests being performed by the toxologists showed otherwise, the ME was going to call it death by natural causes.

Now, said the ME, I suppose you'll want to see the morgue. I scanned my notes hopefully, but there was nothing more to say and I was about to face what I had been dreading all day. I had never seen a morgue and I didn't want to start now, but to turn a first draft into a full draft meant I had to surrender that particular innocence.

My host, who was to accompany me into that nether region, asked if the body had been removed from the table after the post. The ME and his assistant, who looked as if they had a very pleasant afternoon planned as soon as we got the hell out of their office, assured us it was in the cooler. That was fortunate, my host mentioned as we approached the morgue entrance, because an autopsied body was a grisly sight.

He was putting it mildly.

A garage door flipped open. Ten feet in front of me was a horribly mutilated corpse. Great red slashes, hastily stitched with big loops of thick black thread, ripped across the naked man's chest. He was lying on his back and his arms were locked above him in a defensive posture. One of his elbows was laid open like a crown roast in a butcher shop and he looked as if he had been chopped to death by a mad swordsman, but what really hit me was the way he held his arms. It was as if he had raised them *after* death, not to save his life, but to protect his soul.

My host apologized that the corpse had been left out. It was the man I'd been hearing about all day. The slashes were autopsy incisions, wounds inflicted after death. Then, as I edged past the body my eyes drifted from its filthy feet to its face, and I got a second shock.

I knew the man!

It was incredible, but I knew him. It took a moment to make the connection, then I got it. He had been a handyman, years before, in the town where I had grown up. I recalled that he had had a reputation for telling particularly offensive lewd jokes.

Flustered, I retreated to the security of my notebook and penciled a bright entry comparing a morgue to a railroad station where death in transit waits at the junction between life's local and the eternal express. I know; but you had to be there.

My host continued to guide me through the underground facility, which reeked sweetly of formaldehyde. He was a quiet, confident man and he surveyed the Medical Examiner's domain with professional admiration, saluting its aspects: the autopsy tables with channels and drains, as well as overhead mikes for the note-taking ease of the performing pathologist; the curtained viewing room; and the drawer slabs. The drawers are only used for long-term storage in a modern morgue, despite their dramatic reputation from a thousand detective movies. They've been replaced by a cooler, and a quick opening of the door to that refrigerated room has left me to this day with a vivid memory of a *crowd* of dead people.

My host reached for a slab pull. I braced myself. The contents of the drawer, he said, might interest me. He pulled it halfway open. Sickened, and trying to pretend that I wasn't, I glanced in. The body was mummified, little more than a skeleton in a sack of brown-paper skin and rotted clothing. It had been autopsied a long time ago, by the look of the stitches. The impact of death, as we all know, is largely a product of time and this aged corpse held fewer horrors for me.

My host was right. The story was fascinating.

The body, looking much as it did now, had washed up on the beach, autopsy cuts and clothing included. Talk about mystery deaths—this one had stumped both Homicide and the ME. The dental work was Russian and kidney failure was the apparent cause of death, but nobody could figure out how the body had reached the east coast of the United States, until an assistant ME had discovered several tiny marks on one of its boots. They were identified as cyrillic letters which translated to the word "Riga," which someone else figured out was the capital of Latvia, which made no sense at all until someone else realized that Riga was the location of a boot factory that specialized in fisherman's gear, and therefore the man had been a Russian seaman, who died at sea, was autopsied, buried clumsily, and had floated free of his shroud.

The mystery solved, nobody wanted the poor soul. The Russians wouldn't respond to the ME's offer that they reclaim their man, the Coast Guard said it was out of their ken, and the county police boats were too small to venture far enough into the ocean to give him a decent burial. If nothing happened soon, the Russian sailor was doomed to a second rest in a county welfare cemetery.

I was having trouble breathing the cloying air. My host remarked that I looked pale. Would I like some fresh air? I would. I got as far as the attendant's lounge, a smoky locker room, and collapsed on a wooden bench. When I could walk again, I was led outdoors.

I wrote the book. It was packed with fascinating information about drowning in fresh and salt water and had a marvelous little subplot about returning a lost Russian fisherman to a watery grave, as well as clever insights into the nature of policemen and pathologists.

The handyman?

Last I heard the case was still open. In fact, the elite homicide squad recently returned to the scene and asked his neighbors why they thought he was strange. The word is the DA is preparing charges.

The killer?

Seems one of the neighbors finally told the cops that when Mom visited, she pranced around her son's house in a sheer negligee and spike-heel shoes. Seems they had a thing going. Seems they had a lover's quarrel. Seems she hit him with a blunt instrument.

JUSTIN SCOTT has written, among other novels, *Many Happy Returns* and *The Shipkiller*.

"Before I Kill More"

Lucy Freeman

AT THE AGE of eighteen William Heirens, who had just completed his freshman year at the University of Chicago, was convicted in three separate cases of murdering a little girl and two women—Suzanne Degnan, six years old, Mrs. Josephine Ross, forty-three, and Frances Brown, thirty. In lipstick he had scrawled across the beige wall of Miss Brown's apartment the words:

> For heavens
> Sake catch me
> Before I kill more
> I cannot control myself

There were similarities in the three killings. Each of his victims was nude. He had not raped them. He had remained with them for an hour or so after they were dead.

He had carefully washed away all the blood on the bodies, even the little girl, whom he had dismembered, throwing parts of her body—including her head—into nearby sewers.

All Chicago had been gripped by panic after the three murders, which took place within months of each other. Heirens had been trapped in an unexpected way. He was caught in a routine burglary and his fingerprints sent to Sergeant Thomas A. Laffey who, for six months, had been checking more than seven thousand sets of prints against ones found on a ransom note sent to the little girl's parents. Examining the latest burglary suspect's prints, Sergeant Laffey noticed the little finger on the left hand matched the one on the ransom note.

Heirens confessed he had been involved in more than 300 burglaries, starting at the age of thirteen when arrested as a juvenile delinquent and sent to Gibault, a Catholic institution for wayward boys. Now the court gave him three life sentences to run consecutively, and a one-year-to-life sentence for the burglaries, to follow the other sentences. He did not receive the death penalty because he agreed to make a full confession. The judge wanted to make sure, however, that Heirens would never be released from prison. This was September 1946.

Eight years later, I was aboard the streamlined Rock Island Railroad Rocket speeding from Chicago to Joliet to interview Heirens. I had been assigned to write a book about the case, called, naturally, *Before I Kill More*. It was to be not only a description of the murders and the trial but an attempt to find out *why* a youth of seventeen had committed such heinous crimes against women.

I am interested in the specific, deep, dark terrors of the mind that may drive a man to murder. I believe if we understand more about why men murder, possibly we can prevent many murders. Also, as we are able to look into the twisted psyche of a murderer perhaps we may understand more of our own aggressive impulses which we repress from awareness because we believe them dangerous but which may erupt in self-destructive ways because we dare not face them.

I wanted to find out what had happened in Heirens's life to cause such fury he could not control his violent urges, as most men do. In the words of Polonius, listening attentively to Hamlet's ravings, "Though this be madness, yet there is method in't." The killings did not spring full-blown at the moment of commission. There had to be a psychic "method" to them.

I would not be starting from scratch. Prison psychiatrists had written extensive reports. Three noted psychiatrists had interviewed Heirens at length before the trial. A fourth had written a report, after giving Heirens an injection of sodium pentothal. Under the drugs Heirens confessed a second personality, "George," had been responsible for the murders. He said, "George cut her up," referring to the little girl, and that "George" made him commit the other crimes. His father's name was George, as was his own middle name.

Joliet, thirty miles southwest of Chicago, is the home of Stateville Penitentiary, where some of the nation's most sensational criminals have been jailed, among them Richard Loeb, Nathan Leopold, and Roger Touhy. The warden had given me permission to interview Heirens, who was willing to see me for the purpose of a book about his life. Herbert Wetzel, his attorney, had been helpful in bringing us together.

"What is Heirens like?" I anxiously asked the warden as he led me through the prison. I was frightened—this was my first contact with a murderer.

The question of questions—what's he like? Believing him a freak, a madman, different from the rest of us, perhaps to reassure ourselves there *is* a difference, we could never commit murder no matter how strong the wish.

"He's just like a lot of others who do their time and don't give us any trouble," said the warden. "He's a model prisoner."

A model of a model prisoner, I thought. Strange, for such a brutal killer.

Heirens was at work in the vocational building, covering one corner of the vast prison. The icy January wind whipped us toward the building and I was grateful for the warmth as we stepped into a room the size of several gymnasiums. A hundred or so prisoners were repairing radios, television sets, and typewriters, setting type, welding or lettering posters.

"There he is," said the warden.

He didn't have to tell me. To the right of us I recognized the face that had looked out at me in hundreds of newspaper clippings in the morgue of the *Chicago American*. I expected to find a monster, to fit the monstrous crimes. Instead, I saw a husky, rather handsome young man of twenty-six, who looked as though he should be out in the fields behind a plow.

His hands were twirling a screwdriver into a television set. These are the fingers that drove a knife into the necks of two women and strangled a small girl, then sliced her apart, I thought in sudden fear. He straightened up, displaying wide shoulders and the chest of a wrestler, too large for his medium-sized body and his five feet, ten inches. I sensed a feeling of repressed power as he hitched up his belt, threw back the broad shoulders.

And then I was sitting opposite Bill Heirens in the assistant warden's office. I knew his desperation lay so deep I could never hope to reach it, nor did I want to try. That was a task only for a psychoanalyst. But I believed superficial questions, if he would answer them, might reveal some of the warped fantasies of his twisted, maddened world.

For an hour at a time, over several weeks, I questioned him about his life. Not his crimes. For he insisted he was innocent. But about his experiences and feelings as an infant and boy. Freud said the urge to commit murder starts in the nursery. From what I knew of the emotional and psychosexual development in a child, as a result of extensive reading and my own psychoanalysis, something had gone very wrong with Heirens's early emotional growth. He might tell, in indirect fashion, of the suffering and horror that lay in the half-sensed, nightmare-tossed part of his mind called the unconscious. The words he would use, the experiences he chose to remember, his thoughts about himself and his mother, father and brother, his fears and dreams, would give clues to the savage, primitive wishes and conflicts of his life. The psychiatric reports stated he had severe sexual conflicts. Evidently his sexual and violent feelings had become fused, he was unable to separate them. He could not give of himself sexually, or take, except through violence.

He had been brought up as a strict Catholic. He had never had sexual intercourse with a girl. He had felt so guilty when he kissed a girl, he said, he would go home and burst into tears. He thought sex "dirty," more evil than committing a burglary or murder. He had never masturbated as a boy, thought it "sinful." He told me, hesitantly, that for the first time, in prison, because other men did it, he was able to masturbate.

But there had to be many other reasons why he was driven to kill. Many men, as boys, feel their sexual feelings are wicked, yet do not kill. There had to be something in the house in which Heirens grew up, something he felt as terrifying, or frustrating, which angered him to the point of murderous fury, that eventually drove him to murder women he desired sexually.

At the scene of the burglaries he would often leave signs of ejaculation, defecation, and urination. His mother told me he had been toilet-trained exceptionally early. When he was eight months old, he went through the night without wetting his bed. At one year, both daytime bladder and bowel control had been established (two years is normal). In a sense, he was getting revenge on his mother for the rigid control he had been asked to exert over his body too early in life—before he could handle it—when he left semen and excreta at the homes he robbed.

His whole sexual life seemed to be one of extreme submission, then extreme repression of the fury that inevitably follows submission. Such extreme repression is the stuff of human explosion. A temperate amount of repression is necessary to be civilized. But when sexual or aggressive feelings become too deeply repressed, they will find an outlet. Heirens seemed to have controlled his urges as long as he could, then all the natural functions of his body tore loose at once at the time of adolescence (he was seventeen when he committed the murders) as he was being exposed to girls at the University of Chicago.

Why did he kill? There is no one answer. The answers lie in the whole of his life, just as the whole of his life merged in the act of murder. Many of his early experiences held an unusual amount of terror and frustration which must have led to violent anger in his infant heart.

One thing was certain—he knew how to repress feelings. He was particularly controlled when it came to physical pain. The psychiatric report stated, "Very early he learned not to whimper or cry when hurt." The psychiatrists said Heirens did not feel the sensation of pain in his entire body (they pricked him with pins). He must have felt it, of course, but what he did with his feelings was another matter. Long years of repressing outcries had taught him to hold back his emotions.

When I made a remark that angered him, he lost his amiable expression, his hazel eyes grew glazed, and he drew an invisible but impenetrable curtain between us. He usually was friendly though underneath the friendliness appeared traces of nervousness and fear. When he became impatient or upset, he twisted his lips in a grimace. His cheek muscles grew taut if a painful subject was mentioned. He lapsed into poor grammar when irritated or excited.

In the book I made the plea that psychoanalysts take on studies of this kind in depth. I tried to show a few of the specific things of his early life I thought might lead to the conclusion that he had been unable to control his primitive, savage unconscious drives and fantasies because of a severely traumatized childhood. Not one of overt brutality, but of a subtle, ever-present, ominous sense of brutality that, day by day, terrorized him so he could never function as a growing male. His psychosexual development had been crippled early in life.

He offered one important clue when he revealed he had slept in a crib in the same room as his parents the first three years and three months of his life, until his brother was born. When I visited that room, I discovered his parents' bedroom was so small, his crib would have been up against their bed.

He also told me, when I asked if he ever thought of marrying, "Yes, but in my house I am going to have the plumbing installed two stories below the basement."

"Why?" I asked.

"So the pumping won't keep me awake all night," he said.

"What do you mean?" I asked.

He would say no more. But what "pumping" was he talking about that kept him awake all night? I could see him as a child, trying to sleep next to his parents' bed. His mother was a slight woman, his father, a hulk of a man, towering six feet, three and three-quarters inches and weighing 245 pounds. One can imagine the boy's fantasies of sex as an assaultive act, seeing that huge father attacking his frail mother. Parents may believe children innocent of nightly activities but children are *especially* aware of sexual intercourse, interpreting it on the only level they know. Since they are not aware of adult, genital sex based on tender feelings, the act of sex becomes to a child an act of violence, from what he sees.

The primal scene does not a murderer make, though it can help. The parent who permits a child to endure the torture of the aroused onlooker who can find no sexual release is apt to be the type of parent who is uncaring, psychologically cruel, who treats the child as a puppet, in his day-by-day psychic battering of the child's ego.

Why had Heirens chosen his particular form of violence? Nothing is accidental, irrelevant, or purposeless in the unconscious. There had to be a reason why he *cut up* his victims, knifing the two women and dismembering the little girl. As well as why he always washed away the blood. This was his pattern, his M.O., as they say.

One day he happened to mention that his father loved to catch fish and would bring home the fish to prepare them for eating. Heirens recalled that, as a child, he would sit in the basement and watch his father cut up the fish, then wash off the blood. This is exactly what he did with the little girl after he strangled her—cut her up in a basement, then washed off all the blood. He knifed the two women, then washed off their blood. Since he was too repressed to perform sexually with a woman, he may have thought he was being a man, emulating his father, substituting the human body for the fish, using violence instead of love. He had been cutting up animals in biology to study their inner organs and perhaps he also had cut up the little girl to discover *her* inner organs, particularly the genital ones, a subject of natural curiosity to all little boys. One student at the university recalled Heirens "always kept a good book on sex in his room," citing Krafft-Ebing's *Psychopathia Sexualis,* and referring specifically to a case where a little girl was cut up, her sex organs destroyed, then her limbs hacked off and discarded. In the act of murder, in Heirens's warped mind, several fantasies were undoubtedly combined.

To the three psychiatrists, who reported he had "a deep sexual perversion," he confessed that upon breaking into a house or apartment he would get an erection, often an emission. At times he stole women's undergarments, took them home, and put them on to get an erection and ejaculate.

"Why did you steal women's panties?" I asked.

He hesitated, then said, "It was the satin."

"What about the satin?"

His facial muscles quivered, his eyes took on that glaze. He replied, "I can't say anything more."

I would have bet my last dollar that, as a little boy, he often saw his mother in satin undergarments. Every boy feels physically attracted to his mother, the start of the feeling that develops in later years into mature love. But to the frightened, angry child, this emotion, like most others, becomes intense, unmanageable, the focus of all kinds of fantasies.

Heirens was undoubtedly overstimulated as a child by witnessing the sexual acts of parents in the bed so near to his that he was practically in it with them. He would have been frightened but fascinated and aroused sexually. He would also feel the fury of the sexual onlooker, who is aroused and has to remain aroused, though the other participants get release. In later years, when anyone interfered with his getting an erection or ejaculation, he became angry enough to kill. He must have felt angry enough to kill as a child, first, watching his parents, then, taught by them that sex was "bad," "evil."

He mentioned "breaking through windows" in connection with being punished as a boy. I said, "What do windows mean to you?"

He grinned and nodded in the direction of the high tower in a corner of the prison, glimpsed through the window, manned by armed guards. He said, "Windows mean just as much as that post up there."

He was equating windows with men standing ready with guns to bring death to any prisoner who tried to escape. When he "broke through windows" it was to get the freedom of sexual release but at the price of committing a crime, one that might get him shot. Again, the emphasis on sex as something forbidden, secret, wicked.

He recalled his father kept a gun to shoot rats in the greenhouse he owned, next to his florist shop, and he also shot cats. His father was reported as bursting easily into tears when upset, indicating he had many conflicts. When I interviewed him, he did not look me in the eye but stared at a spot over my head. Heirens's mother was outwardly affable but there seemed deep, repressed anger within and a childhood sense of unreality. The parents divorced soon after their son's conviction, a sign they had not been getting along for a long time.

As might be expected, Heirens's first days of life, even his prenatal ones, were traumatic. His mother nearly aborted him when she was two months' pregnant. Her labor was long, sixty-two hours, and difficult. Nursing was a painful ordeal for her and for the baby. He refused to eat at first, was a feeding problem for several months, vomited after each feeding, had colic, and cried a lot. He looked sickly and at times she said she wondered if he would live. It is in the act of being fed by our mother that we get our first sense of love and security and Heirens's early feeding experiences were hazardous and precarious.

When he was seven months old, he toppled out of his carriage, over a railing and down twelve cement steps to the basement. His mother heard his cries, rushed out, called a doctor, who said it was not a serious fall, that he had only a slight bruise on his head. Later he had nightmares about falling, talked about "walls closing in on him."

In describing how he felt when he started to commit a burglary, he said, "It seemed as though I was in a dream. I did not have any feeling. It was like walking through darkness and pushing a mist aside." He struggled against the desire to leave his room at night and go out to steal. He would get headaches when he resisted the urge. Sometimes, if he had an emission as he was burglarizing, or after he left the premises, he would black out.

The psychiatrists had asked him, "On three occasions you were surprised by people seeing you and you immediately killed—why did you do that?"

He said, "It was the noise that set me off, I believe. I must have been in a high tension and the least bit of noise would disturb me in that manner."

His mother told me that, when a child, he would sometimes suddenly wake up and cry and explained it might be due to "some unexpected noise." In his confession to the police, he referred to the "noise" made by the two women he killed and the little girl, as they screamed at seeing a strange man in their room. The "noise," the scream, occurred when he was in a state of sexual excitement. The frustration of the fulfillment of his sexual urge might have angered him so that he killed. This frustration may have stirred earlier memories of frustration as a boy, when he was in a state of great hunger and needed food, and did not get it, or would not take it, as his mother recalled.

His sexual and aggressive conflicts were severe; otherwise he would not have stolen like a maddened magpie, let alone take the lives of two innocent women and a child. To the degree he felt brutalized as a little boy, he brutalized others. He often talked of feeling "crucified." He felt crucified as a boy by parents unable to offer him emotional security though they did their best. One cannot blame them, for they were the victims of their childhood traumas too.

We can speculate on why, under sodium pentothal, during which his unconscious thinking came out, Heirens blamed "George" for his wicked acts. This was the part of him that had imitated his father—all children learn by imitating parents. To his emotionally stunted mind, his father appeared a man of violence and cruelty.

All the fantasies Heirens had about sex and murder are common to all of us as children. Children are cannibals, thieves, would-be murderers, sexual perverts in their illusions. Most men never act on these fantasies as they become civilized. Heirens could never grow up emotionally and he acted out some of his most horrendous fantasies.

As I left Stateville prison for the last time, I thought of Wordsworth's lines:

> The meanest flower that blows can give
> Thoughts that do often lie too deep for tears.

No one knew over the years of Bill Heirens's unshed tears, no one heard his cries of terror. Help me, help me, he had been screaming—in the burglaries, in the stealing of women's undergarments, the setting of fires, the hiding of stolen guns in his room. No one came to rescue him. He finally had to scrawl his plea in blood-red lipstick on the wall in the apartment of a woman he murdered.

LUCY FREEMAN, long-time *New York Times* reporter, has written many books including *Fight Against Fears* and *Children Who Kill*.

The Shambles of
Ed Gein

Robert Bloch

"SEARCHERS AFTER HORROR haunt strange, far places,"
wrote H. P. Lovecraft in the opening of his story, "The Picture in
the House." "For them are the catacombs of Ptolemais, and the
carven mausolea of the nightmare countries. They climb to the
moonlit towers of ruined Rhine castles, and falter down black cob-
webbed steps beneath the scattered stones of forgotten cities in
Asia. The haunted wood and the desolate mountain are their
shrines, and they linger around the sinister monoliths on uninhab-
ited islands. But the true epicure in the terrible, to whom a new
thrill of unutterable ghastliness is the chief end and justification of
existence, esteems most of all the ancient, lonely farmhouses of
backwoods New England; for there the dark elements of strength,
solitude, grotesqueness and ignorance combine to form the perfec-
tion of the hideous."

Lovecraft's tale then goes on to describe a visit to one of these
"silent, sleepy, staring houses in the backwoods" inhabited by a
weird eccentric whose speech and dress suggest origins in a by-
gone day. An increasingly horrible series of hints culminates in the
revelation that the inhabitant of the house has preserved an unnat-

ural existence for several centuries, sustaining life and vigor through the practice of cannibalism.

Of course it's "only a story."

Or—is it?

On the evening of November 16, 1957, visitors entered an ancient, lonely farmhouse—not in backwoods New England but in rural Wisconsin. Hanging in an adjacent shed was the nude, butchered body of a woman. She had been suspended by the heels and decapitated, then disemboweled like a steer. In the kitchen next to the shed, fire flickered in an old-fashioned potbellied stove. A pan set on top of it contained a human heart.

The visitors—Sheriff Art Schley and Captain Lloyd Schoephoester—were joined by other officers. There was no electricity in the darkened house and they conducted their inspection with oil lamps, lanterns, and flashlights.

The place was a shambles, in every sense of the word. The kitchen, shed, and bedroom were littered with old papers, books, magazines, tin cans, tools, utensils, musical instruments, wrapping paper, cartons, containers, and a miscellany of junk. Another bedroom and living room beyond had been nailed off; these and five rooms upstairs were dusty and deserted.

But amidst the accumulated debris of years in the three tenanted rooms, the searchers found:

two shin bones;

a pair of human lips;

four human noses;

bracelets of human skin;

four chairs, their woven cane seats replaced by strips of human skin;

a quart can, converted into a tom-tom by skin stretched over both top and bottom;

a bowl made from the inverted half of a human skull;

a purse with a handle made of skin;

four "death masks"—the well-preserved skin from the faces of women—mounted at eye-level on the walls;

five more such "masks" in plastic bags, stowed in a closet;

ten female human heads, the tops of which had been sawed off above the eyebrows;

a pair of leggings, fashioned from skin from human legs;

a vest made from the skin stripped from a woman's torso.

The bodies of 15 different women had been mutilated to provide these trophies. The number of hearts and other organs which had been cooked on the stove or stored in the refrigerator will never be known. Apocryphal tales of how the owner of the house brought gifts of "fresh liver" to certain friends and neighbors have never been publicly substantiated, nor is there any way of definitely establishing his own anthropophagism.

But H. P. Lovecraft's "true epicure of the terrible" could find his new thrill of unutterable ghastliness in the real, revealed horrors of the Gein case.

Edward Gein, the gray-haired, soft-voiced little man who may or may not have been a cannibal and a necrophile, was—by his own admission—a ghoul, a murderer, and a transvestite. Due process of law has also adjudged him to be criminally insane.

Yet for decades he roamed free and unhindered, a well-known figure in a little community of 700 people. Now small towns everywhere are notoriously hotbeds of gossip, conjecture, and rumor, and Gein himself joked about his "collection of shrunken heads" and laughingly admitted that he'd been responsible for the disappearance of many women in the area. He was known to be a recluse and never entertained visitors; children believed his house to be "haunted." But somehow the gossip never developed beyond the point of idle, frivolous speculation, and nobody took Ed Gein seriously. The man who robbed fresh graves, who murdered, decapitated, and eviscerated women when the moon was full, who capered about his lonely farmhouse bedecked in corpse-hair, the castor-oil-treated human skin masks made from the faces of his victims, a vest of female breasts and puttees of skin stripped from women's legs—this man was just plain old Eddie Gein, a fellow one hired to do errands and odd jobs. To his friends and neighbors he was only a handyman, and a *most* dependable and trustworthy babysitter.

"Good old Ed, kind of a loner and maybe a little bit odd with that sense of humor of his, but just the guy to call in to sit with the kiddies when me and the old lady want to go to the show. . . ."

Yes, good old Ed, slipping off his mask of human skin, stowing the warm, fresh entrails in the refrigerator, and coming over to spend the evening with the youngsters; he *always* brought them bubble gum. . . .

A pity Grace Metalious wasn't aware of our graying, shy little small-town handyman when she wrote *Peyton Place!* But, of course, nobody would have believed her. New England or Wisconsin are hardly the proper settings for such characters; we might accept them in Transylvania, but Pennsylvania—never!

And yet, he lived. And women died.

As near as can be determined, on the basis of investigation and his own somewhat disordered recollections, Gein led a "normal" childhood as the son of a widowed mother. He and his brother, Henry, assisted her in the operation of their 160-acre farm.

Mrs. Gein was a devout, religious woman with a protective attitude toward her boys and a definite conviction of sin. She discouraged them from marrying and kept them busy with farm work; Ed was already a middle-aged man when his mother suffered her first stroke in 1944. Shortly thereafter, brother Henry died, trapped while fighting a forest fire. Mrs. Gein had a second stroke from which she never recovered; she went to her grave in 1945 and Ed was left alone.

It was then that he sealed off the upstairs, the parlor, and his mother's bedroom and set up his own quarters in the remaining bedroom, kitchen, and shed of the big farmhouse. He stopped working the farm, too; a government soil-conservation program offered him a subsidy, which he augmented by his work as a handyman in the area.

In his spare time he studied anatomy. First from books, and then—

Then he enlisted the aid of an old friend named Gus. Gus was kind of a loner, too, and quite definitely odd—he went to the asylum a few years later. But he was Ed Gein's trusted buddy, and when Ed asked for assistance in opening a grave to secure a corpse for "medical experiments," Gus lent a hand, with a shovel in it.

That first cadaver came from a grave less than a dozen feet away from the last resting place of Gein's mother.

Gein dissected it. Wisconsin farm folk are handy at dressing-out beef, pork, and venison.

What Ed Gein didn't reveal to Gus was his own growing desire to become a woman himself; it was for this reason he'd studied anatomy, brooded about the possibilities of an "operation" which would result in a change of sex, desired to dissect a female corpse and familiarize himself with its anatomical structure.

Nor did he tell Gus about the peculiar thrill he experienced when he donned the grisly accouterment of human skin stripped from the cadaver. At least, there's no evidence he did.

He burned the flesh bit by bit in the stove, buried the bones. And with Gus's assistance, repeated his ghoulish depredations. Sometimes he merely opened the graves and took certain parts of the bodies—perhaps just the heads and some strips of skin. Then he carefully covered up traces of his work. His collection of trophies grew, and so did the range of his experimentation and obsession.

Then Gus was taken away, and Gein turned to murder.

The first victim, in 1954, was Mary Hogan, a buxom 51-year-old divorcée who operated a tavern at Pine Grove, six miles from home. She was alone when he came to her one cold winter's evening; he shot her in the head with his .32-caliber revolver, placed her body in his pickup truck, and took her to the shed where he'd butchered pigs, dressed-out deer.

There may have been other victims in the years that followed. But nothing definite is known about Gein's murderous activities until that day in November, 1957, when he shot and killed Mrs. Bernice Worden in her hardware store on Plainfield's Main Street. He used a .22 rifle from a display rack in the store itself, inserting his own bullet which he carried with him in his pocket. Locking the store on that Saturday morning, he'd taken the body home in the store truck. Gein also removed the cash register, which contained $41 in cash—not with the intention of committing robbery, he later explained in righteous indignation, but merely because he wished to study the mechanism. He wanted to see how a cash register worked, and fully intended to return it later.

Mrs. Worden's son, Frank, often assisted her in the store, but on this particular Saturday morning he'd gone deer-hunting. On his return in late afternoon he discovered the establishment closed, his mother missing, the cash register gone. There was blood on the floor. Frank Worden served as a deputy sheriff in the area and knew what to do. He immediately alerted his superior officer, reported the circumstances, and began to check for clues. He established that the store had been closed since early that morning, but noted a record of the two sales transactions made before closing. One of them was for a half gallon of antifreeze.

Worden remembered that Ed Gein, the previous evening at closing time, had stopped by the store and said he'd be back the next morning for antifreeze. He'd also asked Worden if he intended to go hunting the next day. Worden further recalled that Gein had been in and out of the store quite frequently during the previous week.

Since the cash register was missing, it appeared as if Gein had planned a robbery after determining a time when the coast would be clear.

Worden conveyed his suspicions to the sheriff, who sent officers to the farm, seven miles outside Plainfield. The house was dark and the handyman absent; acting on a hunch, they drove to a store in West Plainfield where Gein usually purchased groceries. He was there—had been visiting casually with the proprietor and his wife. In fact, he'd just eaten dinner with them.

The officers spoke of Mrs. Worden's disappearance. The 51-year-old, 140-pound little handyman joked about it in his usual offhand fashion; he was just leaving for home in his truck and was quite surprised that anyone wanted to question him. "I didn't have anything to do with it," he told them. "I just heard about it while I was eating supper." It seems someone had come in with the news.

Meanwhile, back at the farmhouse, the sheriff and the captain had driven up, entered the shed, and made their gruesome discovery.

Gein was taken into custody, and he talked.

Unfortunately for the "searchers after horror," his talk shed little illumination on the dark corners of his mind. He appeared to have only a dim recollection of his activities; he was "in a daze" much of the time during the murders. He did recall that he'd visited about 40 graves through the years, though he insisted he hadn't opened all of them, and denied he'd committed more than two murders. He named only nine women whose bodies he'd molested, but revealed he selected them after careful inspections of the death notices in the local newspapers.

There was a lie-detector test, a murder charge, an arraignment, a series of examinations at the Central State Hospital for the Criminally Insane. He remains there to this day.

The case created a sensation in the Midwest. Thousands of "epicures of the terrible"—and their snotty-nosed brats—made the devout pilgrimage to Plainfield, driving bumper-to-bumper on wintry Sunday afternoons as they gawked at the "murder farm." Until one night the residence of the "mad butcher" went up in smoke.

I was not among the epicures. At that time I resided less than 50 miles away, but had no automobile to add to the bumper crop; nor did I subscribe to a daily newspaper. Inevitably, however, I heard the mumbled mixture of gossip and rumor concerning the "fiend" and his activities. Curiously enough, there was no mention of his relationship with his mother, nor of his transvestism; the accent was entirely on proven murder and presumed cannibalism.

What interested me was this notion that a ghoulish killer with perverted appetites could flourish almost openly in a small rural community where everybody prides himself on knowing everyone else's business.

The concept proved so intriguing that I immediately set about planning a novel dealing with such a character. In order to provide him with a supply of potential victims, I decided to make him a motel operator. Then came the ticklish question of what made him tick—the matter of motivation. The Oedipus motif seemed to offer a valid answer, and the transvestite theme appeared to be a logical extension. The novel which evolved was called *Psycho*.

Both the book and a subsequent motion picture version called forth comments which are the common lot of the writer in the mystery-suspense genre.

"Where do you get those perfectly *dreadful* ideas for your stories?"

I can only shrug and point to the map—not just a map of Wisconsin, but *any* map. For men like Edward Gein can be found anywhere in the world—quiet little men leading quiet little lives, smiling their quiet little smiles and dreaming their quiet little dreams.

Lovecraft's "searchers after horror" do not need to haunt strange, far places or descend into catacombs or ransack mausolea. They have only to realize that the true descent into dread, the journey into realms of nightmare, is all too easy—once one understands where terror dwells.

The real chamber of horrors is the gray, twisted, pulsating, blood-flecked interior of the human mind.

ROBERT BLOCH, best known for his novel *Psycho,* is also the author of *Terror* and *Cold Chills.*

The Circumstances Surrounding the Crime

Desmond Bagley

NINETEEN-SIXTY was not a particularly good year for South Africa. January was not too bad, but on 3 February Harold Macmillan, the British Prime Minister, made his famous "wind of change" speech to the South African Parliament in which he warned of the storms to come. This did not sit well with South Africans, particularly those of the ruling Nationalist Party, who regarded it as an interference in South African internal affairs.

Then on 21 March an inexperienced police commander made a grave error of judgment when he gave the order to fire with machine guns on a crowd of demonstrating black Africans in the small town of Sharpeville.

Within thirty seconds the death roll was sixty-nine and many of those killed and wounded were women.

On 30 March a State of Emergency was declared in South Africa, and on 1 April the United Nations Security Council adopted a resolution deploring the shootings at Sharpeville which were categorised as a massacre.

On 4 April the Union Expo at Milner Park opened its gates to the public.

By this time Johannesburg had become a magnet attracting the journalistic hot-shots—the international leg-men. World news is where you find *Time* magazine rubbing elbows with *Paris-Match,* both of them trying to get a beat on *Stern.* Noel Barber was there from London, and Robert Ruark represented Scripps-Howard. This was Ruark towards the end of his life—the famous hard-drinking, best-selling novelist and old Africa hand. At this time his idea of breakfast was half a bottle of Scotch and a couple of lightly boiled aspirins. I read one of his two-thousand-word cables and wondered how the desk man back in Chicago was going to make sense of it.

Then there was the brash character who entered the bar of the Federal Hotel, a drinking hole favoured by newspapermen and broadcasters, announcing, "I've come to interview your Prime Minister—Forwards or Backwards or whatever his name is!"

And, of course, there was the home-grown newspaper talent such as James Ambrose Brown. After Sharpeville all the surviving wounded had been put into Baragwanath Hospital around which the Army had thrown an iron cordon. Jimmy Brown penetrated the ring by wearing a white coat, an ostentatious stethoscope, and a preoccupied medical expression. He got his exclusive eyewitness interviews and duly made his scoop. Early 1960 was an exciting time for newsmen in Johannesburg.

And where did I come into all this? I, too, was a newspaperman, freelancing for the *Rand Daily Mail* and the Johannesburg *Sunday Times,* and my one aim in life at the beginning of April 1960 was to cover the Union Expo. I was not interested in political matters and scurried about the feet of the journalistic giants doing my own thing. So let us take a look at the scene of the crime, the Union Expo, which was my beat.

Every year at Milner Park in Johannesburg there is an event called the Rand Easter Show. Originally it was an agricultural show—indeed it is still organised by the Witwatersrand Agricultural Society—but it has been overtaken by industry and taken on an international flavour because a dozen nations have built permanent exhibition halls which are brought into use only once each year for about ten days around Easter.

Here the French push their wines, perfumes, military helicopters, and minor guided missiles; the Germans display Bavarian beer and heavy machinery; the British offer Harris tweed, Scotch whisky, and Stilton cheese; the Japanese are there with transistor radios, the Czechs with Bohemian glass, and the Belgians with Browning rifles. The cattle, sheep, pigs, and goats are still there but somehow they seem lost among all the machinery.

Ironically, 1960, the year of disaster, was the Golden Jubilee of the founding of the Union of South Africa in 1910. The Government had decided that this was an occasion for celebration, so a couple of new exhibition halls were built in Milner Park, artists and sculptors were commissioned to decorate them, and the Rand Easter Show was lengthened to three weeks and rechristened the Union Expo, a coinage to chill the blood of anyone who respects the English language. Attendance was expected to top the million mark.

Long before the gates opened on 4 April I had been busy. The *Rand Daily Mail,* Johannesburg's English morning newspaper, was to run a special daily supplement on the Expo and there were many pages to be filled. And I had hopes of pushing material to the *Sunday Times,* the *Mail's* stable companion. So I was kept busy interviewing exhibitors and anyone else who would provide a good story.

Among these was Kobus Esterhuysen, a relaxed Afrikaner who was an exhibition designer of no mean talent and who was responsible for the Combined Provinces Pavilion. He admitted rather shamefacedly that it was he who had coined the term Expo, and added that he was having trouble with the bats in the Transvaal Pavilion. It seemed he had an animal exhibit and the bats would not hang upside-down properly. It made a paragraph.

By the time the Expo opened I was so busy that I drafted my girlfriend, Joan Brown, into helping me. All that first week we scurried about, me working full time, and Joan in the few hours she could spare from her job in a city book shop.

I had no time to think of the political scene but the politics were there and would not go away. The international pressmen were at the Expo in strength on Saturday, 9 April, because Prime Minister Vervoerd was to be guest of honour and was due to make a speech in the Main Arena, supposedly a "keynote" speech on the State of Emergency.

Just before three I joined them in the arena, standing before the

VIP box where C. J. Laubscher, the general manager of the Expo, was sitting with the Prime Minister, the Mayor of Johannesburg, the President of the Witwatersrand Agricultural Society, and a dozen assorted visiting firemen, including my designer friend Kobus Esterhuysen. Behind us, in the arena, were about 500 prize cattle. There were thirty thousand onlookers in the stands.

I was with Stan Hurst, Features Editor and principle lay-out man of the *Sunday Times*. Stan was a good friend and was to be best man at the wedding when I married Joan later that year. He looked at Vervoerd, and said, "He's got to pull a rabbit out of the hat today. He *must*—the country can't go on like this."

Vervoerd made his speech in both English and Afrikaans, the two official languages of the country. It was of mind-numbing dullness, much to the disgust of the visiting newsmen who were not as hardened as were we locals to the stupefying qualities of South African political discourse. There was not a word spoken that was newsworthy, so when the speech ended they vanished from the arena, some going direct to the airport where they had booked flights for the Congo which was due to erupt at any moment, others back to their hotels, but most drifting into the bar, that haunt of all good newsmen, to swap lies and steal stories from each other.

But for Joan I would have joined them; South African barrooms were for men only.

The next item on the program was for Vervoerd to come down into the arena and inspect the cattle. "A lousy speech," Hurst commented. "Nothing in it for me. I'm going home; maybe I'll take a nap." He looked at Vervoerd who was chatting with Alec Gorshell, the Mayor of Johannesburg. "Are you covering the cattle?"

I shook my head. "I leave that to Terence Clarkson." Clarkson was an elderly reporter on the *Rand Daily Mail;* he knew less about cattle than I did, but he could disguise his ignorance better. I grinned. "He'll look up what he wrote last year and rejig it." I checked the time. "I promised to meet Joan in the Members' Pavilion after the speech."

Stan nodded. "Okay; I'll see you in the office tonight."

He went away, and I walked towards the Members' Pavilion which looked out on to the arena. The only newspaperman left was the photographer from the *Farmer's Weekly* who was stuck with the job of following the Prime Minister as he inspected the bovine regiment in a timeless ritual of South African life.

Joan was lucky enough to have found a table in the crowded Pavilion so I ordered strawberries and cream, dropped a few acid words about Vervoerd's speech, and then we got down to figuring the work plan for the rest of the day.

Less than five minutes later there was a slight disturbance in the arena, merely a couple of shouts and nothing more. None of us heard the gun. A man at the next table stood up and craned his neck, then sat down again. "Nothing much," he said. "I think a bull got loose."

The thought struck me that a bull loose in the same arena as a Prime Minister might prove interesting and, after all, I was a reporter. "I'll be back in a couple of minutes," I said to Joan.

I got into the arena by showing my press tag and headed towards the VIP box fifty yards away. There was a small crowd of perhaps a dozen men at the bottom of the stairs and the people who should have been seated around the box were standing and staring. There was not much noise; just a hum of conversation and the lowing of cattle from the arena.

As I got closer a struggling man was hauled away by two policemen. He was not being handled gently. Another man, a stranger, was lying on the steps, dead or unconscious, with someone bending over him. I touched the elbow of an onlooker. "What's happening?"

"He *shot* him!"

"Who shot who?"

"The bastard shot Vervoerd." The man's tone was incredulous. There wasn't another reporter in sight. "*Who* shot Vervoerd?"

"Someone called Spratt."

"Where is Vervoerd now?"

"Lying on the bottom of the box there."

The photographer from the *Farmer's Weekly* was busy taking pictures. He had problems—three of them. The first was his camera. It was an elderly Speed Graphic five-by-four, cut-film camera, a type I thought was obsolete in the 1930s. Slow to load and heavy to hold. His second problem was that the VIP box was too high for him to see into. He was holding his camera above his head with stiffened arms, leaping into the air, and opening the shutter at the top of each leap in the dim hope of getting a useable picture.

His last problem was the Mayor of Johannesburg who hit him on the head with a rolled-up newspaper every time he leaped up.

I turned and ran back to the Members' Pavilion and unceremoniously scooped up Joan from her table. I said in a low voice, "Vervoerd's been shot; we've got to move fast."

She got the point. "Where to?"

"The press room."

The press room at Milner Park offered jaillike accommodation for frequently protesting reporters. There were a few battered and ink-stained deal tables, a few rickety chairs—and four telephones. In the bar of the Members' Pavilion were half a hundred newshungry reporters, each of whom would cheerfully give his arm for a telephone in the next fifteen minutes, and I was determined to get mine first.

The press room was empty. I said, "Ring *Sunday Times* editorial and tell them Vervoerd's been shot by a man probably called Spratt. There'll be more to follow as soon as I can find an eyewitness. And don't let go of that bloody telephone no matter who wants it."

On the way back to the arena I passed the door to the Members' Bar and hesitated. Maybe I'm not competitive enough and maybe I'm a damned fool but I pushed open the door and went in. There, bellied up against the bar counter, were the Fourth Estate's finest—the international team. Now, because I have a stammer, journalistic legend in Johannesburg has it that I went into the bar and shouted, "Ver-Ver-Ver-Ver-voerd's b-b-b-been sh-sh-sh-sh-sh-sh-shot!"

My version is that I caught the eye of Bennett, a reporter for the *Rand Daily Mail,* went up to him and said, not too loudly, "Ver-Vervoerd's been shhhot."

He grinned at me. "Pull the other leg—it's got bells on it." He went on drinking so I shrugged and left them to it.

I needed an eyewitness and then I remembered that Kobus Esterhuysen had been in the VIP box. He and I had got on well together so I elected him as my eyewitness and went in search of him. He was not hard to find because he was standing just by the VIP box.

"*Hi, Kobus; hoe gaan dit?*"

"*Kannie kla nie.*"

I switched into English because my Afrikaans, while serviceable enough to establish rapport with an Afrikaans speaker, was certainly not good enough for detailed discussion. "Got anything to tell me?"

"What do you want to know?"

"Who shot the boss?"

"Pratt," said Kobus. "David Pratt."

"Not Spratt?"

Kobus shook his head. "I know him. David Pratt of Moloney's Eye."

That brought me up short. "Of *what?*"

"Moloney's Eye Trout Farm in the Magaliesburg. Pratt supplies all the Johannesburg restaurants."

"Spell it," I said, and Kobus obliged. "Did you see it happen?"

"Couldn't help it," said Kobus. "We were just getting ready to go down into the arena when that *skelm,* Pratt, came into the box, said something to the Prime Minister and then shot him in the head twice."

"What did he say?"

"I don't know, he didn't speak loudly. Anyway, I grabbed him, and . . ."

"*You* did?" Kobus was not only a model eyewitness but a participant.

"That's right. He was waving the gun about and struggled a bit. Then someone helped me and we got the gun off him—then the cops took him."

The public address system blatted out, "Clear the arena of all those cattle. Will everybody leave the stands in an orderly manner and don't panic—don't PANIC—DON'T PANIC."

Kobus looked across the arena to the stands on the far side. A restlessness was sweeping across the multihued crowd, and he said dispassionately, "Bloody fool! That's enough to put anyone into a panic."

I said, "Where's Vervoerd now?"

Kobus jerked his thumb. "Still in the box. A doctor's having a look at him."

"Then he's alive?"

"Only just."

"Know anything about Pratt?"

"A bit. He . . ."

"Save it," I said. "I have to get this back to the office. Where can I find you in the next half hour?"

"I'll be here, or in the Members' Pavilion—upstairs."

As I went back to the press room the loudspeakers were still blaring, "DON'T PANIC—DON'T PANIC," until suddenly the voice was cut off in mid-shout. I later discovered that some resourceful soul had pulled the plug on the idiot at the microphone.

The press room was bedlam, crammed with shouting reporters fighting for telephones. Fortunately, Joan had valiantly defended hers against all comers although she must have had a tough time. I had not known her long and her introduction to the newspaper world had come through me, so she had very little knowledge of how to telephone in a story.

She had rung the *Sunday Times* and, luckily, got hold of Maggie Smith, a reporter whom she knew quite well. She said to Maggie, "The assassin's name is Spratt."

"What assassin?" asked Maggie.

"The man who shot Vervoerd."

"Are you trying to tell me the Prime Minister has been assassinated?" said Maggie incredulously.

It was only then Joan realised that she, Joan Brown—intrepid, amateur girl-reporter—was scooping the world press. She froze solid. It took Maggie some time to unfreeze her, and then she had to cope with the thundering herd of reporters who charged into the press room, but by the time I got back she had regained her efficiency.

I set myself in front of her, fending off the flailing hands trying to grab her telephone, and fed her the facts a line at a time which she passed on to Maggie. Then I said, "Tell Maggie I'm going to get more from Esterhuysen and some background stuff on Pratt. It'll be about half-an-hour. Then you can give up the phone."

That telephone was seized very quickly.

When Joan and I left the press room two ambulance men went

trotting by carrying a stretcher. On the stretcher lay Hendrik Vervoerd, his hands held to his face. There was a lot of blood. His eyelids flickered and then opened, and I could see that even with two bullets in his head he was quite conscious.

Again, there was not a reporter or cameraman in sight—and I had no camera.

We watched the men carry the stretcher until they turned a corner, then went in search of Kobus Esterhuysen. We drew a blank at the VIP box so we went upstairs in the Members' Pavilion where a reception had been laid on for the Prime Minister after he had made his speech. The black waiters were still ladling out free booze because no one had told them to stop, and every freeloader in Johannesburg seemed to be present. Joan and I took a welcome brandy each, I scooped up a plate of canapés, and we went looking for Kobus.

We found him with a glass in his hand standing by a window. I asked him if he had spoken to other reporters and he smiled and shook his head, so I did my best to drain him of all he knew, glad that the immediate pressure was off and I had reasonable time to spare.

I asked him what it felt like to tackle a man who was waving a gun. He shrugged and said that Pratt did not wave the gun for very long.

"What kind of gun was it?"

Kobus said, "A .32 automatic pistol."

"I've just seen Vervoerd," I said. "He's still conscious."

Kobus stared at me. "He ought to be very dead. One bullet went in at the right cheek; the other went into his ear."

He did not really know much about Pratt apart from a few general facts. Pratt was reputed to be quite wealthy, was a strong supporter of the United Party, had gone through two wives and had the reputation of being an odd-ball. That bit about the United Party made the questioning a shade delicate because the United Party was largely supported by English-speaking South Africans while the governing Nationalist Party, of which Vervoerd was the leader, was favoured by the Afrikaners. Kobus was an Afrikaner and his leader had just been shot by an English speaker.

But Kobus let me off the hook. "Hell, man," he said. "I have no politics. I'm a painter and a sculptor and have no time for those things." He paused. "I'll tell you one thing, though; I'm glad Vervoerd was shot by a white man and not by a black Kaffir. All hell would have really broken loose then. Natives have been beaten up in the show grounds already and the army is moving in."

That was serious. We already had a state of emergency and we were but one step from martial law and army rule.

There was one point left which puzzled me. I said, "I saw Pratt being hustled away by the cops, and Vervoerd was in the VIP box. You say Pratt fired only two shots, both at Vervoerd. Right?"

"Right."

"So who was the man lying on the steps, and how the hell did he get that way?"

Kobus grinned. "That was Major Richter, Vervoerd's bodyguard. He fainted when he saw the blood."

I thanked Kobus and we went in search of a telephone and found one in an empty office. I rang Maggie Smith, gave her what I had, and said we were returning to the office but not to expect us immediately. I had a feeling that getting to the centre of Johannesburg was not going to be easy.

There had been 120,000 people at Milner Park that day and they were being shepherded out by the police and the army. The traffic jams were catastrophic. Not that it worried us because we had no car and were resigned to a long walk, but we spotted a *Sunday Times* staff car and hopped aboard.

It was dusk before we got to downtown Johannesburg and it would have been quicker to walk, although not as restful. I used the time to sort out my impressions of the day and to lay out a story in my mind. Driving down Commissioner Street we saw that Broadcast House, the city radio centre, was ringed with armed troops, and so were the offices of the *Sunday Times*. There were also armoured cars parked at strategic intersections.

Because I was a freelance I had no official press card, but we still wore the press tags accrediting us to the Union Expo. Those, some fast talking, and the fact that we were able to give authentic news of what had happened at Milner Park got us into the building.

One of the first persons we saw was Maggie Smith. "Where is Stan Hurst?" she demanded. "I thought he was with you."

"He went home after Vervoerd's speech."

"Oh, God!" she wailed. "Half the paper is being remade, everyone is screaming for Hurst, and he has to go home."

"Ring him."

"Can't," said Maggie. "He's just moved house and his telephone hasn't been installed." More telephone trouble. Maggie hurried away to give someone the bad news.

Joan said suddenly, "I know his next-door neighbour—she has a telephone." I stared at her. That was the first coincidence; in a city of over a million people Joan just happened to know Hurst's next-door neighbour.

I took her by the elbow, steered her into Hurst's office, and pointed to the telephone, then I appropriated his typewriter and began to put words on paper. Ten minutes later when Stan came on the line he sounded muzzy and was disgruntled at being woken up. "Stan, you'd better get back to the office. Vervoerd was shot this afternoon and the paper is being remade."

He didn't believe it.

More urgently. "Stan, you must get back. You have your own cables to get out to Australia." Hurst was the Johannesburg stringer for a chain of Australian newspapers.

"Is this straight?"

"I wouldn't joke about a thing like this."

"When did this happen?"

"Five minutes after you left."

"Who shot him?"

"A fellow called Pratt—David Pratt."

Something happened to Hurst; his voice was suddenly alert. "Not David Pratt of Moloney's Eye?" he said incredulously. There was a lot of incredulity about that day, but Stan had real reason for his.

"That's right."

"My God!" he shouted. "Pratt's mistress is my ex-mistress. I'm going to see her."

That was the second coincidence. Who in hell would ever suppose that the Features Editor of the *Sunday Times* and a political assassin could be linked in such a way? If I put a thing like that into a novel my publisher would scream.

"Aren't you coming into the office?"

"This is more important." He slammed down his phone.

I looked at Joan and grinned. "It's a small world."

To everybody who asked we said that Hurst was on his way back to the office. It was true, even though he was taking a detour and, after all, it was his exclusive story. The groundwork he had laid must have been delightful even though it was damned fortuitous. He strolled into the office three-quarters of an hour later and beamed at me. "Good lad!"

"That didn't take long."

"I went up to her flat," he said. "I supposed you can call it her flat even though Pratt pays the rent. I hadn't been there more than twenty minutes before two very tall, very broad, Afrikaner Special Branch cops pitched up and tossed me out on my can." He winked. "But I got what I wanted."

"What did she tell you about Pratt?"

"He's bonkers," said Hurst. "A nutter who is really round the twist—but I knew that already. She told me that he took her to Klosters in Switzerland where they were hob-nobbing with Aly Khan, among others. Then suddenly he announced that he was broke, so they went to London. Pratt booked in at the Savoy and then told her to go out and get a job. What do you think of that?"

"Was he broke?"

"Of course not. Just bloody eccentric." Stan shook his head. "Pratt won't hang for this—I don't think he'll even stand trial. And there's a hell of a lot of juicy stuff we won't be allowed to print."

He sat at his desk and started work.

I was pretty busy myself and Joan was drafted into a strange job for a newspaper office. The news of the shooting had been telephoned to the airport and most of the newsmen who were on their way out cancelled their flights and came streaming back into town. The chattering telex machines also told of others who were flying in.

All these men had to be found hotel rooms; and hotel accommodations in Johannesburg during the Union Expo were as scarce as hen's teeth. So she sat with the telephone book open at the yellow pages and rang every hotel in town and got most of the boys a room. Someone ought to have thanked her for what she did that night but I can't recall that anybody did. She certainly was not paid for it.

In spite of the strange hazards associated with the project the photographer from the *Farmer's Weekly* had got his picture—just *one* good picture. It showed Hendrik Vervoerd, Prime Minister of South Africa, sitting on the floor of the VIP box and leaning into the corner. Blood streamed down his face.

That night, in a bedroom in the Langham Hotel, the picture was auctioned off by Terence Clarkson, acting as a disinterested neutral. The bidding was brisk but too rich for local blood, and at last there were only two bidders left in the ring—*Time* magazine and *Paris-Match*. The price crept up by jerks to R2,000 (about $2,800), then *Time* shrugged, looked at *Paris-Match* and said, "What say we split it?" *Paris-Match* agreed and so the *Farmer's Weekly* photographer was a good deal richer than he had been that morning. I hope he bought himself a new camera.

The presses rolled at midnight and five minutes later the first copies were distributed around the *Sunday Times* newsroom. This was a time for relaxation; the first edition was out and away and the pressure was off. Stan brought out a bottle and we drank brandy from paper cups while scanning the front page.

Someone had written an atmosphere piece, the first paragraph of which read:

All is peaceful as the sun sets redly over the Main Arena at the Union Expo. The crowds are gone and all is quiet, and there is nothing to show of the tragedy that happened here this afternoon; nothing, that is, but the Prime Minister's head which still lies on the floor of the VIP box.

I pointed out the error to Joan and she shared my laughter, then I said, "Hey, Stan; here's something that needs changing. There's a clown on the staff who can't spell hat."

I turned back to Joan. "You know; we never did get to eat those strawberries."

"Which strawberries?"

"Those we ordered in the Members' Pavilion."

EPILOGUE

Hendrik Vervoerd survived the half-centenary of the founding of the Union of South Africa. And so did the Union—but just barely. The following year, by referendum of the white population, the country voted by a narrow margin to leave the British Commonwealth of Nations and became the Republic of South Africa.

Stan Hurst was right; David Pratt never stood trial. He was found unfit to plead by reason of insanity, and placed in the Old Fort, the high-security section of the Oranje Mental Hospital in Bloemfontein. There, on the evening of 1 October 1961, he took a bed sheet and tied it to the leg of a bed in two places. Inserting his neck in the loop so formed he rotated his body, thus committing suicide by strangulation.

Hendrik Vervoerd, still Prime Minister of what was now the Republic of South Africa, lived until September 1966. In the House of Assembly in Cape Town he was stabbed to the heart four times by a Greek immigrant named Dimitrios Tsafendas, also known as Tsafendakis, Stifianos, and Chipendis. Tsafendas ascribed his action to a huge tapeworm inside him which he variously described as a demon, a dragon, and a serpent.

He did not stand trial, either, being "detained at the pleasure of the President of the Republic." He is now (April 1977) in the psychiatric wing of Pretoria Prison, studying computers and computing, and still complaining about his tapeworm.

DESMOND BAGLEY's novels of adventure and suspense include *The Snow Tiger, The Freedom Trap,* and *The Mackintosh Man.*

I Remember
Nightmares

Richard Martin Stern

I SHUDDER to think what modern electronic reporting would have made of it. God knows, the newspapers were bad enough.

To anyone today who was alive, even semiliterate, and living in Los Angeles fifty years ago, the name Hickman would have to ring a bell. To me, although I had no actual part in the tragedy, the name brings back memory of unease and apprehension which grew into sheer terror.

William Edward Hickman, described as a "nice-looking young man," walked into the Attendance office at Mount Vernon Junior High School in Los Angeles late on the morning of December 15, 1927, with the story that a man named Perry Parker had been seriously injured in an automobile accident.

Hickman represented himself as a friend of Parker's and a fellow employee and asked to take "the Parker girl" to her father.

I was twelve years old at the time, a fat little boy in the ninth grade at Mount Vernon. It was my first experience with public school after three years in private military schools. As a result, my curriculum was somehow out of whack, and since I would only be at Mount Vernon for that one year before I went off to high school, apparently the school authorities didn't want to make the effort to get me back on track because for one period each morning I was assigned to work in the Attendance office instead of going to class.

I had finished my stint and left the Attendance office that morning no more than fifteen minutes before Hickman walked in. Was that important? I still don't know.

Because I knew that there was not one "Parker girl," but two—twins—Marion and Marjorie, as apparently the kindly lady I shall call Miss Hill, head of the Attendance office, did not.

If I had been there, might I have asked in all innocence if Hickman, who apparently was also unaware that there were twins, wanted both girls? I have no idea; nor do I know if it would have mattered if I had, although crimes planned by amateurs, and indeed by professionals as well, have been thrown completely out of gear by lesser surprises.

But I was not there, and Miss Hill, presumably after looking in the files, merely asked Hickman if he wanted Marion, whose name would have appeared first; and when he said yes, Marion, alone, aged twelve, was summoned from class and sent off in Hickman's charge.

That midafternoon Parker, who of course had been in no auto accident, received a telegram at work. It read:

DO POSITIVELY NOTHING UNTIL YOU RECEIVE SPECIAL DELIVERY LETTER. MARION PARKER (GEORGE FOX)

Parker called the school immediately, and after some confusion was told what had happened. He called his home, learned that Marion was not there, and promptly notified the police. That was the beginning.

In 1927 Los Angeles was still in many respects a small town, thinly spread, very much in the shadow of San Francisco, which was considered "the city." Kidnappings in Los Angeles were almost unknown, and the Los Angeles Police Department bore little resemblance to the splendidly equipped force it is today. Much of what happened later can be explained by these facts.

The police discovered that the telegram had been sent from Pasadena. It was their first lead, and they gave it *and all of the other facts* to the newspapers which then were in active competition, Chandler's *Times* versus Hearst's *Examiner* and *Herald-Express*. The competition took the form of glaring headlines and "extra" editions, and no slightest tidbit was missed.

By evening the entire city knew what had happened, the obvious inference was kidnapping for profit, and it seemed to me that events were coming uncomfortably close to home.

In the first place, I knew the twins, Marion and Marjorie Parker, but only casually and I do not even remember how or why; they were my age, but behind me at Mount Vernon. But what I had not known and learned from the papers was that they lived only three blocks from me, and that fact, coupled with my near-miss at actually seeing the kidnapper in the Attendance office, somehow took me out of the pure-bystander category, although if I had been asked, I am sure I could not have said why. Kids feel these things; they do not require logic. There was also an even closer connection.

Until I saw the newspapers, I had no idea who Mr. Parker was or what he did; parents belonged to their own world, not mine. Then I learned that he was a clerk at a branch of the First National Trust and Savings Bank of which my father was Executive Vice-President—and that made a big difference.

All at once it was no longer a personal-acquaintance-neighborhood-and-same-school affair; it was far more sinister. Adult lives were intertwined, Marion's family and mine, and who could say where that might lead? (I was making up fiction even then, although I had not yet reached the stage of putting it down on paper. Perhaps that made the what-if? scenarios all the more real.)

I don't remember that Marion's disappearance was mentioned at our dinner table that night. I am sure I didn't bring it up, and I doubt if either my father or mother would have. My one older brother who was home—the other was away at college—was five years older than I, just finishing high school, and interested in sports almost to the exclusion of everything else. I doubt if he even knew which junior high school I attended, so he would have seen no connection between the Parker story and me; and even if he had seen a connection, I think his reluctance to make the younger brother the center of attention would have overcome any curiosity he might have felt.

But I do remember thinking a great deal about the entire busi-

ness, and wondering what my father might be feeling about this
thing that had happened to one of his employees. I don't remember reaching any conclusion. When I was twelve, my father
was a distant figure who talked about things like stocks and bonds
which I didn't understand, or care to understand, and whose
thoughts I couldn't even guess at.

Our house was in an enclave called Berkeley Square, a private
street two blocks in length with gates at each end, one of which
was always kept closed to prevent through-traffic. There was a
night watchman named Mac who carried a gun, probably empty,
but who was *there* at night, which was a comfort, even if, as I
knew from Halloween experience, he was easy enough to avoid in
the dark.

I remember thinking about the day's happenings in bed that
night and being glad that I had not been in the Attendance office
when the kidnapper (the only name we knew him by then was
George Fox, from the telegram reprinted in the newspapers) came
in to ask for Marion, and being glad that I lived in Berkeley
Square where Mac walked around at night. The Parker house,
three blocks away, seemed in another world. When I got up to go
to school the next day, the entire affair had receded in my mind.
But the newspapers had not forgotten it.

The night before, Parker had received his Special Delivery letter
at his home. It said:

Marion secure. Interference with my plans dangerous. GEORGE FOX

And that morning Parker had another letter, at the top of
which, as in all later letters, was the word "DEATH," spelled out,
I remember, in ornate quasi-Greek characters:

P. M. Parker:
Use good judgement. You are the loser. Do this. Secure 75 $20 gold
certificates—U S currency—1500 dollars—at once. Keep them on
your person. Go about your daily business as usual. Leave out the
police and detectives. Make no public notice. Keep this affair private.
Make no search.
Fulfilling these terms with the transfer of the currency will secure
the return of the girl.
Failure to comply with these requests means—No one will ever see
the girl again—except the angels in Heaven.
The affair must end one way or the other within 3 days, 72 hours.

You will receive further notice. But the terms remain the same.
                                    FATE
If you want aid against me ask GOD not man.

Parker gave this letter to the police who despite the letter's warnings gave it to the newspapers, all of which printed it with a picture of Marion on their front pages. One must assume that their circulation figures benefited.

Throughout Los Angeles there were no longer any doubts about the nature of the drama that was in progress.

School, of course, was buzzing that day with rumors and all kinds of manufactured tales. I don't remember for sure, but I doubt if Marjorie, Marion's twin, came to school that day. I do remember that a number of kids were driven to school instead of walking or using the streetcars as they normally did. Miss Hill was absent from the Attendance office.

But things went on more or less as usual—except that the pretty red-headed teacher who taught algebra wore a serious and faintly apprehensive look instead of her usual smile—and Friday was the day when I did another of my extracurricular chores, which consisted of taking the typed copy for the school newspaper down to Polytechnic High School to be printed. (As I look back, it seems to me that the Mount Vernon authorities went to a great deal of trouble to keep me occupied during that single year. At the time I thought nothing of it. I was not a rebellious type, and if three years at military schools had taught me little else, they had convinced me to do what I was told, without questions. Once only had I tried objections—but that, as Mr. Kipling wrote, is another story.)

And so on that Friday I rode the Washington Boulevard street-car all the way to Poly High School, perhaps a half-hour ride, and it was during that ride that I saw the "extras" on the street saying that Mr. Parker had had yet a third letter, this one with an enclosure from Marion herself. I spent some of my lunch money to buy a paper.

The letter, headed by the word DEATH:

P. M. Parker:
Fox is my name. Very sly, you know. Set no traps. I'll watch for them. All the inside guys, even your neighbor Isidore B., knows when you are playing with fire there are always burns. Not W J Burns and

his shadowers either [W J Burns was a Los Angeles private detective agency]. Remember that. Get this straight. Your daughter's life hangs by a thread and I have a Gillette ready and able to handle the situation.

This is business. Do you want the girl or the seventy-five $20 gold certificates U.S. Currency? You can't have both. There is no other way out. Believe this and act accordingly. Before the day is over I will find out how you stand. I am doing a solo so figure on meeting the terms of Mr. Fox or else—

                    FATE
If you want aid against me ask GOD not man.

Marion wrote:

Dear Daddy and Mother:
I wish I could come home. I think I will die if I have to be like this much longer. Daddy please do what this man tells you or he will kill me if you don't.
Your loving daughter,
                    Marion Parker
PS.   Please Daddy I want to come home tonight.

Friday was usually a splendid day, and this Friday ought to have been something special because, as I remember it, the accident of the calendar was giving us two full weeks, instead of a customary ten days or so of Christmas vacation; no school the next week, *or* the week after, and there ought to have stretched ahead in my mind thoughts of Christmas Eve with the tree and presents and the *feel* of the holidays in the air. But what had happened and was still happening had changed all that.

In the three months since that school year began I had made some new friends in my class at Mount Vernon, but they were all older than I, and the inner differences between twelve and fourteen or fifteen approach differences in kind rather than degree. Confidences are for equals or strangers, and it would never have occurred to me even to try to explain to my new friends how *close* I felt Marion's kidnapping had become because logic played very little part in what I felt.

In the first place it was the kind of thing that happened to girls, not boys; girls were forever being protected for reasons I hadn't even thought much about. I had no sisters, and girls were mysterious and apparently fragile; in stories they were always getting into trouble.

I sympathized with Mr. Parker, but I suppose I really assumed that he would get the money and pay it and somehow everything would turn out all right. Amongst my new friends that was the conventional wisdom.

No, I think what really chilled me was the tone of the letters. My mother had taught me to read before I even started school, and reading had always been almost a vice. What I found in George Fox's letters was fiction at its wildest, and most bizarre— but close to me, and real, not make-believe; something that was actually happening which could not be shut out by closing a book.

I don't claim prescience, but I was more disturbed by the *tone* of the whole affair than I tried to let anyone know; and I remember a feeling of vast relief that Friday afternoon when I came home from school and walked into Berkeley Square through the reassuringly heavy wrought-iron sidewalk entrance gate and pretended that I could feel it closing behind me.

The broad street was empty and safe. The houses set well back from the sidewalk were all familiar. Even the palm trees that lined the street between sidewalk and curb, usually enemies because their stiff, sharp spines could puncture the bladder of a badly kicked football with ease—even the palm trees seemed friendly, and protective. Sanctuary.

I don't remember what I did that Friday night; it couldn't have been anything special. But I know that others must remember because throughout the Los Angeles area parents of young girls were either keeping them at home or else carefully escorting them wherever they went. And yet there was no general panic—so far.

But what I do remember are some fleeting and exceedingly uncomfortable thoughts in bed that night.

I had my own bedroom. The windows of my room looked down on a small patio covered by an arbor and heavy vines. Even I, fat as I was, had on occasion managed to clamber up arbor and vines and come in through the window of my room. Now, suddenly, in my own home, I was *vulnerable*. That was what I thought about before I went off to sleep.

What the Saturday-morning paper told of what had been happening since George Fox's last letter with its pitiful enclosure from Marion made matters far worse.

At five o'clock Friday afternoon Parker had a telephone call. It was a man, and Parker did not recognize the voice. The voice asked if Parker had the money, and if there were any police around. It said that there would be another phone call shortly, with instructions.

Parker called the police immediately. It was thought that the call had come from a drugstore. The police rushed to it and found no one. (Somehow, in a gruesome kind of way, the Keystone Kops come to mind.)

At half past eight that night, Fox called again. "Come to Tenth and Gramercy in your car alone. Dim your lights, and bring no police if you want to see your daughter alive."

Gramercy was the street at the foot of Berkeley Square; Tenth Street was not all that far away. I noted these facts in the paper and wished I hadn't.

Parker drove to the intersection—and *the police followed him openly*. (Again the Keystone Kops come to mind, but they have long since left the realm of slapstick and are now into tragicomedy.) The kidnapper did not show. Parker at last drove home again. How must he have felt?

Special Delivery in 1927 meant *special* delivery, and Saturday morning another letter arrived from George Fox, again with an enclosure from Marion. Together they brought the nightmare into sharp focus.

Fox's letter read:

P. M. Parker:
When I asked you over the phone to give me your word of honor as a Christian and honest man not to try a trap or tip the police you didn't answer—? Because when those two closed cars followed your car north on Wilton to Tenth and stopped shortly off Wilton on Tenth and then proceeded to circle the block on Gramercy, San Marino, Wilton and Tenth I knew and you knew what for. One was a late model and the other had disc wheels; then later, only a few minutes, I saw a yellow police car speeding toward your neighborhood—of course, you don't know anything about these facts—and that is sarcasm.

Mr. Parker, I am ashamed of you. I am vexed and disgusted with you. With the whole damned vicinity throbbing with my terrible crime —you try to save the day by your simple police tactics.

Yes, you lied and schemed to come my way only far enough to grab me and the girl too. You'll never know how you disappointed your daughter. She was so eager to know that it would be only a short while and then she would be freed from my terrible torture and then you messed the whole damned affair.

Your daughter saw you, watched you work and then drove away severely broken-hearted because you couldn't have her in spite of my willingness—merely because you, her father wouldn't deal straight for her life.

You are insane to betray your love for your daughter, to ignore my terms, to tamper with death. You remain reckless with death fast on its way.

How can the newspapers get all these family and private pictures unless you give them to them? Why all the quotations of your own self, Marion's twin sister, her aunt and school chums? All this continued long after you received my strict warning.

Today is the last day. I mean Saturday, December 17, year 1927. I have cut the time to two days and only one more time will I phone you. I will be two billion times as cautious, as clever, as deadly from now on. You have brought this on yourself and you deserve it and worse. A man who betrays his love for his own daughter is a second Judas Iscariot—many times more wicked than the worst modern criminal.

If by 8 P.M. today you have not received my telephone call—then hold a quiet funeral service at your cemetery without the body—on Sunday the eighteenth. Only God knows where the body of Marion Parker would rest in this event. Not much effort is needed to take her life. She may pass out before 8 P.M., so I could not afford to call you and ask for your $1500. for a lifeless mass of flesh.

I am base and low but I won't stoop to that depth especially to an ungrateful parent. When I call, if I call, I will tell you where to go, and how to go, so if you go, don't have your friends following. Pray to God for forgiveness for your mistake last night. If you don't come in this good, clean honest way and be square with me—that's all.

FATE FOX

If you want aid against me ask GOD not man.

Marion's note:

Dear Daddy and Mother:
Daddy, Please don't bring anyone with you today. I am sorry for what happened last night. We drove wright by the house and I cryed all the time last night. If you don't meet us this morning you will never see me again.

Love to all,
Marion Parker

Saturday afternoons there were movies at both the United and Arlington theaters, only a few blocks from Berkeley Square, usually westerns for the kids, Tom Mix, Hoot Gibson. . . . I didn't

go that Saturday afternoon. We were close to the winter solstice,
and dusk came early, and although I wouldn't for the world have
admitted it, I knew that the walk home after the film would be far
from pleasant.

Mind you, at the time I had no *real* reason to be afraid of the
unknown George Fox. The connection between Marion's father
and mine was most tenuous. As far as I knew, they did not even
know each other. And I had *not* seen Fox in the Attendance office
at school, although—and here, I suppose, is a warning that I was
already headed toward make-believe as a career—what if he
thought I had, and could identify him? Things like that happened in stories.

But unless I took a roundabout route to and from the theater, I
would pass even closer to the Parker house than I had been up to
now, and I wanted no part of that. Who knew whether George
Fox might not be watching again? No Tom Mix or Hoot Gibson
for me that Saturday afternoon.

Parker in the meantime was pleading with the police to stay out
of it, and he had Marion's note as well as Fox's rambling letter as
an argument. At last the police agreed to let him go alone to the
next rendezvous, although they did mark each twenty-dollar bill,
which is one of the few light spots in the whole, dark, sordid business. Parker went home to wait.

The inference from Marion's note was that the next telephone
call would come that morning, but it was not until evening that
Fox did call, and then his instructions were terse. Parker was to
drive to an address on Manhattan Street, pay the ransom and pick
up his daughter.

Radio was not new then, but neither was it the ubiquitous medium it became a few years later. I think that the news of what
happened at the rendezvous that night was put on the air within a
matter of minutes of the time it was known, but I did not hear it.
We had a radio in the house, a console monster, but mine was a
reading family and the thing was rarely used, so it was not until we
saw the morning newspaper that we knew about the grisly denoue-
ment that drove the entire city into a state of shock, and by evening left me more frightened than I ever want to be again.

Parker obeyed the telephone instructions. He drove alone to the rendezvous, parked, dimmed his lights, and waited. It was not long before a blue coupe pulled alongside.

Parker saw a man with a handkerchief mask over the lower part of his face. Next to the driver, Parker could see Marion. She seemed asleep.

The driver pointed a sawed-off shotgun at Parker and asked about the money, and when Parker held out the packet of bills the man jumped out of the car, grabbed the money, and jumped back in.

Parker heard the man say, "Don't follow me. I'll drive up there and put her out and you can get her."

The blue coupe drove ahead some distance, and stopped. The man got out and carried the girl to the large lawn of a house. He shouted, "There she is!" jumped back in his car, and drove away.

Parker started his car and drove to the spot, stopped the car, got out, and ran to the child. She was unmoving as he bent over her in the dim light from the street lamps. He had one close look, and then he screamed and fainted.

Marion's torso was partially wrapped in a blanket. Arms and legs had been hacked off. A wire was wrapped around her neck so tightly that it cut into the flesh. Her hair had been neatly combed, her face powdered, and her eyelids sewed open with black thread.

It is difficult to describe that Sunday. Los Angeles went from shock to mass hysteria. Literally thousands joined the manhunt without the faintest idea whom they were looking for. Parents forbade children to go out of doors. I read that churches were filled and prayers were offered—many of them, I suspect now, for vengeance. The newspapers did their screaming best to keep everyone informed.

In the midst of all this, the police found the blue coupe in a parking lot at Ninth and Figueroa—how they managed to pick it out, I never have been able to understand, because Figueroa was "automobile row" and even in 1927 Los Angeles was a city of wheels. But they did find it, identify it beyond doubt, and from the rear-view mirror take fingerprints which identified the driver as William Edward Hickman.

Also on Sunday in Elysian Park some distance away from the

rendezvous, someone found bloody packages containing the missing parts of Marion Parker's body, the suitcase which had been used to carry them, and bloodstained towels, one of which came from Bellevue Arms, a Los Angeles apartment house. Police rushed there and found Hickman's apartment. Hickman, of course, was gone.

Once William Edward Hickman was identified as the monster, the newspapers went to work digging into his past and speculating on his motives. That was when my real fright began.

Hickman had worked under Parker at the First National Trust and Savings Bank, *my father's bank,* had been fired for forging a check, had been given a parole, tried to return to the bank, and was refused.

Police and the newspapers agreed that Hickman's motive for the kidnapping *and the murder,* was not money, but revenge.

Nothing else seemed to fit. Kidnapping then was not a capital crime. Hickman could have taken the money and returned the girl safely. But he had not, and he was on the loose, and if his grudge against the bank had driven him this far against the daughter of a bank clerk—then what about me, the twelve-year-old son of the Executive Vice-President? (Tell me, doctor, have I been trying to exorcise these phantoms ever since? Is that what drove me to crime-writing and membership in the Mystery Writers of America?)

The newspapers had a story they were not going to let go. They published pictures of Hickman, as had been reported "a nice-looking young man," with dark, curly hair; and the papers even went so far as to write of "citizen's arrest," urging whoever saw anyone resembling Hickman to hold him any way he could.

A number of young men with dark curly hair were held, some beaten before the police could intervene. One man who bore a remarkable resemblance to Hickman, arrested for a robbery, was beaten by his jailmates and later found hanged in his cell.

Hickman was seen in Venice, in Long Beach, in Hollywood, driving through Cucamonga Corners, eating in a drugstore in Manhattan Beach. . . .

I believed none of this. I knew where Hickman was, right where no one would think to look for him, in the neighborhood of the Parker house—and Berkeley Square.

I am sure that I slept Sunday night, although at the time it didn't seem that I could close my eyes without hearing something that had me instantly awake again.

Always before the distant quarter-hour chimes of the grandfather clock on the front stairs landing had seemed comforting. Now those chimes were marking off the time left in my life. Jim Hawkins and *Treasure Island* were out of it; it was "The Pit and the Pendulum" now.

My mother had had planted a poplar tree on the rear lawn, and it had grown to considerable height. The slightest breeze set its leaves to rustling. I heard them time and time again that night, stealthy sounds, almost impossible to locate.

Despite the maid's cat, there were small night creatures that used the ivy beneath my window as their jungle. I heard them; I heard *something,* and when I looked I was almost sure that I could sometimes see a shape at the window. It came and went, and that only made it worse.

All houses creak. The back stairs came up across a narrow hallway from my bedroom door, and I tried to identify amongst all the other faint sounds the particular squeak that meant someone had stepped on the fifth tread from the top—something I had discovered after reading Heaven only knows what story which spoke of such things.

My older brother was heavy, and when he turned over in his bed on the sleeping porch, I had to reassure myself that I knew the sound and that it was harmless. But was it? Might I be mistaken?

I was usually a sound sleeper, and I had not listened to, or been aware of, too many of the sounds I heard.

For example, I don't remember dogs in Berkeley Square although I am sure there were some, but I heard dogs barking that endless Sunday night. And in the dark and the quiet, to my imagination at least, those dogs reminded me of stories, probably by James Oliver Curwood or perhaps Jack London, of sled dogs howling to announce death, or was it *impending* death?

In print now fifty years later the fright I felt then seems unreasonable and unreasoning. And so it was. I was sure then, as I am sure now, that my parents would not have understood it. If they had ever known, and perhaps my mother had once upon a time, what it was like to make up stories that became real in your mind, they had long since forgotten as they settled into, and fitted so well, the grown-up world of facts and finance, committees and clubs, the pre-1929 world of a rising stock market and Sinclair Lewis's *Main Street*.

God knows, I was no neglected child. I had all the love and affection anyone could ask for. Nor in the accepted sense was I misunderstood. My parents had raised two children ahead of me, both boys, and I was nothing new.

But because of the vagaries of the educational system, I was twelve years old instead of fourteen or fifteen as my classmates were, and I see now, and understood sufficiently then, that I could not have it both ways: if I wanted to be able to do the things my new friends did, as of course I did, then it would follow that I would be seen as one of them, and for them the Hickman business held awe and adolescent morbid fascination; produced a great deal of pretense of the "there he is! I saw him!" kind; perhaps, no probably, a healthy apprehension in dark places at night; but certainly no terror.

Reasonable or not, I considered myself alone, unique—and already marked as Hickman's next victim.

But perhaps my parents understood more than I thought, or else had other motives well hidden from me, because that was the Christmas vacation when my father asked if I would like to go downtown with him and be his office boy at the bank, and I jumped at the chance.

The bank building at Sixth and Spring streets in the heart of downtown Los Angeles was as banks were then supposed to be, no nonsense about openness and informality; strength and security were the themes. And my father's office was on the eleventh floor, further protection. From the time I left our house each morning riding in the rear seat of the car beside my father, while he of course read the financial news in the morning paper, until we came home at night, I was safe. It was only after darkness came, and lasted and lasted and lasted until it seemed that morning would never come again, that the terror returned.

The papers of course were still filled with stories of Hickman. Cash rewards were offered for his capture. The City of Los Angeles, the County of Los Angeles, the State of California, the Mayor of Los Angeles, the Hearst morning paper, three radio stations, *and* Aimee Semple McPherson all got into the act, and the amount of money offered totaled a staggering $56,000! Even in pre-Crash days, that was riches.

Sightseers and souvenir hunters swarmed over the Bellevue Arms which had been a perfectly respectable apartment house and now was tainted forever.

Hickman was seen here and seen there. More curly-haired young men were picked up, some beaten. All roads leading out of Los Angeles were blocked, trains and buses searched, the big red trolleys of the Pacific Electric interurban system carefully watched. Hickman had vanished.

Monday passed, and Tuesday, to me their nights, like Sunday's night, interminable. I led a kind of Jekyll-Hyde existence. By day I was very much in the open at the bank, protected by its sturdy structure and its enveloping sense of security which in my mind was typified by the great vault in the basement with its massive, intricate door, and the mirrors exposing every inch of the vast concrete bed on which the vault was set. By night I became like Rikki-Tikki-Tavi's muskrat friend, terrified of open space, seeing menace in every shadow, every unidentifiable sound.

Hickman was too smart for the police; to me that much was evident. In a city in which concealment would seem impossible, he was, nonetheless, evading detection, lying low, waiting until the furor died away. And then? Obviously it would not be the same tactic he had used before of simply walking into the Attendance office at school. No, it would be something else, probably something equally simple, impossible to anticipate. I discovered for the first time that I could not look all ways at once. Do I sound craven? I was.

Wednesday, December 21, six days after the kidnapping, came the first real break. One of the marked twenty-dollar ransom bills appeared in a store in Seattle, Washington, a thousand miles away. I read and reread the newspaper account, absorbing the implications like soothing balm—until the doubts began to set in. Call it the curse of a storyteller's mind.

The mere presence of a twenty-dollar bill, even one which was known to have been in Hickman's possession, did not by any means prove that Hickman himself had been in Seattle, or any-where near it. My friend Joe Stein, head teller at the bank, had ex-plained to me how you could tell where Federal Reserve notes had been issued, some of them thousands of miles away. Money and men were very different things indeed; money traveled effortlessly, and without detection; Hickman's twenty-dollar bill could very well have been passed originally right here in Los Angeles. It probably had.

Somehow, once your hopes are raised and then dashed again, you sink lower than before into despond, or terror. Wednesday, I think, was my worst night of all. Night sounds seemed louder, more threatening; shadows came and went at my window; I was sure the night would never end—for me.

But the lead of the twenty-dollar bill was not viewed in the same way by the authorities. And other leads began to turn up. A man resembling Hickman had used the bill to buy some items in a haberdasher's. Then two young hitchhikers in Portland, Oregon, told a tale of being given a lift by a similar-looking young man driving a green Hudson sedan near the California-Oregon line; they identified Hickman from his photograph. An investigation disclosed that a green Hudson sedan had been taken at gunpoint from a man in Los Angeles on Sunday, December 20, the day the bloody packages had been found in Elysian Park. The Hudson owner also identified Hickman from his photo.

If I knew of all this, I was still unconvinced. Too many young men resembling Hickman had been overpowered—and turned loose again. The man himself was still at large.

There were reports that Hickman had been seen *south* of Seat-tle, apparently doubling back. But he had been "seen" before, in spots all over southern California, and there was no assurance as far as I was concerned that these new reportings were any more reliable.

They did do one thing, however. They aroused Oregon and Washington almost to the state of hysteria that still existed in Los Angeles; papers all up and down the Pacific coast had carried the stories with the grisly details.

Then, back in Oregon again, a man in a green Hudson sedan cashed another marked twenty-dollar bill. I wanted to believe, oh, how I wanted to believe that the obvious implications were true! This time, mercifully, they were.

On Thursday, December 22, two police officers from Pendleton, Oregon, spotted a speeding green Hudson sedan, gave chase, caught it, and arrested Hickman. That was all there was to it.

In the car he had a revolver and the sawed-off shotgun with which he had threatened Parker, but he made no resistance. Nor did he deny his identity, and, in fact, boasted of having been stopped and released by four different Los Angeles police officers as he left the city.

His capture took place exactly one week from the day when he had walked into the Attendance office at Mount Vernon, missing me by only fifteen minutes, and asked for "the Parker girl."

It was over. This time the news was real, and final. I tried, and failed, to find possibilities for mistake. The police had him, identification was positive, and that was that. The sense of relief almost made me sick.

That night, for the first night since Sunday, I slept. If there were night sounds, I did not hear them. What shadows there may have been came and went unnoticed. It was as if the nightmare had never been.

There would be Hickman's confession, his trial beginning in January 1928, and his execution in San Quentin that October. They meant little to me. As far as I was concerned, the Marion Parker–Hickman kidnap and murder case ended that Thursday, December 22. Almost.

The following evening after dinner, following my family's custom on the night before Christmas Eve, we put up the Christmas tree. I suppose a branch needed trimming, I don't remember, but I was sent out to the garage workshop to fetch a hatchet.

It was already dark outside. No matter. And then, as I was coming back toward the house, the poplar tree rustled suddenly, and for a moment I could feel those mice feet scampering up and down my spine again.

But the moment passed, and instantly, no longer threatened, I was bold, defiant, heroic in the face of any odds. If Hickman *were* to come at me now, *this* is what I would do! I swung the hatchet with both hands.

I still have a small scar on my right ankle where the hatchet landed before I could stop it.

Is there scar tissue on my psyche too?

Author of *The Tower* (the novel on which the film *The Towering Inferno* was based in part), RICHARD MARTIN STERN has also written numerous novels of mystery and suspense, including the well remembered *Cry Havoc*.

---

211 DOSSIER

John Ball

IT WAS a little after eight on a Sunday evening in April 1976; the house was quiet and I was alone, bent over the typewriter, when the doorbell rang.

Like a ringing telephone the doorbell is almost impossible to ignore; I got up and answered it.

Under the entrance light stood a huge man, several inches over six feet with the physique of a bull. He had massive shoulders, an enormous belly, and a thirty-eight automatic pointed straight into my face.

It wasn't the first time I'd seen him.

With one thick hand he rammed me back from the doorway. *"Make one sound and you're dead!"*

Then he raised the gun over my head as if to bring it crashing down onto my skull.

For three intense seconds I weighed the odds and tried to measure the chance of resistance. I hold a karate black belt that once before had saved my life. To take him I would have a possible element of surprise for a half second or so; but I would have to give away more than a hundred pounds and some thirty years, and go up against the S and W automatic that was held hard in the man's right hand. The gun was aimed straight between my eyes and the odds were too long against me. Good sense, I hope, and years of dojo training told me that I would have to take my chances the other way. Later, if he turned his back for a moment . . .

The man slammed me down onto my davenport. With the gun still on me he pulled out a roll of wide masking tape and ordered, "Put your hands together."

I laid one on top of the other, remembering something I had once been taught in a Chicago dojo, well before the war.

The gunman locked his left fingers around my wrists like a rigid clamp while he took nine turns of masking tape around my hands and lower wrists. Then, going behind me, he wound eight turns over my mouth and up until my nostrils were almost smothered in the sticky adhesive. In desperation I pulled my lips into my mouth, breaking the close seal of the tape, so that I could breathe. He didn't see me; he was taping my ankles together. When he had finished, I was immobilized.

"You move, you turn around, you make one peep, you're dead."

From his jacket pocket he pulled out a pair of gloves and put them on. Then he took out the gun, held it in his palm, and looked at me, making up his mind.

All I could think of was to roll my eyes, up, let my head loll on one side, and try to suggest that I was about to pass out.

I don't know whether it did any good or not. He slapped me and demanded, "Where's the jade?"

It was not time to show resistance; I nodded to the cabinet behind him.

He forced the door open, then disappeared down the corridor toward the bedroom and came back with a pillowslip. With one huge, gloved hand he began to grab off the shelves delicate jade carvings, some of which I had carried back from the Orient on my lap to guard them against breakage. Pat and I had been building that collection for almost twenty-five years, and into it had put study, love, care, meticulous selection, and a very substantial amount of money.

The gunman dropped the jade pieces into the pillowcase. When one fell from his fingers and broke, he swore viciously and moved toward me, as though he could somehow take the loss out of my hide.

In eight minutes he had emptied the jade cabinets of their precious contents. Then, the filled pillowcase in one hand, he came to where I sat, raised the gun once more, and put it against my head.

The total horror of that moment will never leave me. I was certain I had only a second to live: I used that fragment of time to ask God to look after my wife. . . .

I shut my eyes; at that instant of death I wanted merciful darkness. Then I heard the vicious voice again. *"You move, you yell, you go outside, YOU'RE DEAD."*

I let my head fall to my knees as though I had passed out.

The gunman yanked out the telephone cord and ran out the front door.

It was 8:18 and I was still bound and gagged as he had left me a few seconds before. The constricting tape around my face made it impossible to draw a normal breath and I was dizzy. Because I had been taught how years before, I got my hands loose and worked the tape down off my mouth (at the expense of some skin). Then I rolled over and over on the floor, out into the kitchen, and the extension telephone where I dialed 787-1122, the emergency number for the Los Angeles Police Department.

I rolled back into the living room and peeled the tape off my ankles; I was ready to stand up when Pat came in the front door, all smiles after her dinner out. She took one startled look and from that point on I had help.

Two black-and-whites responded: not immediately because I had not reported the 211 (armed robbery) in progress. I had given a quick description of the gunman over the phone, not too well because I still didn't have enough air in my lungs and my self-possession was a little cracked.

Presently the doorbell rang; Pat opened it to two uniformed patrol officers and a sergeant who was quiet, young, and visibly capable. I gave them a quick account of what had happened. The sergeant asked me to estimate the loss; when I replied that it would be somewhere between fifty and eighty thousand dollars, obviously that made it a different ball game. The sergeant returned to his car while the two officers began to take a detailed statement.

I turned to Pat. "You'd better make some coffee," I told her. "Use the big pot."

"The one that makes thirty cups?"

Twelve years of working with the Pasadena Police Department, of which I was technical staff advisor, had taught me what to expect. "Yes, and get the back-up ready. We're probably going to have more company."

Policemen came and left in a steady stream. At the door IDs were flashed, a somewhat unnecessary gesture under the circumstances. Pat served up the coffee to half of the Valley Division (West) which was good because it kept her from thinking about what had happened.

Once more the doorbell rang.

"Mr. Ball?"

"Yes."

Two IDs were held up for my inspection. The taller man, who had stepped right out of the pages of Peter Cheney, did the talking. "Investigator Yost. This is my partner, Investigator Scott."

It was already an ungodly hour and the house was half full. "Come in, gentlemen," I invited. "Before we start in, how do you take your coffee?"

Once more I went over the story, supplying every detail that I could, and admitting my lapses. For one thing, I couldn't describe the suspect's shoes and there was no excuse for an oversight like that. The fact that I hadn't expected to live through the experience was no excuse, and I knew it.

"Had you ever seen this man before?"

"Yes."

That surprised them. Then I told how, two days before, I had received a telephone call asking me to verify a piece of jade. When I had explained that I didn't do that, but could recommend a good man, the caller pressed and, as a credential, mentioned the name of a mutual friend (or so he said).

A half hour later the giant had shown up, a slab of hardstone in his hand. I never got to see it. A phone call from a confederate drew him away immediately, pleading an auto accident. It was all very plausible at the time. Later I realized there were several people in the house: obviously he had come to pull the job, but turned away when he saw that the time was not right, using the prearranged phone message as an excuse.

"Did you see his car?"

"No." But I thought my ward might have glimpsed it. I knew she'd seen our giant visitor that day.

"Did he give any name?"

"No."

"How did he behave?"

"Like a savage—a wild animal just before feeding time."

I wasn't trying to be funny; it was the best way I could describe him.

Once more the doorbell rang.

"Mr. Ball?"

"Yes."

A different kind of ID this time. "May we come in, please? We're from the FBI."

Pat started the back-up coffee maker and reloaded the first.

At a quarter after six we got to bed and slept until seven-thirty. The doorbell was ringing and there were more policemen. Right behind them came Investigators Yost and Scott. They had not been to bed. And they had instructions.

"A lot of TV people are coming to interview you," they said. "All of the major networks, and several local stations. We want you to cooperate with them all. Now, sit down and we'll tell you what we want you to say."

They were still briefing me when the doorbell rang. And the telephone. The call was from New York; someone had heard a news flash about the robbery. He had a marvelous jade collection for sale: for a hundred thousand dollars he would give me a fine assortment of pieces; he was still in the midst of his sales talk when I hung up—my temper was a little short that morning.

I ate breakfast off my lap as the careful briefing went on. After that the deluge began. Reporters swarmed into the house, TV cameramen and crews set up in every available spot. Lights were hauled in and cables connected. How my wife stood it I don't know.

The TV and radio interviews went on for several hours without a break. As quickly as one crew got out of the way, another set up. I was asked to change clothes, to stand beside my books, and once to please remove the bust of Hitler from my mantlepiece. I explained with as much patience as I had left that the bust in question was of Edgar Allan Poe and that it was going to stay right where it was.*

We ate lunch with half a dozen police guests and tried to unwind. After that Yost and Scott turned up again. Something had developed in the case and they had Officer Rick Brown with them. Armed with a shotgun, the officer looked impressive. Then we were told that until further notice there would be an armed police guard in our home around the clock. We were also told that twenty-eight policemen, investigators, and specialists were working full time on the case.

As Brown went through the house, checking every possible entry and place of concealment, Yost and Scott announced that they would like us to come to the police station with them—and to bring our ward with us.

Our ward is a rather special young lady. She speaks eight languages, five of them with native fluency. Her name is Kesang Dolma Ngokhang and she was born in the highest permanently occupied community on earth: Phardi, Tibet. She has since become our daughter-in-law. Her marriage to our only son, John David Ball, is believed to be the first Tibetan-American union.

At the police station, a young police lieutenant was waiting to meet Kesang. He quickly put her at ease and explained that he was a hypnotist. He proposed that he put her under to see if she could then recall any details about the car she had just glimpsed three days before.

After he took her away we sat and waited. I closed my eyes and fell asleep. It had been a long night.

An hour later Kesang came back. "She's a remarkable girl," Lieutenant Gaida said. "Under hypnosis she was most cooperative, and she certainly has a brain. She gave us a good description of the car, even a partial make on the license."

That was stimulating news. There is a computer in California that can work with fragmentary clues like that and produce answers.

* Ball refers to the best-novel Edgar Award statuette bestowed on *In the Heat of the Night* by MWA—Ed.

But that wasn't all. "I know your police background," the lieutenant went on, "so perhaps you'll be interested in the new Smith and Wesson composite identikit technique. It ends up not with a drawing, but with a simulated photograph of the suspect."

He handed me a composite board and there, staring at me, was the unmistakable face of the savage gunman who had committed the armed robbery. "It's dead on," I said. "How did you manage it?"

"With Kesang—under hypnosis. She was able to do much better that way. Do you buy it?"

"Totally. Put it on the wire."

We went back to the house and our armed guard. Rick Brown, shotgun at his side, proved a stimulating dinner guest.

At two o'clock in the morning the phone rang: it was Detective Vince Scott.

"Would you like to see the guy who robbed you?" he asked, quite pleasantly. "We've got him in a cell."

"I'll be right over."

"No, he'll keep until morning. We'll want you to identify him in a show-up. Be here at nine."

At nine, in the West Valley Detectives Division, I was taken into a small office and the door was closed. Then, in total privacy I was shown a card. It was about eight by ten and on it, mounted in symmetrical order, were the photographs of six men, all of whom superficially fitted the description that I had given. But the center face in the bottom row leaped out at me. "That's him," I declared.

"How certain are you?"

"Positive, no qualification."

"Would you testify to that in court?"

"Yes."

"Turn the card over and sign your name opposite the proper number on the back. Then send Pat in here. Don't say anything to her when you go out, and don't give her any signals."

I went out, weak in the knees, and sat down. Somebody handed me a Virgil Tibbs book. "While you're here, Mr. Ball, would you be willing to put your name in this?" At that point for the LAPD I would have signed anything including a blank check.

That evening Tim Yost and Vince Scott, over dinner, filled us in. Some parts of the story remain confidential, but I now have permission to report all of the essential details.

The partial description on the car used in the robbery, and the fragment of its license, began a thorough search for the vehicle. The computer came up with a list of possibles; this was quickly pared down by careful investigative work until the deductive finger began to point toward one of the California beach cities south of Los Angeles.

Meanwhile the FBI had taken my photographs of the missing jade pieces, duplicated them, and sent out bulletins throughout the country and the world. Fine jade carvings are unique and any one of the stolen pieces could be recognized and identified. Every jade mart was covered. The LAPD got out a flyer with pictures of the principal pieces taken.

The composite photograph of the suspect was circulated widely throughout the Los Angeles area. Because of the developing clues regarding the car, a particular effort was put on in Orange County, which lies just south of Los Angeles.

In an Orange County Sheriff's Station a deputy coming on patrol checked the bulletin board, saw the composite, and recognized a local nightclub bouncer who had a heavy record—he had done time for armed robbery and was currently on parole.

The deputy IDed the photograph. "That's Bear Zabala," he said.

From that moment attention focused in on Zabala. And he had a close associate who drove a car that fitted the partial description obtained under hypnosis. Four very capable and well-prepared officers went to Zabala's house and got him outside on a pretext. They knew his size and ferocity, and his claim to be a karate black belt. (He does not appear in the official directory. Also, qualified karatekas will tell you that it would be impossible for such a man to reach that rank in any recognized dojo in the world.)

When Zabala emerged in front of his house, one of the officers held a revolver on him while he was told that he was under arrest for armed robbery. Despite the fact that the officers were armed and one gun was already pointed his way, Zabala appeared ready to resort to the violence that was his stock in trade. Then, knowing that his position was hopeless, he capitulated and was cuffed. Tim

Yost, who is at least six feet two and a notable athlete, said that he felt like a midget beside him.

In the meantime, word was out on the street that I was to be hit to keep me from making an identification. (Hence the twenty-four-hour armed guard.) At one time, six undercover cars and a helicopter covered a suspect car for forty miles through the maze of the Los Angeles freeways and cleared up another crime in the process.

By meticulous investigation possible receivers of the stolen jades were checked, street rumors were painstakingly picked up and checked out, and much other work of a confidential nature was done. Within three days of intensive activity the case was cracked, some of the stolen property recovered, and three of the four suspects taken into custody. It was a textbook example of first-class police procedure and the kind of detective work that represents the highest state of the art. Here is how we reconstructed the story:

A friend of mine talked about my jade collection in a bar. He was overheard and the robbery was planned.

The "alleged instigator" was Edward Watkins, Sr., fifty-six, a man with a very long and heavy criminal record that included many convictions for major crimes. He had been repeatedly paroled as reformed. Crime, according to his record, appeared to be his sole means of support.

Allegedly, Watkins hired the giant Zabala to commit the robbery and Robert Vaughan of Garden Grove, California, to drive the getaway car. (Vaughan was another Orange County nightclub bouncer who also claimed high karate rank.)

Edward Watkins, Jr., the son of the man accused of planning the robbery, received the stolen merchandise. He subsequently tried to extort several thousand dollars from me for its return. During this period my telephone was wired, with my consent, and the call was recorded.

At the preliminary hearing I testified against Zabala who was present in court. His humble, injured attitude, and his new beard, did not deceive the court. The defense attempted to prove that I was not able to recognize a gun in the suspect's hand and that my eyesight was defective. Fortunately I had just passed my commercial pilot's physical examination the previous week, and that included a considerable number of eye tests. The claim that I could not recognize a gun was answered by the fact that the preceding week's MWA meeting had been entirely devoted to various types of firearms and their uses.

The judge bound all defendants over for trial, with the following dispositions:

Edward Watkins, Sr., alleged to have planned the entire operation and to have hired the actual holdup men: at liberty. He had not been arrested at the time of this writing.

Edward Watkins, Jr., pleaded guilty to having received the stolen property. Watkins, Jr., returned some of the stolen jades and claimed fervently that he wanted no more of crime. In view of his family situation (a wife and two small children), and the possibility that he had been forced into the operation by his father, he was allowed to plead to a misdemeanor. He was fined $500, given a year's probation, and ordered by the court to make restitution.

Robert Vaughan, twenty-five, while wanted was turned in by his attorney. He pleaded guilty to driving the getaway car and was sentenced to one year in jail. He stated that he had been paid $1500 for his part in the robbery; he gave it all to his attorney for his defense.

Daniel "Bear" Zabala, twenty-four, attempted to plea-bargain but was refused. After the preliminary hearing, at which he was bound over, he finally confessed to armed robbery. He was then on parole for a similar offense and had a three-year parole tail at the time (years of supervised parole yet to serve). Zabala was paid $3500 to pull the robbery. The next day he spent the money to buy a motorcycle. Immediately after his arrest, the motorcycle was stolen.

He has been sentenced to serve ten years to life for armed robbery and is now in prison.

The jade collection cannot be rebuilt and I have no intention of trying. I did escape with my life, and at the time that seemed enough. The insurance company, after legal action, paid off the loss.

But the beauty that once graced our home in the jade cabinet is gone and with it a considerable portion of our lives.

JOHN BALL is the author of *In the Heat of the Night* and many other novels and stories about Detective Virgil Tibbs.

From the Grass Roots Up

Lawrence Treat

AS A MYSTERY WRITER for most of my adult life, I've been accustomed to putting imaginary characters in imaginary predicaments, to accuse them unjustly of crimes and then watch them work their way out. And, although I was neither accused of murder nor of a major crime, nor was I exactly a fugitive from justice, nevertheless—

Let me give the background. The town of Gay Head, population a few hundred, is situated at the eastern end of Martha's Vineyard. It is an area of windblown hills and shrub-covered moors that slope toward the clay cliffs that loom over the beaches. There are no stores, no industry. Since 1870 the town has been governed by the Wampanoag Indians, and they have retained tight political control. With a few exceptions some years back, all the important town offices have been held either by Indians or by their spouses.

In the twenties and thirties substantial numbers of summer people began arriving, buying land from the Indians and constructing vacation homes, and by the fifties and sixties the problems of the outside world had filtered in. But summer people don't cast their

votes in Gay Head, and the Indians continued to run the town
without any appreciable interference.

In the spring of 1976 one Harold Montamat decided to run for
treasurer. He is not an Indian. He is a retired diplomat, experienced in finance and accounting. He tears around the island on a
motorcycle and has cleared some five acres of land with his own
hands, plus a machine or two. He has a military mustache and he
looks like a British sahib leading a cavalry charge with drawn
saber, and he spouts the King's English with a rhetorical flow
worthy of a Gladstone or a Macaulay.

His candidacy was a definite threat to the ruling faction, whose
treasurer once, after a mistake had been pointed out in her financial report, rose at a town meeting and said quietly, "If I was paid
more, I could add better." And she sat down. Under such circumstances, Montamat thought he could do a better job for the town,
and my wife and I, together with one Tom Seeman, were among
those who signed Montamat's nominating petition. Mrs. Beverly
Wright, an Indian, was running against him, and it was generally
agreed that the election would be close.

But for the fire, I would probably not have been involved. I
would have cast my vote, had my say at the town meeting, and
gone back to a neighboring town and to the apartment that I'd
been renting every winter for the past four years. Since my wife
and I owned a beach house in Gay Head where we spent five or
six months annually, we'd chosen Gay Head as our voting residence and had voted there for the past several years.

I'd been active in Gay Head community affairs. I was on the
zoning board of appeals and on the finance committee. I'd been an
officer in the community council and I'd worked for a zoning ordi-
nance. I spoke up at meetings and my views were well known. I
felt that I was on friendly terms with virtually everybody in Gay
Head, Indian or non-Indian. I lined up with no faction.

On Thursday, November 20, we had already moved to our winter quarters in the town of West Tisbury, about ten miles from
Gay Head. That was the night of the fire.

It apparently started in the southwest corner of the cellar, where
the wind was in the most favorable direction to spread the flames,
and our house was burned down to the last venerable stick. No

outsider was ever even suspected of being guilty. This was strictly a home-town torch job.

We were unable to provoke any real investigation of the cause of the fire, although almost everyone in Gay Head believes he knows who was responsible. The police chief lived about a hundred feet away from our house. He made no investigation whatsoever. I had to initiate the request to the state fire marshal to come to the island. He arrived eighteen days after the fire and asked me my name, rank, and serial number, or the equivalent thereof, and then went home. The insurance adjuster knocked on my apartment door while the embers were still smoldering, and in a fatherly voice he asked a few seemingly harmless questions. I know of no provable corruption in the matter. I know of no money that changed hands.

In the phantasmagoria of events that took place the following spring, sometimes it was necessary to force oneself to remember that Gay Head had an atmosphere and a background, a tradition peculiar unto itself. Its government had an opera bouffe quality in which the impossible was almost normal. The government had a relaxed quality about it, like a horse grazing with no fixed purpose except to nibble here and there. Law enforcement ranged from a state of suspended inanition to abrupt spurts of paranoiac activity. Life in Gay Head varied from the frustrating to the amusing, according to the extent of your own involvement.

So much, then, for background. On the evening of May 11, 1976, some six months after our home was destroyed by fire, my wife and I walked into the town hall to attend the annual town meeting. We sat down on folding chairs in the center section reserved for voters. We chatted for a few moments with some of our neighbors. Several of them condoled with us on the matter of the fire. We were feeling secure, and somewhat proud to be a part of a traditional New England town meeting. This was democracy, where everyone could speak up and have his say.

Then one of the town registrars walked over to us.

He leaned down and told us we couldn't sit where we were. I asked him why, and he said that on the previous evening the Board of Registrars had decided to take our names off the voting list. I asked for what reason, and he said because we no longer lived in Gay Head. I said how could we, when somebody had burned down our house. I said the whole thing was ridiculous, nobody could disqualify us *ex parte,* without even a hearing, and I refused to leave.

He called the police chief, who backed him up. I repeated my statement, pointed out that deprivation of our vote was patently illegal and might make the entire proceedings of the meeting questionable, and that the election and every action taken tonight might be nullified by the courts. The chief merely repeated the order to leave. I asked him whether he'd use force to eject us, and he said he would. I told him that under those circumstances we'd submit, but first I wanted to lodge a formal protest.

Mary Harris, the unsmiling clerk, was seated at a table at the front of the room. With her shoulder-length hair and her long, doleful face, she looked more like a teenage dropout than a responsible town official, but in her quiet way she has the self-confidence of a Muhammad Ali. She is an *ex officio* member of the Board of Registrars, but she looked up at me with an air of innocence, as if I were a passenger who'd unaccountably gotten on the wrong bus.

She listened to me while I explained what had happened. She said she'd called Boston that day and they'd told her I couldn't vote. I asked whom she'd spoken to and precisely what the conversation had been, and she replied that it was perfectly obvious that we had no right to vote, and so we'd better leave. I said I wanted to make a formal protest, in writing. She consented, picked up a sheet of paper and started to scratch out the words, "The Treats insist on trying to vote, even though—"

I stopped her and pointed out that I, and not she, was making the protest. She threw the pencil at me and shoved another piece of paper in front of me. I leaned down and wrote, in a rather shaky hand, "I protest being disenfranchised because my house was burned down." Then I returned the pencil.

My wife and I left the hall under the escort of the police chief. There is a sense of shame in being conducted from a public place by the police, as if you were being sent to prison. I remembered that years ago one of the grand old men in the labor movement in the South told me I'd never be truly free as long as I had the middle-class fear of going to jail, whereas he accepted injustice as part of life. His last term of prison had been served for trying to read

the Constitution of the United States on the steps of the Mobile
city hall. It was one of several imprisonments for his civil-rights
stands, and he had no bitterness. On the contrary, he said prison
gave him a chance to catch up on his reading.

Although I've never been in jail, except as a visitor, I can see
his point. I should have gone proudly, as if into righteous battle.

Actually few people realized what was happening. Two of our
neighbors, however, caught on and they followed us out to express
their indignation. One of them was crying. We urged her to go
back and vote.

Subsequently I learned that Tom Seeman, who also had been
signatory to Montamat's nominating petition and was also a Gay
Head voter temporarily living in the next town, had been disqualified in the same manner as we had.

My wife and I went home in a daze and tried to absorb what
had happened. The next morning we turned on the local radio and
heard the news. Ninety-two votes had been cast in the election for
treasurer. Forty-six were for Montamat and forty-six for Mrs.
Wright. Mary Harris, the town clerk, stated that the votes had
been counted twice, with due care.

Our three "disqualified" votes would have made the difference.

In Gay Head, however, nothing is certain. A day later clerk
Mary Harris "found" another ballot marked in ink and with Beverly Wright's maiden name written on it. The clerk decided that
the vote was valid and the tie broken. She immediately declared
Mrs. Wright the winner and swore her in as the Gay Head treasurer.

Our candidate, Montamat, reacted by stating that three voters
had been illegally disqualified, and he demanded that they be restored to the voting list, their votes accepted, and a recount ordered.

I spent the morning in the law library at the county courthouse.
Chapter 51, Section 37, of the General Laws of the Commonwealth of Massachusetts reads as follows:

They [the registrars] will strike from the register the name of each
person who has died, and the name of each voter who has removed
from the city or town and as to whom they have received notification
from the registrars of such voter's new place of residence that he has
been listed there. *They will remove no other name from the current*

*register, however, and they will not change a place of residence
shown for a voter on such register, until they have sent the voter notice of their intention to do so, setting a date when he may be heard.*
[Italics are mine.]

Chapter 56, Section 22, provides the penalties for violation of
the above as "a fine of not less than five hundred nor more than
one thousand dollars or by imprisonment for not more than one
year or both."

I sent a copy of Chapter 51, Section 37, to the Board of Registrars, calling their attention to the requirements of the law and
stating that I intended to bring the matter to the attention of the
Attorney General to see what remedies I had. I sent the letter
from West Tisbury by registered mail, return receipt requested.
The West Tisbury and Chilmark post offices, the latter of which is
the mailing address for Gay Head, are five miles apart. Eight days
later the Board of Registrars signed and returned my receipt. They
did not answer my letter, and they did nothing further in the matter.

Nevertheless I felt triumphant. I had the law on my side. Once
the facts of my disenfranchisement were made public, I expected
the righteous indignation of an aroused community to burst forth
with the splendor of a Fourth of July fireworks. I thought that in
this bicentennial year celebrating the cause of freedom, the full
power of the state would sweep into action, restore our votes, and
transform us from victims of injustice into national heroes, or at
least local ones.

Nothing like that happened. Nobody followed my naive mys-
tery-writer's script. I felt as lonely and as vulnerable as if I'd been
swimming in the middle of the Atlantic Ocean without clothes and
with no ship in sight.

Obviously the forces of justice were on vacation and needed a
nudge. A letter or two ought to do it, so I picked up the Boston
phone book and found the address of the Attorney General, Civil
Rights division. I outlined the facts and asked for advice. To my
surprise, I received no answer, but meanwhile I'd written to the
Massachusetts office of the American Civil Liberties Union. They
answered in due course and advised me to request a hearing before
the Board of Registrars, which was the very board that had disenfranchised me. To me, this seemed like asking the man who'd
mugged me to decide whether he should punish himself and return

my money. I therefore wrote a second and more eloquent letter stating what seemed obvious to me—that a citizen of the United States had an absolute right to vote and that I'd thought the ACLU's job was to act whenever basic civil liberties were violated.

I received no answer.

I'm a writer. I'd rather write a thousand letters than make one phone call, but I was finally reduced to dialing the Attorney General's office and talking to someone I couldn't even see. He informed me that my letter was on file but that the civil-rights division of the Attorney General's office didn't handle election matters. The Secretary of the Commonwealth, Elections Division, was the proper place in which to lodge my complaint.

The New England chapter of the Mystery Writers of America was due to hold its monthly meeting the following week, so my wife and I decided to push our claim while we were in Boston.

We had no trouble finding the Elections Division office. It was located on one of the upper floors of the state office building, and the view of Boston and the Charles River was magnificent. We spoke to a charming girl and her legal assistant, who was a law student at Boston University.

In the course of a discussion of an hour or so, they maintained that, while they sympathized with us, they could do nothing. No jurisdiction.

But who had jurisdiction? Ah! That, they didn't know.

I quoted the constitution of the Commonwealth of Massachusetts, Article XI: "Every subject of the Commonwealth . . . *ought* [italics mine] to obtain right and justice freely, and without being obliged to purchase it; completely and without any denial; promptly and without delay; conformably to the laws."

The Elections Division set up an interview for us with one of the assistant attorney generals. He listened to our story. He was courteous and he said he'd look up the law, which he did. He wrote me later on, quoting a case and concluding that "the Attorney General is not the proper party to seek relief in cases such as yours."

I ask, who then?

On their part, Seeman and Montamat were also trying to get action. Montamat sought an appointment with one of the registrars in order to see what could be done to remedy matters. The registrar refused to involve himself in anything so formal, but he did happen to meet Montamat at the town dump. I quote from Montamat's notes on the conversation.

Montamat: "The statute gives them [the Treats] the right to be heard before you can disqualify them."

The registrar: "You don't need no goddamn law. Everybody knows the Treats can't vote."

Meanwhile Seeman was making valiant attempts to speak to District Attorney Philip Rollins concerning the criminal aspects of the case. Regularly, Tom got as far as the DA's switchboard. For reasons that baffle me, Rollins took a dislike to Tom, accused him of being interested in his rights only because he hoped to get some money out of it, and practically kicked Tom out of the office.

Tom took the matter philosophically and rolled with the punch. Tom is in his thirties. He is slim, strong, clean-cut, with dark intense eyes that burn with sincerity and seem to reflect some goal that lies too deep for utterance.

I sometimes wonder what would have happened but for the local press. Gerald Kelley of the *Grapevine* and George W. Adams of the *Vineyard Gazette,* both of them able journalists, took up the case. They headlined it, interviewed the town clerk and quoted her verbatim. Some of her remarks printed in the *Gazette* and the *Grapevine* were as follows:

> If I'm supposed to do everything by the book, I'll have to be paid $10,000. I use my own judgment on those things. . . . I send out those questionnaires about voting status only to the obvious ones. . . . The Treats listed Gay Head as their voting residence and that's why I didn't accept it. . . . The Board of Registrars can question anybody. If they have doubts, they don't have to accept a person on the voting list.

(Chapter 51, Section 48 provides that the Registrars *must rely on their records, and that before removing a name from the voting list, there must be a hearing* at which the voter may be represented by counsel and all witnesses may be cross-examined.)

The articles in the local *Gazette* and *Grapevine* were taken up by the *New Bedford Times-Register,* by the *Cape Cod Times,* and finally by the *Boston Globe.* For my wife and myself, that was the week that was. Our phone rang all day long. Reporters, friends, all the force and strength of an aroused community finally were brought to bear.

Two of the registrars resigned.

And the DA finally stirred.

We spoke to him in an office in the stately brick courthouse which had become famous at the time of the hearings on the Chappaquiddick affair. But there were no TV cameras and no newsmen hovering outside the small smoke-filled room where we had our interview with Philip Rollins, the well-fed District Attorney.

He sent for the green volume containing the General Laws of the Commonwealth of Massachusetts and, after reading the relevant statute, turned to the section setting out the penalties. He said that the right to vote was sacred, and was at the foundation of democracy itself. He said his father had been a town official and would have turned in his grave if he'd heard our story. He said he'd investigate.

The result of his investigation was a court order to show cause why a criminal complaint should not be issued against the registrars.

At the subsequent hearing the registrars sat in the courthouse like small subdued children caught talking in class and sent to the principal's office. They were scared little creatures, and they looked it.

Just before the scheduled hearing, we told the DA that the matter appeared to be far more serious than we'd originally realized, because it now seemed that the motive was fraudulently to deprive us of our votes in order to ensure Montamat's defeat, and that Montamat had evidence on the point. The DA promised to look into it. (He never interviewed Montamat.) Then, for reasons beyond me, the DA moved to continue the hearing in recess for two weeks.

Two weeks later, a half hour before court opened on the morning of the postponed hearing, we had another interview with the DA.

He said he didn't feel that he could prove the graver charge of fraudulent intent to influence an election.

I asked whether he nevertheless intended to pursue the original Chapter 51 charge of illegally depriving us of our vote.

He said yes, he would press the matter in court later on in the morning. We said we stood ready to testify to the facts as we'd presented them to him.

He thanked us and informed us that he was trying to work out a settlement of the matter; he asked us whether we'd attend a meeting that evening with the selectmen and a special town attorney, appointed for this night only. The regular town attorney, Rollins explained, had represented Seeman and had therefore disqualified himself. The proposed compromise settlement, according to Rollins, was designed to give us absentee ballots. We said we'd cooperate to the extent that we could without prejudice to our statutory rights, if we were restored to the voting list and if our possible actions had no bearing on this morning's hearings.

We parted with the firm assurance that the criminal aspects of Chapter 51 would be prosecuted, and that we'd be perfectly free to do as we wished about any proposals to be made that evening. We then went out for a short walk and returned to the courthouse, where we watched a succession of teenagers answer to various charges of driving without a license, driving without proper insurance or safety stickers, and sleeping on the beach.

Our case was announced without fanfare just before noon. The order to show cause was read.

Then—bombshell!—DA Rollins stepped to the bench and asked that the motion be dismissed!

The judge asked if the complainants had agreed to the dismissal. The DA said no.

Despite our opposition, the judge granted the motion.

We were shocked, horrified, dismayed. We tried to find out what had gone on behind the scenes and why Rollins had reversed himself so completely. We told reporters that this must be some kind of a deal and was conscienceless.

A half hour later I chased the DA down the street, only to see him duck into a doorway. I lost him.

Subsequently he wrote me a letter of "explanation." I quote it, written under date of July 1, 1976: "It was sufficient warning to the officials at Gay Head that they had better start obeying the General Laws."

How? I wondered. By not enforcing them?

The comedy, however, was not yet played out.

At 7:00 P.M. we arrived at the town hall for the conference that the DA had set up. It took place in the selectmen's room, a bare plaster-walled room with one desk, nine folding chairs, and steel bookshelves containing town reports and an abridged version of the General Laws of the Commonwealth of Massachusetts. Present were the three selectmen, (the first time they'd concerned themselves with the matter) three registrars (two new ones to replace the resigners), the temporary town attorney, and the ubiquitous town clerk.

The temporary attorney, Richard Walton, was a small chunky man who existed somewhere behind a brown bushy beard. He took charge of the proceedings. I sat next to one of the registrars who kept leaning toward me and speaking in an alcoholic whisper: "I love you, I love Mrs. Treat."

Lawyer Walton opened the proceeding by suggesting that the three of us be allowed to vote absentee ballots.

I objected to being "allowed" to vote, and insisted that this was my absolute right, which he could neither grant nor withdraw.

After some discussion, Walton said his proposal was not strictly legal and was open to objection, but that he'd go ahead with it anyhow.

He then disclosed the astonishing fact that the former registrars had never been sworn in, and never been told what their duties were. He said he now had obtained state-issued pamphlets outlining their duties and he would have the new board sworn in *after* they'd studied the instructions.

I asked how on earth the old board had been appointed. One of the selectmen said he'd simply called them on the phone and asked whether they'd like to serve as registrars. When they said they would, he told them to come on up to the town hall, which they did.

It followed therefore that they'd never been registrars, that none of their actions had any legal force, and that the registrars who'd resigned had resigned from jobs they'd never held.

Equally, it followed that the registrars, not being registrars, could hardly be prosecuted for violation of duties which they were incompetent to perform.

It was a lovely loophole, worthy of Dan'l Webster.

The case of Mary Harris, however, was quite different. She'd been properly sworn in as town clerk, and among her duties was that of serving as a registrar. She therefore could have been prosecuted to the full extent of the law.

I recalled, then, that her attorney had conferred with Rollins this morning shortly after he'd solemnly promised to go through with the case.

Thoughts such as these went through my head while the new registrars were duly sworn in. By some hocus-pocus, the process apparently restored us to the voting list, and thereafter nobody questioned our eligibility. We were suddenly first-class citizens again and Walton asked us whether we'd agree to filing absentee ballots for the preceding election.

Seeman refused, citing the illegality of the proceedings. The election was long past. Walton told him he was making a mountain out of a mole hill, but Seeman left nevertheless, carrying his mountain along with him.

It was now apparent that the two Treat votes would elect Montamat, and that Mrs. Wright would somehow have to be unsworn, or sworn out, when Montamat was sworn in as treasurer.

I went into Mary Harris's office, where she handed me an envelope containing an absentee ballot.

We were very formal. She looked down her nose while I read the printed matter on the envelope. I crossed out most of it as not conforming to the facts, such as that I had been absent from the area at the time of the election. I then marked and signed my ballot, which she put in the ballot box.

It was an old-fashioned, wooden box with a hasp for a padlock. I admired the box as a relic of long ago, and I noticed the padlock, although I don't recall whether or not it was locked. Later, the *Grapevine* quoted the following exchange between Montamat and Mary Harris on the subject of that box.

Montamat: "Did you reopen the ballot box at the time you declared Mrs. Wright elected by that one vote?"
Harris: "No."
Montamat: "The box was locked and sealed, though?"
Harris: "No."
Montamat: "Then it could have been opened any number of times?"
Harris: "Yes."

After the events in the selectmen's office, after my wife and I had cast our votes, we went home bewildered but a bit more confident.

I was not present at the final recount on the next day, but it was held publicly for a change—in the presence of police, selectmen, attorneys, tellers and the redoubtable Montamat.

The count showed Montamat the winner by 50 to 49, *after* which our absentee votes were added. The original count, when the vote had tied, had showed a total of 92 votes cast. The recount showed 101.

One of the tellers was overheard to say, "It's certainly a wonderful thing that we called for a recount."

Isn't it.

If there's a moral to this story, and I love morals, it is a simple one. A wise man should learn to accept a certain amount of injustice, but not too much.

LAWRENCE TREAT is the author of *Big Shot* and of *V As in Victim*, described by the late Anthony Boucher as the progenitor of the police procedural genre.

Getting Busted

Lawrence Block

IT WAS the summer of '58. I had just turned twenty and was tentatively approaching the age of reason. After a year in the employ of a marginally disreputable literary agent, a year during which I spent my time encouraging the continued literary efforts of earnest souls who couldn't write their names in the dirt with a stick, I had decided to visit Mexico.

My companion was Steve, my best friend and erstwhile college roommate; I'd be returning with him to college after the summer. We bought traveler's checks, had ourselves inoculated against a full complement of diseases, stocked up on kaopectate and penicillin pills, and got on a plane for Houston.

We hitched from Houston to Laredo, and as I recall it took us thirteen rides and almost as many hours to cover the distance. We got a room in a grungy hotel in Laredo and walked across the border to Nuevo Laredo, the little cesspool conveniently located on the other side of the Rio Grande. Word had it that Nuevo Laredo was a great place to buy marijuana, which we hadn't had all that much experience with, and to get laid, which was another area in which we felt we could use some refinement.

Getting laid in Nuevo Laredo was about as tricky as getting warm in Hell but scoring marijuana proved more difficult. Here's how we managed it. We crossed the bridge, made our way to the public square, and were immediately approached by a dude with a sombrero and a horse-drawn cab who wanted to take us to his favorite whorehouse. *"Actualmente,"* I said, *"deseamos comprar alguna marijuana."*

After I translated this into English for the cat he frowned and shook his head. "No, no, señor," he said. "Marijuana illegal in Mexico."

We walked another four paces and another hack driver hit on us. This time I skipped the old Español and pitched him directly in English. "No, no, señor," he said. "Marijuana illegal in Mexico."

Steve and I looked at each other and shrugged. I said, "This isn't going to be all that easy."

We continued circling around the plaza. We walked no more than a hundred yards when a chap with a mustache and what he must have thought were snappy clothes sidled up to us and winked. "Hello, there," he said. "I understand you boys would like to buy a little marijuana."

No kidding.

We bought three or four bombers from our new friend, who announced that his name was Ernesto. We took them back to our stateside hotel and smoked them. I think they cost fifty cents apiece or thereabouts.

The next day we crossed the border again and ran into another Ernesto who knew a really sensational whorehouse that he'd be delighted to show us. We repaired there. The next morning I caught Steve checking out the want ads, looking for job opportunities in beautiful Laredo. "I think I'm in love," he said.

I got our tourist cards processed and dragged him onto a bus for Mexico City. "Someday I'll thank you for this," he said. "But not just yet."

The girl's name was Letitia.

On the bus we both had stiff necks from sleeping under a fan. We sat next to a girl named Dorcas who was on her way to a Quaker encampment near Cuernavaca. Dorcas was no Letitia and neither of us fell in love with her.

Mexico City was terrific. A tout zeroed in on us at the bus sta-

tion and told us he had just the hotel for us. I think his name was
Ernesto, too, but I don't expect you to believe me.

Someone had hipped us to a friend who was studying at Mexico
City College on the GI Bill, and through him we met a lot of beat
types and learned to drink Dos Equis beer and smoke Delicado
cigarettes and hang out at the whorehouse at No. 9 Medellin.

I think we were in Mexico City for about a week. We drank a
lot and managed to fit in a little sightseeing in the off hours.
We hooked up with another Stateside friend named Phil and
dragged him around to the house on Medellin. Later that night he
ate up all our penicillin pills, but to no avail. He came down with
some form of galloping clap that baffled a team of Park Avenue
urologists for a year and a half. He also drank all our kaopectate
and that didn't do him a lot of good either.

But we led charmed lives. Loved and ate whatever looked good
and didn't catch so much as a cold.

Then we went to Guadalajara and the roof fell in.

It seemed a good idea at the time. Mexico City was expensive
compared to the rest of the country. Besides, we had it on good
authority that it wasn't the "real" Mexico. Guadalajara, however,
would be a step toward the real Mexico, and we could take a further step from there by crossing to Puerto Vallarta on the Pacific
coast.

We took a bus to Guadalajara, got a hotel room, and went out
to visit a man I knew through correspondence from my days at the
literary agency. He was a prize guppy, conned into "collaborating"
with my employer, which merely meant that he sent in an outline
which was criticized by me, then did a first draft, then revised it as
I told him, and ultimately was assured that his manuscript was in
perfect shape and was being marketed. What happened was they
cached his hopeless script in a filing cabinet and left it there
throughout eternity.

So we went to see him and he turned out to be a paraplegic in a
wheelchair, and that visit did not turn out to be one of the happier
times of my life.

We didn't stay there long. Steve spent the afternoon watching a
John Wayne movie with Spanish subtitles. He said it was better,

all things considered, than watching a foreign movie with English subtitles. I spent the afternoon reading *The Brothers Karamazov* until Steve came back from the theater; and I stopped reading and we went out and had dinner.

The restaurant we chose was on the opposite side of the plaza from our hotel, a few blocks away down a side street. We walked through the plaza on our way to dinner and, naturally enough, intended to walk through it again on our way back to the hotel.

But in the meantime somebody started a riot.

At this time Mexico was getting ready to have an election, which is evidently something they do every now and then as a matter of form. I don't know why they bother. The PRI party always wins these elections. At the time the head of the party, and thus the President of Mexico, was one Adolfo Lopez Mateos. I have no trouble remembering his name even unto this date because I saw it everywhere I went in Mexico. All the barns and rock outcroppings and sundry surfaces that say *Chew Mail Pouch* in America said *Adolfo Lopez Mateos* in Mexico. There were other political parties and no doubt they were running candidates in opposition to Adolfo, but I don't know much about them.

I do know one thing. One of these parties, a right-wing group of some sort, was known as the PAN party. That acronym spells the Spanish word for bread, and I'm sure it stood for something, but whatever it stood for the PAN party was having a south-of-the-border version of a rally-cum-fundraiser, which is to say they were holding a riot.

The plaza was circled by public buildings, and the PAN enthusiasts were heaving bricks and rocks through the windows of these buildings and shouting slogans and shrieking and generally contributing to the furtherance of the democratic process.

The police were meeting this challenge calmly and professionally by lobbing tear-gas shells all over the place and firing rifles over the heads of the crowd. (At least that's the presumption. We didn't see anybody get shot. But then it wasn't possible to see very much because of the tear gas.)

A little perspective. This was 1958. Eisenhower was in the White House. There was no such thing as SDS. There was such a thing as Vietnam but stamp collectors were the only people who had heard of it. The only urban guerrillas were housed in cages at the Bronx Zoo. Tear gas was something the cops used on television. Cops, for that matter, were something on television.

We were very excited about the whole thing. It would be terrific to tell our friends about. We felt sorry for poor Phil back in Mexico City, sitting on the toilet and missing out on all this.

Of course the tear gas was extremely unpleasant, and it really worked in practice the way it was described in books; and enough, sooner or later, was enough. By the time one enormous cop pointed a finger in our direction and told us to get the hell away from there, we were only too anxious to comply.

But that wasn't the easiest thing in the world to do. Whenever we started in one direction, somebody dropped tear gas in front of us and a mob of people began running toward us and we had to go with the flow or get trampled. And in no time at all we lost whatever sense of direction we had possessed and didn't know which way was the hotel, or even which way led away from the core of riot activity.

At that point the cop who'd yelled at us before came not exactly to our rescue. He got us off to one side, asked us who we were and what we were doing, and demanded our identification. We explained that we were students, that we were trying to get back to our hotel, that our tourist cards were at the hotel. Meanwhile we showed him such things as drivers' licenses.

Thereupon he bundled us into the back of a police cruiser, drove us to a building a mile or two from the action, and, before we really knew what was going on, led us to a cell and slammed the door on us.

Things apparently were beginning to get a little hairy. After all, who hadn't heard stories of people vanishing into Mexican jails and languishing there for the rest of their lives?

I yelled in Spanish for someone to come around who spoke English.

Nothing happened.

We called out the same request a few times in English, with similar non-results, and then we decided to shut up lest we aggravate somebody.

It was still something of a lark. I suspect it was our stupefying innocence that made it seem frivolous. We were decent middle-class kids from good homes and we lived in what we were sure was a well-ordered universe. In an hour or certainly by morning the men in charge would realize that they had made a mistake. We would be returned to our hotel and released—perhaps with a warning, more likely with an apology. Naturally, in the heat of the moment, arresting us might have seemed like a good idea: after all, we were foreigners; we were dressed a bit scruffily; we had beards, albeit tentative ones. And we had ignored a direct order to leave the area. We'd tried to obey the order, but perhaps El Jefe had been unaware of that. Assuredly, señores, there was a certain amount of justification for jugging us, if only for our own protection. Assuredly.

The jail itself was not the sort of stuff nightmares are made on. I don't recall that it was terribly clean, and the sanitary facilities were limited and generally foul, but I don't recall an all-pervading stench or anything that would constitute the last word in squalor. In retrospect I think we were probably in a tin can of a jail where they put people who'd gotten drunk or fallen behind in alimony payments or something about that dangerous to the community.

It was the only jail we had and we made the most of it, pacing back and forth like Rubashov in *Darkness at Noon,* then searching our persons for incriminating documents. I found two pieces of identification in the name of Leonard Blake. One was a Social Security card and the other wasn't. I can't recall why I'd ever thought to provide myself with them in the first place. "If they find these," I said, "they'll think I'm some sort of agent."

Steve checked his own wallet and turned up his NAACP membership card. "If they find this," he said, "they'll think I'm a Communist."

We giggled at both notions—agent, Communist, sure. But why be careless when it's so much more dramatic to be careful?

We ate these incriminating documents forthwith. Just as well, too, because it was all we got to eat that night. De Maupassant, I have been given to understand, ate some human flesh once so he'd be able to describe it. Unhappily I can't remember what the cardboard tasted like. Probably it tasted like the *plat du jour* in a fast-food joint.

Of course no one ever checked our wallets. Not to look for false ID, anyway. But I don't want to get ahead of my story. . . .

There were a dozen cells like ours circling a large empty room. I seem to remember that they let us out sometime during the night to exercise in the large open area. Most of the other cells were unoccupied. Of our few fellow prisoners, none seemed conversant with English. For the most part they appeared to be drunks sleeping it off.

I suppose we slept a little.

In the morning it seemed there was a problem. Someone had checked our hotel and we did not seem to be registered under the names we'd been booked with. Oddly, we had forgotten this altogether, and it had come about for a curious reason. The beat-generation type we'd palled around with in Mexico City had tried to borrow money from us, and had muttered something about dropping in on us in Guadalajara, and we saw him as a possible source of future annoyance. To duck him—and, I don't doubt, out of a desire to dramatize ourselves—we had used last names different from our own in signing the hotel register. We were only going to be in Guadalajara a couple of days, we reasoned.

We explained this to the cops. Our friend from the night before was present, and it might be a good time to describe him. He seems to have been eight feet tall and built like King Kong, but I'm sure memory has distorted reality. I know that he was very large, very gruff, and that he spoke perfect English. He told us something about having served in the American Army during the war but he did not say he'd been educated at UCLA.

He wasn't delighted with our explanation of the false names. In fact he took pains to make this look like a serious offense, and at the time I thought it really disturbed him. Then he and his partner, who looked like an accountant, accompanied us back to our hotel room where we were to be searched and questioned.

And that was when the feces and the fan really collided.

The first thing the search disclosed was my diary of the trip. This was a very sketchy account of things, as I've never been temperamentally inclined to keep a detailed diary, but it did disclose that we'd visited a whorehouse now and again. This threw the cop into a frenzy. Here we rotten Yanquis had come south to ruin the sacred virgins of Mexico. He really seemed livid about this.

Next he got hold of our tourist cards. There's a blank there for religion, presumably so they'll know what sort of last rites to give you if the dysentery does you in. I'd put Jewish and Steve had put none. The cop read all this out loud and didn't know whether to defecate or go blind. "To be Jewish is bad enough," he announced, "but to have no religion is even worse." Steve and I couldn't even bear to look at each other. Clearly we'd both flunked that test.

But the worst revelation was yet to come. A systematic search of our belongings yielded up the literature we'd brought along, my copy of *The Brothers Karamazov* and Steve's edition of *Ten Days That Shook the World*. "My God," the cop roared, "you're Communists! Agitators from Moscow! Reading Russian books! Coming here to stir up the poor peasants of my country!"

Let me tell you something. It sounds a lot funnier in print, and in retrospect, than it ever did at the time. Because this son of a bitch was one hell of an actor, and even though it was fairly obvious that he was acting, it was also eminently possible that he'd get carried away with the role. By this time he had his gun out of his holster and was waving it around the room. He was really into the part he was playing, condemning us as Jew pervert Communist bastards, and we weren't too innocent to know how easy it would be for him to report us as killed trying to escape, or something of the sort, and . . .

I don't think he actually hit us with the gun. He swung at us a few times but I don't think he connected. And I don't remember what if anything we said in our defense but I'm fairly sure it's nothing we'd be terribly proud to remember.

After what was probably only a few minutes of this deliberate rage he calmed down and his partner, who looked embarrassed, explained that he thought he might be able to reason with the monster. Of course there were problems, there were expenses. He'd have to see just how much cash we could scrape together and if it would be enough.

They knew how much money we had because they'd searched us. We had six hundred dollars' worth of traveler's checks between us. You know about traveler's checks. They're better than cash because you don't have to worry about losing them and they're accepted everywhere. Well, the second part of the statement is true enough. The fuzz in Guadalajara couldn't have been happier than to accept our traveler's checks. We signed them over one by one, and the good cop solemnly held us at gunpoint while the bad cop trotted off to cash them. I figured if the bank didn't turn those checks into pesos we were going home to our parents in plastic bags.

While we waited the partner felt silly pointing a gun at us and put it away. Then he got me to show him how the camera worked. They'd had to confiscate it, of course, on the chance that we might have taken subversive photos, and since it was confiscated he wanted to know how to operate it in case he felt like taking a couple of photos of his mother.

Then, he frowned and asked why that particular model didn't come with a case. I found the case under the bed along with some unexposed film. He packed it all up and couldn't have been happier.

When the big guy came back with our money he promptly made another confiscation—my pornographic diary and our three subversive Russian books. He also went through our wallets, leaving us bus fare to the border and a few odd pesos for Delicados and tacos en route.

The two of them drove us to the bus station and told us we had twenty-four hours to get out of the country. After that we'd be subject to arrest, imprisonment, and God knew what else. Summary execution, I suppose.

It occurred to us, while we waited for that bus, that there was almost certainly an American consulate in Guadalajara and that we could most likely go there and pitch a bitch. We decided that this was not a safe and sober thing to do. We had the feeling we were being observed, that some official all-seeing eye would stay on us until we boarded that bus. A single step outside the station was more risk than we were prepared to take.

We did learn something, though, while waiting for the bus. We picked up a copy of the local paper and I had enough Spanish to dope out what had happened. The PAN party had indeed rioted, and twenty-seven rioters had been duly arrested by the heroic police. Then in another article there appeared a list of twenty-five rioters who had been carted off to jail—not our jail but another one.

It seemed pretty clear that we'd been singled out for special treatment from the start. The police were busy busting up a riot, all right, but they were willing to take time off in the middle of it to jug a couple of Americans who might turn out to be a good source of cash.

We also found a picture of the enormous bastard who'd waved his gun in our faces. The caption identified him as the chief of the district police or something of the sort.

The rest is a blur in memory and I think it was pretty much of a blur at the time. Our bus was a local, taking forever to carry us eastward as far as San Luis Potosi, where we waited four grim nighttime hours for a connecting bus to the border. We sat in a grimy café sharing out the Delicados to make them last—Delicados were six cents a pack at the time, but they hadn't left us with abundant cash. Our bus finally did come, and it did take us to Laredo, and we got back across the border and did indeed stoop to kiss the ground of Texas, an act I for one had never expected to perform.

One hideous moment. The Mexican border guard gave our luggage, such as it was, only the most cursory sort of search. But he did take his time opening Steve's tobacco pouch and helping himself to a good hearty sniff of its contents. Now we'd been dumping our roaches in with the tobacco earlier, and had forgotten about this altogether in the course of our prison experiences, and I think that's as close to cardiac arrest as I care to come. But he evidently didn't smell anything more authoritative than tobacco and we were on our way.

Our parents wired money and we flew home the following day. We made an attempt through the traveler's-check company to get our money refunded, arguing that we'd signed over our checks under duress, and a fat lot of good that did us. The company chap told us, as diplomatically as possible, that he figured we lost the dough in a crap game. I can understand his position and I suppose it's one I'd take were our roles reversed, but it'll be awhile before I buy traveler's checks again. Perhaps as long as it'll be before I return to Mexico.

Remembering all this, certain things occur to me. I guess the most striking is the realization of just how massive a source of guilt this entire experience was for us. In spite of the fact that we were certain we'd been marked as pigeons the minute El Jefe laid eyes on us, I've never been able to dismiss the notion that it was our fault. Couldn't we have gotten away from the riot area, at least after our warning? Shouldn't we have had the sense not to bring Dostoevsky and Reed with us? And Barry Ulanov, for God's sake? Where did I get off mentioning whorehouses in my diary? Why hadn't we thought to list ourselves as Catholics on our tourist cards?

And what power had so possessed us as to lead to our registering at that hotel under false names? That's one detail we didn't bother mentioning to our parents.

Another guilt suggested that, given the situation, there should have been some way we could have acquitted ourselves more manfully. I don't know just what we might have done—I certainly had few fantasies of overpowering that gorilla and taking his gun away from him.

I had dreams about that cop for years, daydreams in which I slipped into the country with a rifle and blew his head off.

I can't say what I gained from the experience, or what it may have cost me besides a couple of hundred dollars, a camera, and a typewriter. I have, since that Mexican trip, written more cops-and-crooks stuff than anyone should have to read, let alone write, but if I've ever drawn on the experience I did so subconsciously and still don't know about it. I'm left with prejudices—that people named Ernesto are shady but reliable, for instance, and that civilization stops at the Rio Grande. I suppose one of those theories makes about as much sense as the other but I prefer to go on believing both of them just the same.

A lot of forms contain the question, *Have you ever been arrested?* For a while I answered *Not in this country,* which invariably led to some interesting conversations, but that got to be too much of a hassle. So I just put in *No,* and so far I've gotten away with it.

And time does fly, and heals wounds. Phil's a VP at an ad agency now. Steve's a college dean, and at the very institution where we once roomed together. I find that slightly incredible, but not much more incredible than the fact that my eldest daughter is very nearly the age I was when I took that trip.

Why, those cops may well be dead by now.

I certainly hope so. And I hope they died hard, the bastards.

LAWRENCE BLOCK, author of *Deadly Honeymoon* and the Matt Scudder mystery series, is also known as Paul Kavanagh, a name under which he wrote *Such Men Are Dangerous* and *The Triumph of Evil*.

A Time Bomb with a Forty-Year Fuse

Madelaine Duke

BEFORE 1938, when I was a child in Austria, few families thought of the art objects in their homes in terms of cash value, especially when those objects had been passed down from generation to generation.

My family lived near Vienna, in a house superbly well designed by my father who was a lawyer and a senior civil servant. The paintings he had inherited, the collection of fine Oriental and Aubusson carpets which my mother had brought into the marriage, were as natural a part of our life as the cutlery on the dinner table and the towels in the bathroom. We took good care of them, but took them for granted. To a small child, paintings by Canaletto or Ruysdael, a portrait by Botticelli or a cheerful inn-scene by Teniers were bound to be an integral though subconscious factor in her life and character.

That my world collapsed and disintegrated forever was due to the annexation of Austria in 1938 by the Nazis.

There are two scenes, indelibly imprinted on my mind, which epitomize the beginnings of the destruction which finally affected the greater part of the world's population.

My young artist friend, Simon, and I had gone to the Second District of Vienna—the Jewish quarter—to select a frame for his portrait of me.

The craftsman who had been making Simon's frames had disappeared overnight.

The sign, with the single word *Levi* on it, had been torn from the wall and was hanging by one nail. The little show window was broken and someone had painted a yellow star of David on the door. The walls of the yard had been disfigured with crudely painted swastikas and graffiti. *Tot den Juden, Jude verrecke. Heil Hitler* . . . Death to the Jews . . . Jew perish. The yard was littered with the wreckage of those poor apartments.

I picked up a piece of crushed pewter; a small menorah—the seven-branched candlestick—which is as holy to a Jewish family as a rosary to a Catholic.

As Simon and I walked out of the yard, we heard a piercing scream. It seemed to go on for minutes. Then, suddenly, it stopped. *"Kumm schon!"* a man shouted in Viennese.

"Hast net gnua ghabt . . . Haven't you had enough?" Five men in black SS uniform came pushing out of a door, yelling obscenities and laughing. One big lout was buttoning his fly.

As Simon and I got closer we saw that another SS man was holding a small boy. The child, about eighteen months old, was dangling head down, screaming with terror.

Simon broke into a run. He was about twenty meters from the men when the fellow holding the child suddenly changed his grip. Grasping him by the ankles, he swung the boy backwards across the sidewalk and dashed him against the wall of the house. There was a thud, which reminded me of the breaking of an earthenware jar of honey, and the child dropped to the ground.

The men turned away. "One Jew less. Let's go, Kameraden. . . . I'm hungry. Time for Sunday dinner."

They piled into the truck and roared off toward the Prater fairground.

Simon picked up the small body and cradled it in his arms. The child's eyes were open . . . clear, dark eyes. Inside the doorway I saw the body of a young woman, her cotton dress torn down the front. She too was dead.

I took the body from Simon and placed it beside the woman.

Then I tried to raise Simon to his feet. The blank look on his face frightened me. He was staring at the blood on his sleeve, shaking all over.

We had guests for tea—Simon and a timorous middle-aged man by the name of Direktor Haberl. My mother was cutting a cake when the front-door bell rang. Simon offered to answer it, returning with a young man who went by the nickname Aff. With his big loose-limbed body, his small eyes and jutting lower jaw he did in fact look like an ape. Before the German take-over of Austria Simon had recommended him as a picture restorer and Aff had spent weeks at our house, cleaning our paintings. Aff was a northern German who had passed himself off as a refugee from the Nazi regime. Now he was wearing the black SS uniform.

He addressed my father. "I have certain orders. If you cooperate with us you have nothing to fear."

Four other storm troopers entered the drawing room, guns drawn.

"This show of strength is unnecessary," said my father. "What is it you want?"

"We have orders to confiscate some of your paintings."

Aff was not shamed. "You'll help us collect the pictures on this list."

"As you will. But ask your men to put their guns away."

Aff nodded and three of the storm troopers returned the guns to their holsters. The fourth did not comply.

Simon went back to the tea table while my father led Aff and his three men out of the room. The fourth stormtrooper remained with us, still covering us with his gun.

We sat still, listening to the jackboots on the stairs, the moving of heavy furniture overhead, to Aff's orders in the hall, the seemingly endless procession to the front door.

At last the men returned.

"The rest's in here." Aff consulted his list. "The Florentine Lady by Botticelli . . . the Cranach Adam and Eve . . . the Rembrandt self-portrait and the Ruysdael pastoral. Take them down." (He stared at my father with his pale expressionless eyes.)

"That's all, except for the contents of your safe. You do have a safe?"

There would have been no point in denying the existence of the safe which housed among other important documents, the histories of our paintings. The safe was behind the Ruysdael pastoral.

One of the storm troopers tried to remove the painting from the wall, but it was fixed to the door of the safe by a special device. The man gripping the carved frame was wrenching at it viciously.

"Careful," warned my father. "You'll damage the picture. Wait . . . I'll take it down." As he raised his arms the SS man with the gun cracked the butt down on his left hand.

I heard the bones snap. The pain must have been excruciating. My father made no sound, but his face turned ashen. My mother, ignoring the looters, helped him to a chair.

Before my parents sent me to England in January 1939 I witnessed a succession of such raids, some more brutal than others. Gradually our home was stripped of some sixty paintings, superb carpets, antique china and silver.

Why didn't we seek help from the police? Because it became crystal clear from the moment the country fell into the hands of the Nazis that the Austrian police was at no time prepared to protect the life and property of any Jew. Murder, maiming, and looting became accepted everyday events.

In 1942 my parents and twelve other members of the family were deported to Minsk, a concentration camp inside Russia. Later the Red Cross informed me that they were presumed killed.

It was not until 1946, when I went to that concentration camp, that I discovered how my parents had died.

In the winter of 1942 the Nazis had forced the prisoners to strip naked, driven them to the perimeter of the camp, made them dig their own graves, then mowed them down with machine guns. Russian prisoners shoveled the earth over the dead and nearly dead.

Thus far my story is a familiar one. My family shared the fate of millions. Had it not been for certain events that took place many years later, indicating that the murderers are still among us and enjoying the fruits of their crimes, my story would have remained personal and private.

The first of these events happened in 1945 when I returned to Austria as a member of the Allied Occupation Forces. About the same time my father's friend, Haberl, returned to Vienna from the Theresienstadt concentration camp. As an art historian he had taken an interest in my parents' collection of paintings. He persuaded me to think of the future. Masterpieces did not just disappear from the face of the earth. Some, if not all of them, were bound to have survived the war because the man on whose behalf they had been looted would have been powerful enough to protect them.

I could not argue against Haberl's reasoning, especially when he put it to me that my parents would have expected me to save whatever I could of the family's civilized heritage. Between us we compiled lists of the looted paintings and, on his advice, I registered our losses with the Austrian Fine Arts Department (Bundesdenkmalamt) in Vienna.

The official who accepted and filed my claim told us that nothing was known about any of the paintings, but her Department was busy sending details of looted art treasures to national galleries and major dealers throughout the world. Sooner or later some of them would come on the market and when this happened her office would inform me.

After 1945 the extent of Nazi crimes against humanity became general knowledge. Nine million men, women, and children shot, gassed, and tortured to death.

Carrying out a lethal operation on such a scale required a vast administration. At the collapse of Germany in 1945 a handful of the *administrators* were caught and brought to trial. But the majority of the murderers, one hundred and sixty thousand killers who are on file at the Ludwigsburg Justice Department (which was originally set up by the Allies), either escaped abroad or remained at liberty in Germany and Austria. They have been shielded ever since by former comrades and sympathizers. The protecting of so large a number of Nazi criminals, and the resulting conspiracy of silence, has inevitably led to corruption in private circles and in the public life of the former Nazi homelands.

In a small population, at least a quarter unshakably Nazi even today, any political party bidding for government power needs the Nazi vote and will carefully avoid any action that would upset the Nazi public.

In 1946 another aspect of the Third Reich came to light. While their minions had committed mass murder the Nazi leaders had pursued a more personal interest—the acquisition of wealth. That Hermann Goering amassed art treasures is widely known. What remained unknown until I exposed the facts in my book *The Bormann Receipt* is that Hitler's deputy Martin Bormann did equally well in the art-acquisition stakes.

While Goering had openly lived like an obscene playboy, Bormann—a colorless, dour man who hated and envied Goering—had prepared for a wealthy future.

After the war Goering was brought to trial and committed suicide. Federal Germany, stating publicly that she was the legal heir, took possession of the fortune in art that Goering had amassed, keeping some art treasures and giving others to the State of Bavaria.

But Bormann, having managed to move the bulk of his loot to South America, escaped.

Bormann has become a legend. Despite determined efforts by his friends in Germany to stage a proof of his death in 1945, the American authorities who examined the evidence remain unconvinced that he perished while the Russians were capturing Berlin. Not surprising: the skull that was exhumed near the Lehrter Station in Berlin was identified as Bormann's by no other than Hitler's dentist. Since then Bormann has been seen in Chile by a number of credible witnesses.

I personally did not spend any thought on Martin Bormann. And from 1946, when I registered the loss of my family's paintings at the Austrian Fine Arts Department, until 1969 I deliberately pushed the thought of our lost art treasures out of my mind. In those twenty-three years the last people who had known our art treasures well had died—my mother's only surviving sister, her husband, and Haberl.

On 7 September 1969 the past caught up with me. My husband found a paragraph in one of our Sunday papers, stating that the Austrian government had tried for years to trace the owners of art treasures looted by the Nazis. Unless such owners claimed their property by the end of the following year the art treasures would go to Austrian museums. Austria claimed that it had returned a number of items to their former owners.

Eight years later Austria is still refusing to answer one simple question: what art treasures have been returned and to whom have they been returned? It is quite an important question to which the British Foreign Office has failed to receive any reply.

The piece in the Sunday paper persuaded me to set the legal wheels in motion. I obtained a list of the 1,231 art treasures in Austria's keeping. For obvious reasons the descriptions of paintings on the list were incomplete. Owners like me had lost all written proofs of ownership—the contents of our safes had been thoroughly plundered—nothing but an accurate and detailed description of each painting could prove our rights to it. As twenty-four years had elapsed since the end of the war and this first announcement that the looted art treasures still existed, many valuable witnesses had died.

It seemed the Austrian government had invented a restitution law. If my claim to paintings should be thrown out I was to fight for the paintings in Austria's civil courts.

My claim was to be automatically opposed by the Ministry of Finance. The expert witnesses for the Ministry of Finance were to be drawn from my old friends at the Fine Arts Department. I managed to find two witnesses of the prewar era, neither of them art experts, who testified that my parents had owned a house full of fine carpets and paintings.

There followed a series of court hearings in Vienna, before Judge Wagner. I had claimed five paintings which were also being claimed by other private persons, by the State of Austria, and the State of West Germany. After exhaustive questioning I was taken to the Monastery of Mauerbach near Vienna, and shown the paintings. Four out of the five had in fact belonged to my family. The fifth, as I immediately recognized, had not belonged to us and I gave up my claim to it on the spot. I believe that other perfectly honest claimants stepped back when they saw certain paintings and recognized that they were not theirs. At the end of the rounds with Judge Wagner the Judge observed that none but the owner or the thief could have given so detailed a description of the pictures after so many years and assured my lawyers and me that the four paintings would be returned to me within six months.

All seemed fair and straightforward until, shortly before the paintings were due to be returned to me, Judge Wagner was replaced by a new judge—a young man by the name of Otto Fritscher. Dr. Fritscher decided that he had to institute his own, new investigations. After about four years of court proceedings I was back to square one.

Meanwhile some fascinating questions arose. I discovered that the American Forces in Austria had found the looted paintings as early as 1945 and handed them to the Austrian Government for return to their rightful owners. Why had the Fine Arts Department not informed me of the find? What had happened to the paintings after they were taken from us and in the period between 1945 and 1969? Enquiries by the British Foreign Office and *The Times* and *Guardian* newspapers yielded no answers.

I seemed to have arrived at a dead end when I was once again bidden to attend a court hearing in Vienna. On my arrival my lawyer informed me that the hearing before Judge Fritscher had been cancelled.

I insisted on seeing the Judge in chambers. As my lawyer was a senior member of the Austrian State Legislature, the interview was readily granted.

In the Judge's chambers I was granted my first view of my own file. While the Judge and my attorney discussed another case I gained insight into the complexities of mine. Then, suddenly, I came upon Germany's claim to my pastoral by Ruysdael. It was based entirely on a bill of sale from Berlin art dealer Lange, made out to Martin Bormann, who was supposed to have bought the picture through a Munich go-between.

I immediately realized that the breakthrough had come at last. The names on the receipt would provide a basis for research into the fate of the Ruysdael since the theft.

When I showed the receipt to the Judge he pronounced in all sincerity that it was a good piece of evidence in favor of Germany's claim to the painting. I suggested that the receipt was phony; Hitler's deputy could have gone to any art dealer, and—unless the dealer was prepared to perish in a concentration camp—he would have issued a bill of sale.

Why should Bormann have bothered? Probably to make his acquisition of the painting appear legal in case he ever wanted to sell it to a respectable collector.

The Judge couldn't see it. His understanding of the Nazi system was nil.

It did not surprise me that he refused to let me have a copy of the Bormann receipt. I did not press the point. I found my own way of acquiring a copy.

The Bormann receipt led to years of travel and investigation. The Berlin dealer who had issued it was dead, of course; killed in a Russian prisoner-of-war camp according to his friends, murdered by Bormann's henchmen at the end of the war according to other witnesses. Michaelis, the middleman, who had advised Hitler, Goering, and Bormann on the paintings worth acquiring, had succeeded in remaining a good German civil servant—like so many of his good Nazi colleagues—and died in 1953.

But through countless interviews with Germans and Austrians and often accidental pieces of information the jigsaw puzzle finally came together. I even succeeded in acquiring further receipts made out to Martin Bormann in 1942, which prove without a doubt that it was he who acquired the other three paintings I am claiming plus other masterpieces which are on my list of losses. There were of course the lists I had filed with the Austrian Fine Arts Department but they, curiously, had disappeared without a trace.

Meanwhile Judge Fritscher continued the court hearings. I saw my four paintings once again in 1975 at the Monastery of Mauerbach. On the Judge's instructions they were brought one by one into the heated cell that was serving as a courtroom. When I'd seen them the first time they had been in good condition. On that second occasion, which took place on a bitterly cold November day, they steamed up like mirrors the moment they arrived in court. All four had deteriorated and it was perfectly obvious that they were being stored in intolerably bad conditions.

I pointed this out to the court—no one was denying it—and I

warned that these great paintings would have to be moved quickly if they were not to suffer irreversible damage or even total destruction. (To my knowledge, years later, these masterpieces are still moldering at the Monastery.)

The Judge, however, was encouraging at the time of the viewing. After the hearing he told me that he believed my evidence and that the paintings should be returned to me within a few months.

Judge Fritscher, however, was transferred and a new judge, Dr. Kremtsow, took over the art-restitution cases. His ignorance of art was matched only by his determination to begin the investigations once again, from scratch. So far the *scratch* has lasted two years or more.

In November 1976 my Austrian opponents, the Ministry of Finance, showed a certain weariness in the courts. They said that they could see no reason why at least one of the paintings—the least valuable one—shouldn't be returned to me. Austria was no longer claiming it, no one else was claiming it, and the British Embassy in Vienna was pressing for the conclusion of my case. The judge reluctantly agreed and I was promised the return of the painting within six weeks. A year later that delightful little picture of a painter at work is still imprisoned at the Monastery in Mauerbach.

When I recently wrote to my attorneys, asking them to speed up the hand-over, they replied that the picture could not be restored to me without another court hearing and unfortunately the Judge was sick.

Bungling or deliberate obstruction by a Germany and Austria still riddled with people who are anxious to cover up what a young German journalist, writing in a Swiss paper in 1965, called "The Biggest Art Robbery in History?"

My collected evidence, published in *The Bormann Receipt*, points to a grand cover-up.

What had happened to our paintings after they had been looted and passed into Martin Bormann's hands is no longer a secret.

Bormann and other Nazis had evacuated their stolen art treasures to places they assumed to be safe from the ravages of warfare and bombing. In 1945, while Bormann was staying with a Spanish family, the American Forces in Austria found the art treasures and returned them to the Austrian government for return to their owners.

President Renner of Austria was an honorable old man; but the administration and the civil service remained in the hands of loyal Nazis.

The paintings remained in Austria for several years, until Martin Bormann and his lieutenants Barbie-Altmann and Schwend had safely settled in South America. Then the Nazi bosses sent their orders to the Austrian minions.

The American Forces had set up a collecting depot for looted art at 10 Meiserstrasse, Munich—a kind of storehouse which finally contained billions' worth of art treasures.

It was convenient for Bormann and company. As Austria is landlocked, large consignments flown out of the country would have attracted attention. To send consignments of art treasures out of Germany would be much simpler. With years in hand, when Austrian art experts were supposed to be busy assessing the authenticity and value of the art treasures, vast numbers of them were gradually taken to the Munich depot. From there they were removed in easy stages to Hamburg. And from Hamburg, a busy world harbor, they went by ship to the original thieves in South America. Bulky consignments in large ships can travel relatively unobserved.

By 1965, when the Allies placed the Munich depot in Federal Germany's hands, the greater part of the masterpieces had quietly left the country—restolen by Bormann's associates. Had it not been for the murder of an industrialist in Peru, no one would have been the wiser.

The brutal stabbing of Señor Cruz alerted the Peruvian police and reactivated American investigations into the illegal activities of Nazis resident in South America—the drug trade, gun-running and the highly profitable sale of paintings by world-famous artists. No one believed that the killing of Señor Cruz was the act of local bandits, especially as his latest neighbor turned out to be Bormann's henchman, Barbie-Altmann, a man who had been dealing in fine art among his other business interests.

The Bormann receipts must have come into Cruz's possession in the course of these deals. Cruz must have become suspicious of his art dealer and sent the receipts to a relation in Hamburg, a Bolivian diplomat. That diplomat—and this was a much-reported scandal in Germany—was found murdered in Hamburg harbor.

From Hamburg the receipts blundered on, somehow escaping a relay of Nazis who tried to recover them, until they arrived in the hands of an official of the Federal German Ministry of Finance whose job it was to disperse the last of the looted art treasures.

About 1966 the Austrians, who had sent the paintings in their charge to Germany, got cold feet and demanded the paintings back from Germany. New, young officials—ignorant of the history of such men as Bormann—duly returned the paintings as requested. And why not? They could always reclaim them in the Austrian courts on the strength of art-dealers' receipts made out to the *late* Martin Bormann. As German Arts Minister Dollinger had publicly stated that Federal Germany regarded herself as the heirs of the Nazi leaders and had taken possession of Goering's collection, the young officials could see no reason why they shouldn't substantiate their claims with the Bormann receipts.

Many of them believe to this day that the tales of Nazi mass-murders committed by their elders are anti-German propaganda.

When I faced my attorney with my findings he gave me a world-weary smile. What was so extraordinary about my story? Didn't we all know that there hasn't been an end to Nazi corruption yet? Not to worry; the Austrian legal machinery was grinding on. And what about the art treasures which are being destroyed through bad storage? My attorney promised to consult with an art expert and with Judge Kremtsow.

Meanwhile a spectacular case of looted art treasures in Holland is stimulating worldwide interest.

One day both Austria and Germany may be forced to answer the questions which I have asked all along. It is perfectly clear how Austria will meet the challenge. She will say that the restitution cases are still *sub judice;* she will kick Judge Kremtsow upstairs and appoint a fourth judge who will duly scrub the investigations of his predecessors and begin his own enquiries. If Austria can postpone the answers there is a fair chance that curious people like me will drop dead. It hasn't yet occurred to Austria that there are young people who are my heirs who will continue to ask questions and to demand long overdue justice. After forty years the fuse of the art-theft bomb planted by Martin Bormann and his armed gangs is still burning.

DR. MADELAINE DUKE is the author of *The Bormann Receipt*, published by Panther Books in England.

Billy

Christianna Brand

I LIKE TO THINK that my home in London was originally designed for some deliciously naughty lady of the Regency days when it was built. It shares a garden wall with one of the huge mansions in Hamilton Terrace where a family of a dozen or more children might be splendidly housed; and Paterfamilias had then but to nip over the wall to visit this little house built for no more than one or two. There would be a sufficiently large and elegant drawing room and similar dining room and, upstairs, the master- (or mistress-) bedroom and two or three smaller rooms for the lady's maid and her work. Madame's pretty little carriage would be housed in what is now our garage with its cobblestoned entrance, and we can still see the woodwork of the stalls where the horses were stabled. In the basement would be the big kitchen, and accommodation for the rest of the staff.

This basement has since been converted to a self-contained, furnished apartment; and this I am in the habit of offering free of rent to a couple, the wife doing my housework in return, the husband going about his usual occupation. "Middle-aged couple," runs my advertisement, and concludes, "regret, impossible to accommodate children."

So why did I take on Billy, age twenty-four, with his young wife, Hannah, and their three-year-old daughter? Even though they did swear that they proposed to bring no more children into a world as hard and difficult as the world was now.

Billy! I see him now—dark, slender, eager, alert, and so passionately anxious to have the place. He had come down from the north of England, giving up his job as porter in a block of flats for old people, because his mother had suffered a stroke and needed looking after. Now the mother had died and he had lost his home with her. He had been staying with his sister but she couldn't keep them much longer; he was desperately in need of a job that would give them accommodation—homes are desperately short in London these days.

Hannah was used to work, looking after the old people; he himself had done all the handyman work of the flats and would be only too thrilled to do any odd chores in his spare time. He had a good situation as driver in a hire-car firm run by an elderly gentleman of the improbable name of Mr. Lilypad, and his son. These were the things he told me. Mr. Lilypad would speak for him, and so would Mr. Prentiss who had owned the block of flats in Lancashire.

And so indeed they did. That very evening, Mr. Prentiss rang me up from wherever it was. He said Billy had telephoned and begged him to plead for him. Mrs. Prentiss, long a wheelchair invalid, had recently died and he himself was in a bad way, and indeed his voice was choked with tears, poor old boy. But this was such a wonderful young couple, he felt he must speak for them; I could have no idea of what a job the two of them had done on the flats. The old people had loved them. Billy had even received some award for fighting off two men who had tried to beat up one of the tenants. Hannah had found time to come and help his own poor wife in her last illness. And please to excuse him now, because . . . His voice failed and he rang off. I often spoke to him later. He was a dear old man.

And Mr. Lilypad rang up. Billy had asked him also to speak a word. Well, he had to say that this was really an excellent young chap; in fact already he was thinking of promoting him to personal chauffeur to Lilypad junior. He couldn't too highly recommend the boy.

And Billy rang up. He rang up every day and pleaded and pleaded. They came round to see me again, I went over it all a dozen times and eventually the alertness, the evident ability and willingness prevailed. As they left, the child put its little hand in mine and said, "I like this house."

How could I refuse? They moved in.

Dear old Mr. Prentiss was thrilled. He rang up, this time less tearfully and thanked me and said I would never regret it. And Mr. Lilypad Jr. rang up and asked to speak to Billy but meanwhile said to me what a fine young chap he was; and Billy came back from the telephone absolutely glowing. Mr. Lilypad had duly invited him to become his personal driver. A Rolls!

He used to drive it home sometimes and, most typically, had soon sorted out a corner, visible from the house, where he could safely park it. It was a beauty; he pointed it out to us, standing shining there.

The girl, however, was useless; she seemed vaguely ailing, listless, and overanxious. I spoke to Mr. Prentiss about it on one of his phone calls and he said he would come down one day and see them; they were like a son and daughter to him and this was worrying. I didn't see him when he came; but he left gifts for me, hoping I wouldn't be offended—a dress and coat which had belonged to his late wife, hardly worn; and some shoes. But as a result of whatever he may have said to them, there was no improvement in Hannah's usefulness. I began to get worried about keeping them but I hadn't the heart to tell Billy.

He came upstairs one day, radiant with excitement. Mr. Lilypad was giving a dinner at the Playboy Club for all the drivers. But the thing was . . . He didn't know . . . I was a proper lady, I understood all these things. . . . What was one supposed to wear? And all them knives and forks . . . And he didn't drink, wouldn't that be embarrassing, when they offered him things . . . ? He had this sort of plum-coloured velvet jacket—

I said that that would do splendidly, with a nice shirt to go with it, and explained the simple rules of dealing with knives and forks. As to the drinking, he was a driver, everyone would respect him for avoiding it; just ask for tomato juice or something at the bar, and at the table ask the waiter quietly for a glass of water.

Off he went and on the great evening appeared in the jacket with a white frilled shirt looking absolutely marvelous; and next day was delirious with the success of it all. What was more, Mr. Lilypad was going to give another such dinner at Christmas and I and my husband were to be invited. And indeed that very day Mr. Lilypad Sr. rang up and in stately numbers remarked upon the triumph that the evening had been and how honored he would be if on a future occasion we might be prevailed upon to attend: he understood that my husband was a famous surgeon and I a famous writer.

Anybody less likely than my dear husband to find himself at the Playboy Club could hardly be imagined, but with many private reservations I replied that of course when the time came we should be delighted. . . .

A few days later, Billy came upstairs again. He carried a small cardboard box. In the box were some trinkets—of no great value— a string of imitation pearls, a brooch, earrings. He said, "Please let me give them to you. They belonged to my mother and I'd like you to have them." Tears came into those bright brown eyes of his. "You've been so good to me," he said, "like the other day, helping me about the dinner, a real lady like you. I feel you've been like my mother. She'd have liked you to have them. Please accept them."

How could one refuse? I don't adorn myself with them, any more than I wear Mr. Prentiss's late wife's bequeathals, but I have them still.

So the weeks passed and we all became very pally on the telephone and then one day Lilypad Jr. rang me up. He said that a curious thing had happened. As I must know, Billy never took a drink; but that morning, he had had "half a pint" and then confided to one of the other drivers that Hannah was four-months "gone." He thought I ought to know.

I faced Hannah with it. "And you must have known this when you took the job."

"Yes," she admitted.

"You assured me that you had no intention of having any more children. But you were already pregnant?"

"We wanted the place," she said, weeping into the washing-up.

I saw Billy that evening. He was miserable. "She never told me nothing."

"Well," I said, "my dear, I'm sorry but I can't have a pregnant girl working for me; there's a lot to be done and already she's not fit for it. And I couldn't give all this work to a mother with a small child and then a new baby. You'll have to find something else. I'll help you, and until we get something, of course I shan't turn you out of your home."

Mr. Prentiss rang up, the Messrs. Lilypad rang up—they were all disturbed about the deception. But the Lilypads, père et fils, were full of helpful suggestion. Junior had room in his home, their resident maid had recently left, they could live *there* and Hannah help with the work a bit, till they found somewhere; and Mr. Lilypad Sr. explained in his rather stately way that he was obliged to part with a couple who had worked for him for many years and would suit me down to the ground. He would arrange for them to call for an interview.

Billy was very happy for me on that score. He said he knew these people well; Mr. Lilypad was a very aristocratic old gentleman and he'd seen how they'd hold his coat for him and hand him his hat as he left the house. Without needing anyone to hold our coats or hand us our hats, I did feel that this type of old-fashioned service would be an improvement upon poor Hannah's languid ministrations.

As to Lilypad Junior's proposal, however, Billy was less than enthusiastic. He had confided to me already how through the driving mirror he had sometimes reluctantly observed that gentleman's conduct—and him a married man—with his secretary on long drives to his various businesses up north—(they were all from roughly the same part of the world; the north of England is in some ways sharply divided from the south and we tend to stick to our own). And the reason the maid was leaving was that the boss had got her in the family way; and he didn't fancy Hannah living in such a situation. What he'd really like would be a job in the country with chauffeur's quarters attached, especially now that he would have two children.

I couldn't turn them out but I was working on a book and desperate to replace them. I put advertisements in endless newspapers, wrote glowing references, without however the inclusion of Hannah's name. Billy went out after jobs, as chauffeur, as porter, as handyman, anything with accommodation included. But nothing.

He fell ill, took to his bed, couldn't get to his work.

Lilypad Jr. was sympathetic but meanwhile he must have a chauffeur, he couldn't go on keeping the job open.

He called round and saw Billy and explained to him. But this seemed the last straw. The boy got worse and worse, he seemed to be going to pieces with the worry of it all; his hands shook, he could hardly stand on his feet. He had no doctor, but I wangled him on to somebody's list and took him along. The elderly doctor spoke a lot of long words and rang up for an appointment to see a neurologist, forthwith.

I fought my way to the hospital, fought my way to an immediate confrontation. It was agreed that the boy was in a highly neurotic condition, the symptoms hysterical. "I could get him into an institution," said the very good and clever young neurologist, "and that would be socially nice and tidy; but I don't know what it would do to him. He regards you almost as his mother. If you would take the responsibility—?"

"Yes, yes," I said. "I couldn't bear him to be shut in somewhere."

"Well, a fortnight of total rest in bed, then, on a very careful diet . . ."

We tottered home; he fell into bed.

Strong smells of frying bacon and sausages suggested Hannah's idea of a very careful diet, so for several weeks I cooked for the invalid myself. When I had got him to sitting-up-in-a-chair condition—in constant touch with his associates including a brother who now put in an appearance—I suggested to all and sundry that Hannah should be sent home with the child to her mother, while Billy found a room for himself, which would be much easier, and could look round, unencumbered, for a job. I handed over a large sum of money for her fares back up north and for a down payment on such accommodation as he could arrange for himself and something to be going on with; and when he seemed well enough, he set off to arrange it all.

An hour or two later, I got a call from Police Constable Hanson at the station in Wimbledon. He had picked up this young man hanging about a large local house belonging to a wealthy gentleman called Mr. Lilypad, and suspected him of "loitering with intent." Moreover the youth had on his person a considerable amount of money. But he seemed in a strange condition.

At first the constable had supposed he was drunk; he walked unsteadily and was almost incoherent; but he had in his pocket such a very good reference with my name and address on it, that it had seemed wise to contact me first.

"It's all right," I said. "The boy's ill; he'll have been trying to see his late boss, and the money is what I myself have entrusted to him." I explained the situation.

P. C. Hanson absolutely turned up trumps. He would send Billy home in a police car, he said—if I would accept the responsibility? —and meanwhile arrange lodgings for him in a hostel nearby the police station, and keep an eye on him. . . .

And in due course Billy appeared, very shaky but grateful to everybody all round.

The day came for Hannah to leave. I was not entirely delighted to see how much of my money had apparently been spent on an outfit for her to arrive home in, but off they went at last in a taxi with their curious assortment of belongings.

My husband offered to drive them to the station but for some reason was prevented.

Billy was to move into the hostel—P. C. Hanson had meanwhile taken him out, on his own free day, for an afternoon at a football match, and was proving a real friend.

That evening Billy rang up. Hannah and the child had duly gone off and the hostel was OK and he'd report progress.

A week passed; the various friends rang up with enquiries but I had no further news for them.

Then Billy telephoned at last, very odd and shaken. He said that Hannah had done with him, five telephone calls to her home had brought only refusals to speak to him. He was in despair. He had been some days "unconscious in hospital." He rang off.

I was really scared. Had he been referring to a suicide attempt? I recalled that the neurologist had considered sending him "into care" and that I had taken the responsibility of looking after him.

I tried to reach the hostel at Wimbledon but couldn't find it. Finally I rang up the police station at Wimbledon.

The Wimbledon police said that there was no such hostel anywhere near them. Nor did they know of any Police Constable Hanson. . . .

OK, so you're there before me? No hostel. No P. C. Hanson, so helpful and kind; no outing to the football match.

No mother dying of a stroke, no accommodating sister.

No kind, weepy dear old Mr. Prentiss with his diffident offerings of his relict's cast-off dresses and shoes. No old-folks' home, no award for courageous defence of its inmates.

No Messrs. Lilypad, senior or junior, no Mrs. Lilypad to be outraged by her husband's behaviour with housemaids and secretaries; no excellent hat-handing married couple who would take the place of departing Billy and Hannah—and I wonder whose Rolls Royce it really was, parked just across the green.

No marriage even: just a girl with an illegitimate child of her own, seduced from her home into which he had been taken and shown nothing but kindness—a young man, encountered in hospital, brought in suffering from a nervous collapse following upon his wife's suicide (no wife, of course, and no suicide).

Nor of course had Hannah ever gone back north; my husband caught sight of them one day as he drove past, Billy and Hannah, walking aimlessly along the street—only flaxen-haired Hannah now appeared as a dark brunette.

And not even any Billy.

Just someone with another name and a long, long record of drunkenness, theft, and violence, "a very, very dangerous young man."

Yet, when they left this house, after many weeks of freedom upstairs and down—not so much as a pin was missing. "You've been so good to me. I feel you've been to me like a mother. . . ." I can only suppose that that at least had been true.

But for the rest . . .

Why? Mr. Prentiss perhaps we can understand, with the strong recommendation that helped Billy get the place; even a Mr. Lilypad also "speaking for him." But once the situation was attained— why on earth all the rest?

Why the phone calls, the chats, the invitation to the Playboy Club, the confidences about Lilypad Jr.'s misbehaviour, a hundred details that I haven't mentioned here. *Why?*

A fantasist, you'll suggest, impelled to act out some second life, to make things up? But not only Billy was involved. Many of the calls came when he was here in the house. All in north-country accents—did that not alert the suspicious mind of the so-clever crime writer?

But as I've explained, north and south stick rather closely together; it would be natural enough for Mr. Lilypad of Yorkshire, for example, to employ Billy from neighbouring Lancashire.

And P. C. Hanson—who spoke for *him?*—so clipped and professional, with the calm tolerance of the true London copper. And again why?

Why the story of Billy's discovery hanging about the Lilypad home—no such place, of course, in Wimbledon or anywhere else; why the story of the visit to the football match? Why the curiously roundabout manner of revealing to me the fact of Hannah's pregnancy? All so spiced with danger: at any moment we might idly ask for a closer look at the splendid Rolls, might check Mr. Lilypad's telephone number or watch for the visitors coming to the private door of the basement flat—Mr. Prentiss, Lilypad Jr., and Billy's brother were all supposed to pop in and out.

And whence came the late Mrs. Prentiss's quite expensive garments, all hardly worn; and the trinkets of the poor departed Mum?

And the breakdowns? "The boy is of low mentality," the elderly doctor had said to me. "No reserves. Trouble and he goes to pieces." Little did we know, he and I, of all these balls kept juggling in the air, with, till things began to go wrong, such happy sangfroid. And he had reeled off all those long, solemn words and sent us off to see the neurologist. The neurologist had proved to be a very keen, clever young man, and much opposed to pseudo-mums insisting upon accompanying the patient; but ladies long married into the medical profession get to know how to deal with keen, clever young men and by the end he was dismissing Billy and asking me confidentially, "What do *you* think is wrong with the boy?"

I remembered the doctor's long words and dismissed them. "I think he's just a young man frantic with anxiety about finding a home for his family," I said, "and the symptoms just hysteria."

"So do I," he said; and then consulted with me about how best

to deal with him. I did just note that as I supported Billy's totter-
ing footsteps home, he grew a little impatient and stepped out
quite smartly for a change. There you are, I thought to myself
smugly, the symptoms are nothing but hysteria!

It gave them a bit longer in the flat, of course, while meanwhile,
outside, those other voices were fixing up an alternative.

Was the whole thing a fraud? It took in a cagey old general
practitioner; and my clever young man would have admitted him
"into care" if I hadn't talked him out of it.

I saw him once again. The bell rang and—there he was, very
spruce and bright-eyed as ever, standing on the front door steps,
with a little car parked near the gate. "Billy!" I said. "What on
earth are you doing here?"

"Well, I came to see you," he said.

"To see *me?*"

"Yes, well—to ask you how you were, and to tell you how I was
getting on and all . . ." He threw out a hand proudly towards the
rather battered little car.

"Billy," I said, "I think I should explain to you that I know all
about you now."

He stared at me in blank consternation. "You know—? I don't
understand. What's there to know?" He grasped at straws. "I'm
not with Hannah any more."

I recollected that accidental sighting in the street. "No," I said,
"you're with a dark girl now, aren't you? Or has Hannah dyed her
beautiful blonde hair?"

I think that he thought I must be a witch. "Well, never mind," I
said. "I know it all now, Billy. I have friends in all sorts of places
and I've enquired and found out. But you never did me any harm
and I know you never would; and I'll do you none. Now—you've
let my dog out and he's got into the next-door garden. Go down
and rescue him for me; and that'll be the end."

He went off next door and got the dog and started it back up
the steps to the house; and standing at the gate, looked up at me
and gave a little shrug, with outspread hands as though to say,
"Well, that's it, then—isn't it?"

I looked back at him standing there—dark, slender, eager, and alert as ever, as I had seen him on that first day; and returned the same little shrug and the same gesture and picked up the dog and went in and closed the door.

I've never seen him again and please God I never shall—that "very, very dangerous young man."

But I still ask myself—why? And who? And again—*why?*

Creator of the mystery-series detective Chief Inspector Cockrill, CHRISTIANNA BRAND is the author of—among others—*Starrbelow, The Honey Harlot,* and *Green for Danger.*

Edgar Smith—The Human Copperhead

Mary Higgins Clark

ON TUESDAY EVENING, March 4, 1957, my husband and I were in the den of our new home in New Jersey watching "Sergeant Bilko" on television. It was a raw night with the incipient chill peculiar to March, a good night to be snugly at home with our four young children. When the program went off at 8:30, we began to chat about how glad we were that we'd made the move to New Jersey. Native New Yorkers, we'd loved apartment living in Manhattan, but the city wasn't the same anymore. Crime was on the increase there. How much better, we agreed, to have decided to raise our family in one of the small safe hamlets in northern New Jersey.

Even as we talked, a few miles away teenager Vickie Zielinski was saying good-bye to her friend, Barbara Nixon. They'd been doing their homework together. Small and slender, Vickie was a cheerleader at Ramsey High School. Her shoulder-length brown hair falling over her school jacket, her thick white bobby socks stuffed into penny loafers, her purse and school books in her arms, Vickie started the ten-minute walk home. Her fourteen-year-old sister, Myrna, was to meet her halfway.

Concentrating on her own homework, Myrna had to be reminded at twenty of nine that she was supposed to meet her sister. She ventured as far as the Nixons' house but nowhere along the way did she see her sister. Confirming with the Nixons that Vickie had left at 8:30, Myrna returned home. Her mother was annoyed but not alarmed. Maybe Vickie had met another girlfriend and gone off with her. Anthony Zielinski, a laborer, exhausted from his day's work, was already asleep. At 12:30, his panic-stricken wife finally roused him. Their daughter Vickie was missing.

The next day, the *Bergen Record,* northern New Jersey's largest newspaper carried the shocking headline, "Girl Murdered in Mahwah." The story began: "Murder overtook a fifteen-year-old girl walking home on a Mahwah road last night. Her mother and father found her body near Fardale School this morning."

So savagely had she been beaten that the Zielinskis thought they were staring down at the back of her head where hair had been pulled from her scalp. Instead they were looking at what had been the face of their pretty second child.

Two young men from the Mahwah area discussed the crime. Twenty-one-year-old Donald Hommell had dated Vickie. Twenty-three-year-old Edgar Smith, an ex-Marine, married, and the father of an infant, knew her too. Occasionally he'd given her a ride home when he saw her walking. Donald said, "When they get this guy, they'll probably hang him."

"No," Smith replied. "He'll plead insanity."

The Bergen County Prosecutor's office began asking about Vickie's friends. Their queries led them directly to Edgar Smith. At 11:30 the night of March 5, he was brought in for questioning. The following morning, he admitted the crime.

The confession. Smith's bloodstained shoes and pants. The bloodstains in the borrowed car he was driving. The bloodstained baseball bat that had been in the car and was found in the sandpit. The evidence was overwhelming. It appeared that the trial would be merely a formality; an open-and-shut case. There were few of us who did not expect Edgar Smith to be found guilty of first-degree murder. In 1957 in New Jersey that verdict could mean death in the electric chair.

Smith's speedy apprehension tended to quell our fears that a killer was loose in our area. But even so, for parents like us it could never be the same. The myth that by moving to the suburbs we could offer our children the quality of life we had enjoyed at their age was shattered forever. As the *Record* pointed out: "There are very few women and girls on the streets after the sun goes down. The residents of the communities are not outspokenly angry at Edgar Smith. Rather they are deeply resentful that he has destroyed the bond of faith and trust that people of small towns place in one another."

The Vickie Zielinski–Edgar Smith case compelled me from the first bulletin. The incredible viciousness of the crime haunted me. Suppose, someday, someone capable of that kind of evil stalked one of my daughters? The wanton selection of the victim. Edgar Smith had no plans to meet Vickie. She simply had had the incredible misfortune to leave her friend's home at the exact moment he cruised down the block. I was interested in knowing more about the mind of the man who was capable of such a monstrous act.

I had just begun my writing career. I could not conceive then how drastically it was to be influenced by the Edgar Smiths of this world.

From the first, the case attracted nationwide attention. Capital crimes often did and this one promised all the elements of drama; the violence of the murder . . . the young girl victim . . . the ex-Marine defendant. Their pictures ran side by side in newspapers all over the country; Victoria, smiling and vibrant in a short skirt and turtleneck sweater, her iceskates over her shoulder; Smith's mug shot portraying a sneering ne'er-do-well. He might have been impersonating a young Burt Lancaster, typecast as the villain.

But when he was led into court, Smith's outward appearance had been altered to fit the image he would portray for the next twenty years. One reporter wrote: "With his dark-rimmed glasses, sports jacket and slacks, he looks like a night school or college student listening to a lecture."

His twenty-year-old wife, Patricia, attended every session. It was the era of the billowing skirt, the tiny hat, the spike heels. Pat Smith, demurely pretty, looked as though she had dressed for church as she came in carrying her infant daughter, Patti Ann, and took her seat in the first row.

Bergen County Prosecutor, Guy Calissi, tried the case. A former assistant prosecutor, John E. Selser, was retained for the defense. Widely respected County Judge Arthur J. O'Dea presided.

The jury selection was a long and tedious affair. The prosecution challenged any juror who did not believe in capital punishment, a usual procedure in a first-degree murder trial. Later journalists, William F. Buckley, Jr., among others, would scornfully suggest that Smith's rights had been violated by *not* including jurors opposed to capital punishment.

Today advocates of capital punishment are fighting to have it restored in many states including New Jersey. Twenty years ago, studying the pretrial publicity, I was struck by the "will he get the chair" aspect of the headlines. Even then, long before I began intensive research into crime, I decided that the death penalty glamorized a murder case. Later in my research I came across a statement of Supreme Court Justice Jackson. "The death penalty," he said, "completely bitches up the criminal law. It ties up the judicial process with endless appeals and trials. It sentimentalizes the judicial process. It sensationalizes justice."

Nowhere were those words to be more clearly proven than in the Edgar Smith case.

The trial began on May 15, 1957. In his opening statement, Prosecutor Calissi told of Victoria leaving her friend's home:

Smith passed her going in the opposite way. He noticed Victoria and she noticed him. He pulled down a short distance, backed into a driveway and came back and picked her up and proceeded down Wyckoff Avenue toward the home of Victoria Zielinski, but instead of going all the way down, Smith turned onto Crescent Avenue Young Road and went down to what is called the sandpit. In the sandpit he pulled right into . . . he went right into the sandpit. They talked. Victoria talked about school but the defendant, Edgar Smith, didn't have school problems on his mind. He molested this girl immediately. He ripped up her sweater and he fondled her breast, this fifteen-year-old girl, and he bit her right breast. She refused his advances and she tried to get out of the car. He grabbed her by the wrist but she still released herself and started running. He finally caught up with her down on Fardale Avenue and he struck her with a blunt instrument. . . . He got her back into the sandpit and crushed her skull with a very heavy implement which we will offer in evidence. Her brains were spattered on the sand. In the sandpit he took that body, that mutilated body, he took it to the top of the knoll and dumped it down at the bottom of the knoll and then he proceeded to get into his car. . . .

By the time the opening statement had been completed, the atmosphere in the crowded courtroom was saddened and subdued. Spectators sitting in the squeaky visitors' seats stared at Edgar Smith who listened attentively to every word or cast furtive glances back at the victim's mother who sat in stony-faced silence in the rear of the room. Everyone wondered what Defense Attorney Selser could possibly say to soften the horror of what they had just heard.

Selser readily admitted that Smith had picked up Victoria and driven her to the sandpit. He explained that Smith became outraged when Victoria told him that his wife was running around with another man. In his fury, he'd slapped her and she ran from the car. According to Selser, Vickie went up the road; another car came along with its lights off and Smith heard a commotion. Afraid that Vickie had been met by her father, he grabbed the baseball bat from the car to protect himself. But it was his friend, Donald Hommell, who returned with a badly bleeding Vickie. Selser continued:

Smith dropped the bat on the ground and said to Hommell, "What happened?" And Hommell said, "She fell and struck her head." Smith looked at her head . . . and it was bleeding badly and Smith said, "Get in the car and I will take you to the doctor. . . ." And she got into the car and laid her head back on the back of the seat of the car. . . . Don Hommell then grabbed her by the sleeve of the jacket she was wearing and yanked her out of the car and she fell to the ground head first with her feet still in the automobile and as she fell, her head bleeding as it was, went upon the right foot and trouser bottom of Smith's trousers and it became saturated with blood. The girl pulls herself up from the ground and Smith and Don Hommell helped her to her feet and Smith said to Hommell, "She should go to a doctor," and Hommell said, "I'll take care of it; I'll take care of her, you go on." Smith then got in his automobile and drove from the scene of the offense and drove on home to his trailer camp. . . .

This was the defense. Edgar Smith, claiming that he had left a bleeding Vickie with an angry Donald Hommell in the sandpit where she met her death, had figured out a better defense than insanity, one that later the prosecutor would label "the foulest, dirtiest legal trick that was ever pulled by a defendant."

The trial lasted two weeks. The spectators heard Mary and Anthony Zielinski describe their search for their missing daughter, their finding of one of Vickie's loafers and her kerchief. Anthony Zielinski told his wife to phone for the police while he continued to search. Joined by a police captain they walked further into the sandpit and found Victoria's red gloves. They came across her broken locket. Then Anthony Zielinski looked down over the bank and cried, "Mother dear, come here. I found her."

The penny loafers, the gloves, the jacket, the tee-shirt, the saddlebag, the scarf, were placed side by side in the courtroom. The Judge looked down at the saddlebag. It was exactly like the one his own fifteen-year-old daughter carried.

But Edgar Smith protested his innocence. He claimed his confession was a lie told because, "I was afraid for my wife, afraid for my child and therefore I gave that statement."

Donald Hommell was called a psychopathic liar by the defense.

Selser: "You had been out with Vickie, had you not?"
Hommell: "Casually, that is all."
Selser: "Do you remember saying to Smith on the drive from Ridgewood to the trailer court, 'Don't forget, you have a baby'?"
Hommell: "Definitely not, sir."
Selser: "Do you remember saying to him, 'It would be unwise to mention my name'?"
Hommell: "Definitely not, sir."

John Selser, an attorney with a fine reputation, passionately believed in the innocence of his client. State Prosecutor Calissi passionately believed in Smith's guilt. But as he later commented, he not only had to convince the jury that Edgar Smith was guilty, he had to prove that Donald Hommell was innocent.

On May 28, 1957, the case went to the jury. It took the twelve men and women one hour and fifteen minutes to return a guilty verdict with no recommendation of mercy. When Judge O'Dea dismissed the jury he said, "I first want to commend you on your verdict. If it had been the Court's decision without a jury I would have found the same as you do. . . ."

On June 4, 1957, Edgar Smith was sentenced to "the punishment and judgment of death at the hand of the Principal Keeper of the New Jersey State Prison at Trenton, New Jersey, during the week commencing Monday, July 15, 1957."

The case was over. But in effect it had only begun. The death sentence was to gain for Smith notoriety and controversy that made him a cause célèbre. If there had not been a death penalty he would have vanished into the obscurity of prison and his many appeals would have gone unpublicized. But the carnival atmosphere that is engendered by the race to see if a man will beat the chair kept Smith front-page news. For the next fourteen years he lived on Death Row, as appeal after appeal was rejected. Excerpts from the endless file of headlines tell the story:

(The first direct appeal to the State Supreme Court was affirmed on June 25, 1958.)

June 5, 1958: *Death House Visit on Wedding Date*
June 25, 1958: *Smith Murder Conviction Upheld by New Jersey Supreme Court*
August 22, 1958: *Smith Case Will Return to State Supreme Court*
April 8, 1959: *Selser Pleads for Murderer—Court Is Cool.* Chief Justice declares case as complete as any he's seen.
May 4, 1959: *Smith to Try Federal Court*
November 3, 1959: *Smith Is Notified of Execution Date*
May 5, 1961: *New Petition Filed by Smith's Lawyers*
June 5, 1961: *Smith to Get Reply in Fall*

A few days later an editorial appeared. It pointed out that "the reluctance to execute speaks for itself."

Significantly the last paragraph read: "Legislation to abolish capital punishment dies year after year in committee. Evidently we are not yet quite ready to formalize our now fully developed horror. We do the next best thing which is to defer our grisly ignominy and hope the judges or at length the Governor can find a way to spare us. In our hesitancy we have let our heart speak for our head. Perhaps the day will come when we shall let our head return that compliment."

March 5, 1964: *Smith Awaits Execution for Murder Seven Years Ago*
March 17, 1964: *Execution of Smith Set for Next Month*
April 18, 1964: *Doomed Murderer Will Appeal Again*
June 3, 1964: *Court Hears New Smith Appeal*

A December 26, 1964, editorial commented: "Now Great Britain has all but abolished the death penalty, perhaps by way of showing that among the civilized nations of the world, she is still the serene sovereign. . . . The United States is still thinking in 19th century terms on capital punishment."

March 29, 1965: *Smith's Time Running Out—Killer of Girl to go to Chair April 27th*
April 17, 1965: *Execution Stay Granted Smith*
July 20, 1965: *Smith Files Seventh Death Stay Petition*

In 1965 William F. Buckley, Jr., conservative candidate for mayor of New York City, author, editor, and television personality, learned that Edgar Smith subscribed to his magazine, *The National Review,* and began corresponding with him. Eventually Buckley became Smith's champion and actively fought to win for him a new trial.

December 25, 1968: *Smith's Tenth Christmas in Death House*

During his years in prison Smith had taken correspondence courses, worked on his own defense, and now had written a book entitled *Brief Against Death* which became a best-seller. Filled with distorted facts and outright lies it arrogantly ridiculed the New Jersey courts but did manage to implant some doubt in many more minds of his guilt. In the book Smith again claimed that Donald Hommell had been with Vickie in the sandpit when Smith drove away.

December 29, 1970: *New Twist in Hearing for Smith*
"Unlike all of Smith's previous appeals, 18 in the last 12 years, this hearing will require appearances by some of the witnesses who figured in the case more than a decade ago. Earlier appeals had been decided based on transcripts of Smith's original trial."
September 12, 1971: *The United States Supreme Court Agreed to Consider Smith's Request for a New Trial . . .*
October 12, 1971: *High Court Boosts Smith Over Hurdle*
February 4, 1971: *Court Says No to Plea of Coercion*
February 10, 1971: *He Couldn't Take It Anymore, Smith Says of Police Tactics*
May 14, 1971: *Smith Granted a New Trial*
October 15, 1971: *Smith Will Be Tried in Bergen*
December 1, 1971: *Kugler Blasts Uproar Over Smith*
"State Attorney General George F. Kugler says there is enough evidence to convict Edgar H. Smith again of a murder committed fourteen years ago.

"In a stinging response to the uproar over the case, Kugler told a press conference in Trenton, 'He just happens to be a clever guy who knows how to get publicity.' "

December 3, 1971: *Man Smith Accused Loses Alibi Witness*
"A strange quirk of fate has killed an alibi witness for the man Edgar Smith says murdered Victoria Zielinski. . . . Hommell testified at Smith's first trial that at the approximate time the fifteen-year-old girl was killed, he was drinking at Pelzer's Tavern in Mahwah. Hommell said he was seen there by a friend, Charles R. Rockefeller of Ramsey. Rockefeller, who corroborated Hommell's alibi, was killed November 21 in Middletown, New York, by a man later charged with drunken driving and manslaughter. Ironically the man who helped send Edgar Smith to Death Row was killed by a man named Smith—Thomas F. Smith of Warwick, N.Y."

Then on

December 12, 1971: *Edgar Smith's "I Did"*
"Edgar Smith rather than go on trial again for first degree murder confessed to the killing of Victoria Zielinski. Judge Morris Pashman asked: 'Did you and you alone kill Victoria Zielinski?' Without pause, in a barely audible voice, Smith answered, 'I did.'"

Resentenced to the time he had already served, Edgar Smith left the courtroom a free man. Outside the courthouse he entered the limousine of his patron, William Buckley, and was whisked to a television studio where on Buckley's program "Firing Line" he repudiated the confession he had made under oath. "What you saw wasn't justice, it was theater," he said, smilingly, and then piously explained that the only reason he'd confessed was that his wife, Pat, was now remarried, his teenage daughter believed her stepfather was her natural father and he would not want to shatter the privacy of the family by bringing Pat back to New Jersey to testify at a new trial.

When he repudiated his original confession, he'd claimed that he feared Hommell would harm his wife and child if he involved him. Now, having confessed to the crime, he was once again using Pat and Patti Ann to muddy the truth.

Once free, Smith was treated with the same acclaim usually reserved for a war hero fresh out of the clutches of the enemy.

One headline read: *A Life Without Bars Awaits.*

One television reporter followed him down the streets of Manhattan, recording his comments on the sights, sounds, and smells of New York.

A year and a half later Edgar Smith wrote a book called *Getting Out* in which he ridiculed the Chief Judge of County Court, the

Prosecutor, and members of the Prosecutor's staff. A reviewer from the *Washington Post* scathingly dismissed the book as "rubbish."

Through it all, the nineteen appeals, the plea bargaining, the follow-up, I stayed doggedly with the case. And reading over and over the details of that desperate uneven struggle in the sandpit, I wondered how Victoria's family could bear to have that scene vividly recreated every few months in newspaper headlines.

I wondered how Don Hommell could live a normal life with that accusing finger constantly pointing him out.

I had begun my own research into sex crimes and was appalled to learn how frequently the sex offender is highly intelligent, a pathological liar, persuasive, capable of deluding even the most astute psychiatrist, and a recidivist.

Edgar Smith seemed to fit that profile. He'd been arrested when he was fourteen for molesting a ten-year-old girl, another crime he'd always denied, claiming the girl was hysterical and—to quote him—"had in the past accused other boys of the same offense, each time relating an essentially similar tale which had always proved to be untrue."

I wondered if we had heard the last of Edgar Smith.

We had not. After his release from prison, Smith enjoyed brief fame as an author and college lecturer, basking in the attention.

But it didn't last. His third book was not well received. The writing assignments dwindled. His desirability as a lecturer faded. He married Paige Hiemer, a twenty-two-year-old girl from Ridgefield, New Jersey, and they moved to San Diego. Once again Smith began bouncing from job to job. He sold advertising copy and did the housework while Paige supported them by working as a bank teller.

Smith began to brood and on October 1, 1976, he drove to a deserted parking lot in Chula Vista, a town not far from San Diego, and waited for a woman to come along. A thirty-two-year-old housewife, Lefterlya Ozbun, finished work and came out to the parking lot where her husband was to pick her up. Wielding a six-inch knife, Smith forced her into his car. Struggling with the woman during a frantic fifteen-minute drive on the freeway, he stabbed her below the breast. She still managed to open the door and throw herself from the car.

Apprehended two weeks later, Smith admitted that he had often visited the Chula Vista sandpit to sit and think about raping a woman. He had once stalked a doctor's receptionist but did not approach her. Finally, as he waited in the parking lot Mrs. Ozbun came along.

Smith pleaded guilty to the California abduction. At his sentencing he also admitted unequivocally that he had killed Victoria Zielinski and that, yes, when he was fourteen, he had molested a ten-year-old girl in Oakland, New Jersey.

It was over. For Edgar Smith the possibility of parole seems unlikely ever. No doubt he will now sink into the obscurity of the convicted long-term or life prisoner who cannot be let loose in society again.

But I hope he has served one purpose. As advocates for capital punishment plead their case in the legislatures of nearly every state, his lesson is one that should be studied. Nineteen appeals . . . endless expense . . . endless burdens on the court . . . endless anguish for the families of his victims.

This is what we're letting ourselves in for again with the reinstitution of capital punishment. We are hoping by reviving it that it will be a deterrent to murder. In 1972 Edgar Smith was asked if he thought it was a deterrent. "I don't think it makes much difference either way," was his answer.

What if Smith, wily and clever as he was, had managed to convince people that Donald Hommell had been the real murderer of Victoria Zielinski? What if Donald Hommell had been found guilty of that crime while the death penalty was in effect?

The Edgar Smiths of this world need to be swiftly apprehended, swiftly tried and sentenced to long prison terms that stick. Proven recidivists like Edgar Smith should never be released to prey on society again. Victoria Zielinski's father is now sixty-five years old. Since Smith got out of jail in New Jersey in 1973, Anthony Zielinski had prayed that he would make some mistake, commit some crime that would put him behind bars again. After the sentencing in California, he said, "A rattler will give you a warning when it's going to strike again. But a copperhead snake will never warn you. It'll strike a second and third time if you let it. Smith is a human copperhead."

I agree. It is now more than twenty years since that evening when my interest in the Smith case led me into crime writing. Now with whatever influence I can exercise as a writer, I intend to protest the reinstatement of the death penalty. I've just completed a new novel. It's about a psychopathic killer who stalks young women. And it's about a nineteen-year-old boy who is going to die in the electric chair for a crime he did not commit.

MARY HIGGINS CLARK is the author of *Where Are the Children?* and *A Stranger Is Watching.*

Odyssey

Dan J. Marlowe

IN DECEMBER 1962 I drove from my home on the shore of Lake Huron in Michigan across Canada to Buffalo, New York. The purpose of my trip was to attend a preliminary hearing in federal court in Buffalo. The hearing was for one of a pair of bank robbers who had been captured the previous month after a two-year assault upon the banks of the country during which they had staged brazen daylight robberies at more banks and escaped with more money than John Dillinger during his entire career.

I arrived in Buffalo a day early and went around to the local office of the FBI where I introduced myself as a writer who had been assigned by *The Saturday Evening Post* to do a lengthy article on the bank robbers, one of whom in a bizarre circumstance had involved himself in my life.

The hearing was scheduled for 11:00 A.M. the following morning. At 9:00 A.M. I received a phone call in my motel room from an FBI agent who informed me that the hearing had been postponed until 2:00 P.M. He suggested that we have lunch together in the interval.

I agreed, and after a leisurely meal I walked to the courtroom where I found that the hearing, far from being postponed, had taken place at the originally scheduled time. The FBI, it developed, had wanted no writers present for a hearing in a case in which the FBI appeared none too favorably even in their own eyes. Twice during the bank robbers' two-year run the FBI had had its hands on one of the pair only to have him talk his way loose.

I appealed noisily to the U.S. District Attorney—now a federal judge—who had acted as prosecutor at the hearing. I stated that the FBI had baldly circumvented the purpose of my trip. I asked for permission to visit the prisoner so my trip wouldn't be entirely wasted. The District Attorney refused permission, declaring blandly that while the prisoner wasn't being held incommunicado, no visitors were permitted.

I had no way of knowing it at the time, but the incident was the beginning of a fourteen-year exercise in frustration during which I became an expert on rebuffs to citizen inquiries by many elements of federal authority, including most particularly the Department of Justice's Federal Bureau of Prisons.

My original involvement in the affair was slight. It was also quirky enough to pique my interest and launch me upon a course of bureaucratic lance-tilting which became a mini-career. The twists and turns that ensued were almost worthy of being included verbatim in my fictional plots.

Writers hear occasionally from their readers, usually by letter, sometimes by telephone. In July 1962 I received a "fan" telephone call from a man in Philadelphia who wanted to tell me how much he'd enjoyed a book of mine which had been published that spring. The book had been a first-person depiction of a professional bank robber, a man who told his own story in self-justified and casual terms.

My fan presented himself to me on the telephone as a frustrated writer who had made a few unsuccessful attempts to get his ideas down on paper. He dissected the story line of my book intelligently, inquired how I had created some of my effects, and asked where I had obtained some of my information.

I answered in some detail, all the more so since my caller was cheerful, incisive, and irreverent, qualities I happen to appreciate. Within a week I received a follow-up letter from him, going over much of the same ground. I answered the letter, heard nothing more, and forgot about it.

In November I was summoned from the typewriter in my upstairs workroom to meet two men who had come to the house to see me. When I descended the stairs, the men were in opposite corners of the room I entered, as far apart as they could get.

"We're from the FBI," the younger man said to me, showing me his opened billfold.

I have friends who play practical jokes as a way of life. I didn't think they were from the FBI. I examined the Department of Justice gold shield carefully, then changed my mind. They were from the FBI. "What can I do for you?" I asked.

The agent produced two Post Office circulars of the Man Wanted type. "Do you know either of these men?"

I looked at the circulars. "No, I don't."

"We think you do."

"Then think again. I don't."

"We think you do," the older agent said, "because this man telephoned you from Philadelphia in July." He pointed to one of the circulars.

I laughed. The most prominent words on the circulars were WANTED, BANK ROBBERY, and DANGEROUS. "Called me? You're mistaken. Certainly no bank robber ever called—say, I did get a long-distance phone call from Philadelphia in July."

"We know you did. We checked it out. And we'd like to hear about it."

I explained the circumstances of the fan telephone call. "That's all there was to it," I said. "Except that he wrote me a letter afterward."

"We'd like to see the letter," the younger agent said.

I found it in my files, and only after both men had read it did the atmosphere begin to relax slightly. I've wondered since what I would have had to do to convince the agents and their superiors that I wasn't a bank robber myself if I hadn't received the letter, because my caller was a professional bank robber who—with his partner—had been written up in *Reader's Digest* as "Most Wanted Criminal Since John Dillinger."

At the time the FBI agents came to see me my fan was already in custody, but his partner, the dangerous one of the pair, was not.

A paragraph in the letter to me mentioned that my fan was going to show my book to a friend who was sure to be interested in it. The FBI was positive the friend was the bank robber's partner. They put a saturation team into the area of the Philadelphia apartment from which the phone call had been made to me, quickly discovered where the partner and his girlfriend had been living, tracked him from Philadelphia to Baltimore, and captured him before the end of the week.

The fact that my novel about a fictitious bank robber had received a written testimonial from a real bank robber created a small stir in the literary world. It gave my writing career a boost at a time it badly needed a boost, and I felt a sense of obligation to my unknown benefactor. Also, I couldn't forget the shiny-bright intelligence and quicksilver good humor of the first telephone call.

I first met Al Nussbaum, the man who made the phone call, in the federal courtroom in Brooklyn, New York, in which he pleaded guilty to the planning and execution of eight bank robberies in Buffalo, Rochester, Brooklyn, Washington, D.C., Philadelphia, and Pittsburgh. We had already been in touch by mail while he was being held in city prison in New York City while awaiting trial.

Sentencing followed Nussbaum's plea, and he was consigned to Leavenworth, Kansas. His partner was sent to Atlanta, Georgia. The Federal Bureau of Prisons was determined to keep the two men as far apart as possible.

By this time I had been able to learn a good deal about Al Nussbaum, whom J. Edgar Hoover himself labeled as the most cunning fugitive in the history of the FBI. I talked to friends, relatives, acquaintances, and victims in the Buffalo, New York, area, his home town, and in Florida and the District of Columbia. A picture began to emerge of an unusual character.

He had been an average student in high school and had gone into the post-Korean War army. He had been a "gun nut" all his life, buying and selling at gun shows in the New York State–Pennsylvania–Canada area. While in Washington he discovered that he could enhance his military pay by selling weapons to military officials attached to various embassies.

He soon had a sizable arms business going as a sideline. His IQ rating on the Army's Binet Intelligence Test was 139, and he was a self-taught locksmith and gunsmith. He also flew his own plane. He went to California after his army discharge and was caught transporting weapons into Mexico in the trunk of his car. He was sentenced to five years in federal prison, served two and a half years in El Reno, Oklahoma, and Chillicothe, Ohio, was paroled, and returned home.

What follows has to be considered in the context of the times. Batista was still in power in Cuba, and it was considered almost patriotic to be smuggling weapons to Fidel Castro, still in the Sierra Madre mountains. Nussbaum didn't hide from his friends his previous gunrunning activities, and he talked to them at length about the money to be made doing it.

Gunrunning is a federal offense, but to the average man it carries little of the stigma attached to ordinary crime. Nussbaum's friends listened to him, and in a small way they began accumulating a store of weapons. It takes money to make money, however, and the master mind became impatient.

Nussbaum, without saying anything to his friends, imported a former penitentiary acquaintance to Buffalo. Capital was needed to operate in the munitions field in style, and with the import's muscle and his own brain, Nussbaum knew how to acquire capital. The first bank jobs were intended as a means to an end, but they succeeded so well, and so easily, that he quickly found himself in a different line of business.

He accounted for his sudden affluence by telling his friends it represented the fruit of successful arms deals. He used his illicitly acquired wealth in atypical ways: he set up friends in legitimate businesses, including an export-import shop, an advertising business with its own print shop, and a restaurant.

Eventually, he found himself no longer able to control his muscle-man partner, and the road turned downhill. Even after the FBI knew the identities of the bank robbers they were looking for, Nussbaum kept the show on the road for two years, part of the time in Mexican border towns where he acquired a working knowledge of Spanish.

Al Nussbaum hadn't been lying when, in his first phone call to me, he'd called himself a frustrated writer. He began to write fiction on lined paper in pencil during the thirteen months he spent in New York City prisons awaiting the trial which eventually resulted in his guilty plea.

He sent his fiction efforts to me, and I criticized them. He asked technical questions, and profited from the answers. He demonstrated from the beginning an aptitude for story construction and for dialogue. I felt from the outset that if he persevered he could make it as a writer, even though he faced the additional complication that while in the federal prison system he wasn't allowed to write about the activities with which he had been most recently connected.

Our lengthy letter-communications terminated abruptly when he was sent to Leavenworth, Kansas, to begin serving his sentence. Previously our exchanges had been on an almost-regular two-or-three-times-a-week basis. Not so after the federal system took over. My letters to him at Leavenworth were returned, and I was informed in writing by the Director of the Federal Bureau of Prisons that only blood relatives could write to inmates.

I made a trip to Washington to state my case that Nussbaum and I should be allowed to continue to correspond. I pointed out that the Bureau of Prisons preached rehabilitation, but in this instance, at least, was failing to practice it. My first visit brought no results, and I learned an important fact of life about bureaucrats. "It's too easy for them to say No," a Washington friend told me. "Because if they do, they don't have to do anything. If they say Yes, something has to be changed, and they might have to justify the change to some government ogre hidden in the woodwork."

The third or fourth time I went to Washington I was given grudging permission to correspond with Nussbaum on a once-a-month basis. It had taken a year. It took another year of campaigning to get the letter-writing permission raised to a once-a-week exchange. Whereupon I began to campaign to be allowed to visit Nussbaum.

The same routine began again. I was informed that only blood relatives were allowed visiting rights. It took another two years before this barrier was breached. If I hadn't been a writer, and thus presumably able to voice publicly my conclusions about the prison system's lip-service-only approach to rehabilitation, I don't know if permission would ever have been granted.

The resumption of correspondence had of course meant the re-

sumption of fiction lessons. The day came when some of Al Nussbaum's material seemed to me worthy of submission for possible
sale. In addition to the worthiness of the material itself, the other
obstacles Nussbaum faced were formidable.

First, anything he wrote for submission had to be sent from
Leavenworth to Washington for approval. This took unconsciona-
ble amounts of time. And second, even after approval from Washington, never a sure thing, anything he wrote could only be submitted once to an outside market. If it was returned, that was it.
Any writer knows what such a proscriptive ruling would do to his
own chances for sales.

The greatest problem, though, was the ban on writing about his
own experiences. Every beginning writer is urged to write about
what he knows, but this avenue was denied Nussbaum. It often
seemed in the early days that innocuous subject matter of small interest to editors was the only material he could get approved.

I wore Washington down finally about the restrictions on their
visiting policy, and I tried to visit Nussbaum twice a year. During
one of my early visits we worked out an arrangement, not without
the usual official problems, whereby I became his legal agent. He
sent his completed material to me, and I moved it around for him.
And, slowly, during his fourth year inside, he began to sell.

Through the years a number of the more restrictive prison regulations have been eased. It's no longer necessary to send material
to Washington for prior approval. It's possible now to make additional submissions after the first unsuccessful one. And it's possible
now for an inmate to make submissions directly without working
through an intermediary.

But none of it happened without kicking, clawing, biting, and
screaming from inside and outside. One of the more frustrating
aspects of the federal penal system is the turnover rate among
prison officials. Wardens move to other prisons. Educational
officers change jobs. Case workers, the men with whom inmates
have their closest and presumably best contacts, move up or down
the prison job ladder. Each time such changes take place, policy is
reviewed. Rules change. Permissions change. An inmate must
often run hard to hold his place in the prison system, without the
time to improve his situation.

Federal Bureau of Prison inmate restrictions have eased during the past fifteen years, as I've indicated, but they're far from perfect. Many rulings are arbitrary and without rational basis. Once Nussbaum began to sell fiction, for instance, the best help I could have given him was to get a typewriter to him inside. He had to use the typewriters in the prison's Educational Department on an if-and-when basis. If available, when not in use otherwise.

Twice a year I wrote Washington, D.C., and offered to hand-deliver a typewriter for Nussbaum's use. It was never permitted. The responses were always the same: (1) It was against official policy, and (2) It would be too noisy for the other inmates.

I rebutted the latter argument rather successfully during one visit to Leavenworth, I thought, but it didn't help. I was given a tour of the prison by the educational officer for whom Nussbaum was clerking at the time. It was a real tour, not just a high-spots once-over. One of the areas I was taken to was the old wing of the prison, built at the turn of the century, still with six-man and ten-man cells, all fully occupied. I noticed that these cells often contained six to eight different musical instruments, and I mentioned, first to the educational officer, later to the warden, that the musical instruments must be much noisier than a typewriter.

It didn't do any good. I wrote additional letters upon my return home, bearing on the same subject, and received no satisfactory answers. I was never allowed to ship or deliver a typewriter to an inmate who could have made excellent use of it.

But Al Nussbaum made steady progress even with only hit-or-miss access to institutional typewriters. He sold to markets as diverse as *Harper's, The American Scholar,* and *Alfred Hitchcock's Mystery Magazine.* He became a steady contributor to the latter. Some of his Hitchcock stories were later selected for Mystery Writer of America anthologies and other annual short-story collections.

He attacked the book-review field and built up a market in the crime and suspense genre which at its peak covered twenty of the larger newspapers in the country, an impressive self-syndication. He accomplished this himself by sheer perseverance with no outside help from anyone.

He told me once that his ambition was to keep himself so busy inside that he never had time to realize where he was. He had himself transferred to a wing of the prison which contained no television. And he never lost his sense of humor. I complained once during a visit that I never had time enough to undertake all the projects I had in mind, and it didn't look as if I ever would.

"It's simple," he told me with a smile. "All you need is one of the federal fellowships I have."

During his tenth year inside we began to talk seriously about his chance for a parole. We had discussed it previously, but always academically. He had received a forty-year sentence, two twenty-year terms to run consecutively, and in the federal penal system serious parole consideration is usually given only after two-thirds of the sentence has been served. Parole would by no means be automatic. It was something to be worked for. We figured that three to four years' planning and legwork would be necessary to bring it about.

Federal parole hearings are of two types. In one, a federal hearing officer, an employee of the Federal Parole Board, goes to a federal penitentiary and interviews a series of inmates, each of whom has five to ten minutes to impress upon this arbiter of his destiny his rehabilitative progress and ability to cope in the real world. The hearing officer makes his recommendations to Washington based upon this brief exposure, and the Parole Board acts upon his recommendation, usually without ever having met the prisoner.

The second type of hearing is essentially the same except that it takes place outside the prison and representatives are allowed to appear to speak for the inmate under parole consideration. What usually comes from both types of hearings is what prisoners call a set-off: they are turned down, but are given another date in the future when they may have another hearing. In the case of long-timers, most set-offs are for an additional two or three years.

The first requisite for a successful parole appeal is an assurance to the Federal Parole Board personnel that the inmate will have outside backup. That he will have a place to go, and reasonable support until he can again become self-supporting. I wrote to Washington, D.C., each year and placed myself on record that in the case of Albert F. Nussbaum I would guarantee to furnish such support.

I didn't do it without a qualm or two. I had known the man for ten years, had worked with him very closely, but did I really know him that well? For all I knew he could be sitting inside planning the biggest job of all time. No one wants to look like a fool by sponsoring an inmate who reappears in the law's toils as if in a revolving door.

The final decision wasn't too difficult, though. I had seen him work hard at acquiring a new skill, one with which he was totally unfamiliar when I first met him. He had made steady progress in his new career—spectacular progress when the individuals who try but never make it are considered. He deserved a chance, another chance.

There was another factor in my decision. My relationship with Al Nussbaum had been no one-way street. I may have helped him, but he contributed measurably to my work. During each visit in addition to discussing his immediate projects and problems, we would also talk about mine, both overall concepts and minute details.

I haven't written a word for years about weapons and ballistics that he hasn't vetted for me. Ditto with locks and bolts and their manipulation. Ditto with safes, vaults, and alarm systems. It's not every writer who is fortunate enough to get his technical information from the horse's mouth. Fictionally, I often found myself leaving out one important detail of a process lest I be accused of writing manuals for crooks.

Nussbaum warned me that the final steps in effecting a parole for him would be no easier than my first attempts at persuading authorities to let us communicate. He was right. The federal penal system rarely bends to accommodate the inmate.

Nussbaum appointed me his representative to speak in his behalf at the parole hearings held outside the prison.

"They won't make it easy for you," he told me with what I felt was unwarranted cynicism. "They'll look up where you live, and the hearings you'll be invited to attend won't be where they're easily accessible to you."

He was right again.

I attended hearings in Baltimore and Chicago, frustrating affairs with no feedback about possible progress. Neither hearing lasted more than fifteen minutes. Half of that time was devoted to questions about my sincerity in affording backup. How do you make the points you feel it's important to make about a man's *positive* rehabilitative efforts when you have the definite impression that you're hitting your tennis ball against a very soft mattress?

Meanwhile Nussbaum had started a backfire. After each hearing inside the prison walls which resulted in another set-off, or after each of my efforts, he made use of the prison law library to bring suit in federal court to make the Federal Parole Board show cause why his next hearing shouldn't be held sooner than the board had scheduled it. Soon he had a string of such suits in progress.

"The courts have become much more sympathetic in recent years to prisoner actions in regard to due process," he told me. "And government agencies are letting some cases against them go uncontested rather than stand up in court and let a precedent be set they'd have to adhere to afterward." He grinned. "Did you hear about the inmate who had so many suits going and was spending so much time in court and tying up so many federal people in the process that they threw his butt out on the street to get rid of him? It's the little drops of water process."

An apocryphal story, no doubt.

In late summer of 1975 I received a notice from Washington, D.C., that I was invited to attend another parole hearing for Nussbaum. The location: Burlingame, California. I wrote and asked if I could appoint a stand-in. The answer came back, no, I couldn't, but Nussbaum could. I suggested to Nussbaum the name of a West Coast writer, Joe Gores, whom Al had "met" through me. I asked Al to appoint him.

I thought of Joe Gores (*Hammett, Interface,* the *File* series) because he had worked on the fringes of the law as a private investigator and felt about it much as I did. More importantly, he was tough-minded, articulate, and patient. Nussbaum and I both primed him with the points we felt he should make during the hearing, and Gores went off to the wars.

The night of Sunday, January 25, 1976, Gores and his wife Dori sat up until 3:00 A.M. polishing the points he would make the next morning at 8:30 before the full United States Parole Board. A lot had been learned during our skirmishes with the federal bureaucracy down through the years, and Gores used it all during the thirty minutes allotted to him before the Board.

He asked, first, that his attorney be allowed to be present. Denied. Then he asked to be allowed to record the proceedings. Denied. Then he asked that Dori, who sat in with him before the Board, be allowed to take notes. Denied. Finally, acting on advice from attorney and fellow-writer Jack Leavitt, Gores stated "For the record" that he was "incompetent to legally represent Mr. Nussbaum."

This set up a *prima facie* case, if the appeal was rejected, for the argument that Nussbaum really hadn't been heard before the Board, because Gores was incompetent to represent him. Gores then went on to make points in three main areas. First, that Nussbaum's prison file contained untrue derogatory information. Second, that the Nussbaum who had taught himself to be a professional writer while in prison was very different from the bank robber of thirteen years before.

Finally, he stated that if the appeal failed, efforts would be all-out and unceasing to effect Nussbaum's release through the court. In retrospect, the third was probably the most compelling to the Board: Gores implied, without really saying so, that there was a vast network of writers working for Nussbaum's release. He hinted that there was no place they could hold a hearing at which some representative, armed with legal counsel, would not appear.

Maybe all our combined efforts finally paid off.

Maybe it was just time, anyway.

Joe Gores telephoned me after the hearing and said the hearing examiner had told him that his recommendation was going to be parole as of July 1, 1976.

I didn't fully believe it until I received the official notice from Washington four days later.

Al Nussbaum is in California now, writing.

Selling.

He sold a movie script to the "Switch" television program, and he's writing educational books under contract while also working on his own material.

Nobody knows whether it will work permanently, I'm sure not even him. Economics will have as much to do with it as anything else. But he *is* outside, and he *is* making it, and I have to feel good about it.

It should be no secret by now that I don't have a high opinion of the rehabilitation program preached by the Federal Bureau of

Prisons. Pious platitudes are given extensive lip-service, while ac
tual help gets short shrift.

There's been one odd side effect from the foregoing.

The sudden absence of strife with various federal agencies has
left a vacuum in my life.

But in this particular instance I'll take it.

DAN J. MARLOWE is the author of the Earl Drake crime novels, including *Operation Flashpoint* and *The Name of the Game Is Death.*

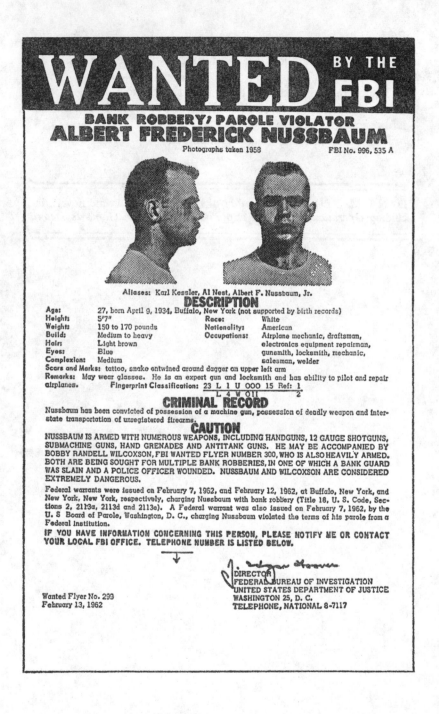

WANTED BY THE FBI

BANK ROBBERY; PAROLE VIOLATOR
ALBERT FREDERICK NUSSBAUM

Photographs taken 1958 FBI No. 996, 535 A

Aliases: Karl Kessler, Al Nest, Albert F. Nussbaum, Jr.

DESCRIPTION

Age:	27, born April 9, 1934, Buffalo, New York (not supported by birth records)		
Height:	5'7"	Race:	White
Weight:	150 to 170 pounds	Nationality:	American
Build:	Medium to heavy	Occupations:	Airplane mechanic, draftsman,
Hair:	Light brown		electronics equipment repairman,
Eyes:	Blue		gunsmith, locksmith, mechanic,
Complexion:	Medium		salesman, welder

Scars and Marks: tattoo, snake entwined around dagger on upper left arm
Remarks: May wear glasses. He is an expert gun and locksmith and has ability to pilot and repair airplanes.
Fingerprint Classification: 23 L 1 U OOO 15 Ref: 1
                            L 4 W OII   2

CRIMINAL RECORD

Nussbaum has been convicted of possession of a machine gun, possession of deadly weapon and interstate transportation of unregistered firearms.

CAUTION

NUSSBAUM IS ARMED WITH NUMEROUS WEAPONS, INCLUDING HANDGUNS, 12 GAUGE SHOTGUNS, SUBMACHINE GUNS, HAND GRENADES AND ANTITANK GUNS. HE MAY BE ACCOMPANIED BY BOBBY RANDELL WILCOXSON, FBI WANTED FLYER NUMBER 300, WHO IS ALSO HEAVILY ARMED. BOTH ARE BEING SOUGHT FOR MULTIPLE BANK ROBBERIES, IN ONE OF WHICH A BANK GUARD WAS SLAIN AND A POLICE OFFICER WOUNDED. NUSSBAUM AND WILCOXSON ARE CONSIDERED EXTREMELY DANGEROUS.

Federal warrants were issued on February 7, 1962, and February 12, 1962, at Buffalo, New York, and New York, New York, respectively, charging Nussbaum with bank robbery (Title 18, U. S. Code, Sections 2, 2113a, 2113d and 2113e). A Federal warrant was also issued on February 7, 1962, by the U. S Board of Parole, Washington, D. C., charging Nussbaum violated the terms of his parole from a Federal institution.

IF YOU HAVE INFORMATION CONCERNING THIS PERSON, PLEASE NOTIFY ME OR CONTACT YOUR LOCAL FBI OFFICE. TELEPHONE NUMBER IS LISTED BELOW.

J. Edgar Hoover
DIRECTOR
FEDERAL BUREAU OF INVESTIGATION
UNITED STATES DEPARTMENT OF JUSTICE
WASHINGTON 25, D. C.
TELEPHONE, NATIONAL 8-7117

Wanted Flyer No. 299
February 13, 1962

Turning Sentences into Words: Writing in Prison

Al Nussbaum

COLE YOUNGER had been a guerrilla officer during the Civil War. Later, he and his brothers joined with Jesse James to form one of the most notorious outlaw gangs in history. However, when the Younger brothers pooled their resources one hot summer day in 1887, they were serving life sentences for their part in the famous Northfield, Minnesota, raid. The fifty-dollar total was used, not for crime, but to help finance a newspaper, *The Prison Mirror,* at the Minnesota State Prison at Stillwater, Minnesota.

That wasn't the first penal publication in the United States. Prison administrators had long found them useful. They provided a way to circulate new rules and let the convicts know about regulations changes. Also, they were one more way to keep men occupied in overcrowded prisons. Then too, it was claimed, though no one really believed it, that prison newspapers and magazines would furnish valuable on-the-job training for would-be writers.

Surprisingly, the 200-odd prison publications in the U.S. *do* spark a certain amount of creativity inside prisons. No matter how poorly produced these newspapers and magazines may be, they give aspiring writers a showcase long before they develop the skill needed for outside publication. And, despite the fact that prison isn't the ideal place to learn writing or any other craft, there have been many successful authors who began to write in prison.

O. Henry, whose byline is synonymous with short stories having surprise endings, began writing while he served a sentence in the Ohio State Penitentiary. Caryl Chessman's *Cell 2455 Death Row* and the books that followed it drew public attention to him while he fought to avoid San Quentin's gas chamber. Steven Linakis, who wrote *In the Spring the War Ended,* began writing in the federal prison at Lewisburg, Pennsylvania; and Frank Elli started writing in the same Stillwater, Minnesota, prison where the Younger brothers helped found the newspaper. Elli's book, *The Riot,* won a $10,000 award, was selected by a large book club, and was made into a successful movie, starring Gene Hackman and former fullback Jim Brown.

And the list has hardly begun. Edgar Smith (who is back in prison on a new charge after a long fight to win his release) wrote his best-seller *Brief Against Death* while in a New Jersey prison and followed it with several other books and articles. Tommy Trantino, another New Jersey prisoner, wrote *Lock the Lock* which was well-received by reviewers. Malcolm Braly, whose *On the Yard* is probably the finest and least self-conscious novel ever written about prison in the U.S., began putting words on paper in a California institution. James Blake, whose *Esquire* story "The Widow Bereft" is the only piece of writing that equals *On the Yard,* has also published *The Joint,* a volume of his letters from a Florida prison. Even without including all the articulate "political" prisoners, and the ones whose names or works I would have to stop and look up, the list is a long one.

I saw my own scribbling first published in *New Era,* a magazine that was produced inside the U.S. Penitentiary at Leavenworth, Kansas; but there's no way of knowing how much influence prison publications may have had on other prison writers. One thing most prison writers probably have in common, however, is a mentor, someone who took an interest in them and devoted countless hours to their development. For Edgar Smith it was columnist and TV personality William F. Buckley, Jr. Malcolm Braly had Fawcett Gold Medal editor, now literary agent, Knox Burger. James Blake was helped and encouraged by writer Nelson Algren. Frank

Elli had a creative-writing instructor from the University of Minnesota to guide him. And I had Dan J. Marlowe, a man who has written over twenty-five full-length suspense novels and hundreds of short stories and articles.

It's impossible to exaggerate the importance of constructive criticism to any beginning writer, but it's all the more important to a prison writer, separated from most intellectual stimulation. A beginning writer must have someone with developed skills or perception to guide him. If a musician hits the wrong note, he knows it; and the artist who paints a red sea or green animals doesn't have to be told he goofed. A writer, on the other hand, must learn to recognize his own errors, and he needs help to do it. Just as anyone will misspell a word forever unless the mistake is pointed out—who looks up a word he thinks is correct?—the beginning writer will continue to make blunders until he learns to avoid the big ones and find the small ones by himself. Most men who try to write inside prison, usually because of senseless restrictions, never get the help they need.

I became a "writer" before I began to write. I was hiding out in Philadelphia's Germantown section while the FBI turned the country on end looking for me. I had to have an occupation that would explain the fact that I seldom left my apartment except to buy food and hair dye, or sneak away to rob another bank. I told everyone I was a free-lance writer. That seemed to satisfy them.

The trouble was, they started asking me questions about writing, questions whose answers required a knowledge of the business and craft of writing that I didn't have. I put everyone off as best I could; then, in order to get the answers, I bought half a dozen books about writing and an equal number of biographies of famous writers. I also subscribed to a couple of writers' magazines and made a habit of letting them protrude conspicuously from my mailbox for a day or two before picking them up.

I bought a desk and decorated it with a used typewriter and a ream of paper, positioning everything so it could be seen by anyone who might ring my bell. I also bought a tape recorder, made a tape of myself pecking at the word machine, and played it most of the day for the benefit of people passing my door.

Just to round out the picture, I began wearing a tweed jacket with leather patches on the elbows and switched to smoking a pipe. If anyone had asked me to write so much as a laundry list, I would have had trouble, but no one asked to see a sample of my writing. I *looked* like a writer.

Then a funny thing happened. I was so immersed in writing lore that I began to identify with real writers. I was able to appreciate many of the difficulties they had faced and overcome; and, alone as I was, it wasn't hard to imagine how a writer might feel, sitting alone in front of his typewriter, confronting miles of blank paper and the danger of snowblindness.

One rainy day I read an especially entertaining book and decided to write the author a fan letter. Not incidentally, the book was about a bank robber. I telephoned his publisher in New York City and was given his agent's number. Somewhere along the trail to the writer, I realized that a semi-literate fan letter wouldn't give him much of a boost. It would be like a tone deaf man praising a musician. So, instead of writing, I telephoned Dan J. Marlowe at his home in Michigan and talked to him about writing for half an hour. A few days after that, I wrote him a long letter, but I had to leave Philadelphia before an answer arrived.

Months later, when I was being held in The Tombs, the New York City prison, Dan Marlowe and I began to correspond regularly. He encouraged me to try to write. He sent me textbooks, gave me as much criticism as I could handle without being crushed under its weight, and praised scribbling that deserved only burning. He once read an 80,000-word manuscript I'd written on long, yellow legal pads with soft, blunt pencils. This piece was so terrible it would have had to be drastically revised before it was good enough to throw away, but he read and commented upon every page.

Writing filled the empty days, weeks, and months while I waited for the courts to get through with me. Then I was sent to Leavenworth with two twenty-year consecutive sentences—a total of forty years. Because of the terms of the judge's sentence, I had to serve only one-third of the first twenty to become eligible for parole. But that was theory, not practice. I had been one of the FBI's ten most wanted men, and the FBI had a lot to say about who was paroled and who wasn't. J. Edgar Hoover was a lot of things, but forgiving wasn't one of them.

Of course, I didn't give up hope. A man with a forty-year prison sentence has to have some hope. But I didn't fool myself very much, either. I spent a lot of time wandering around the prison with escape on my mind. There were always half a dozen plots being worked on, and my sentence made me a good candidate for anyone with a scheme.

I was put to work in the small offset print shop in the basement of the education building. I did as I was told, but only barely. With my long sentence, I had to be careful not to set any precedents I couldn't live with later. So I never did anything I wasn't told to do, and I usually had to be told twice. Printing jobs that would benefit the other prisoners were the ones I took pains with. The others were simply thrown together. No one seemed to notice. Years later one of the guys was organizing a penitentiary work strike and he asked me if I would take part. I told him that, as far as the prison was concerned, I had been on strike for seven years, I just hadn't told anybody. He thought I was joking.

When none of the escape plans showed promise, I decided to spend my time writing. Creative writing was encouraged in some prisons, but Leavenworth wasn't one of them. A man had to have a permit before he could begin a manuscript. Then completed manuscripts had to pass censorship at Leavenworth before being sent to Washington, D.C., for Bureau of Prisons approval. This could take six months or more, but it had to be done before anything could be sent to an editor for his consideration.

But there were other problems, too. For one thing, prisoners could not have typewriters. They had to use whatever machine they could get permission to use. This meant that manuscripts had to be composed in longhand and typed later. Then the mail room had no provision for including a stamped return envelope, and no one was inclined to establish a new procedure for me. Most publishers were good about paying the postage on rejected stories and articles, but that just gave the mail room another crack at them. On the return trip through the mail room (all incoming mail was censored), they were invariably filled with staple holes. Each piece had to be retyped before it could be sent out again.

Worst of all, I was no longer allowed to correspond with Dan Marlowe. At that time, all federal prisoners were required to have an "approved" mailing list, and the officials refused to add Dan's name to mine. No reason was ever given except to point out that he wasn't a relative.

I wrote a first-person story with a female protagonist that was censored because "it may be autobiographical," and another piece was declared "obseen" though I doubt the censor could define the word any better than he spelled it. Another man had a western story turned down because the characters were carrying guns, and he stopped writing.

By this time I could no more stop writing than I could stop eating. It wasn't a habit, it was a necessity. The restrictions slowed me down, but they didn't stop me. Even though it was difficult to get the officials to approve a manuscript for publication, I decided to keep trying to improve my writing whether I could mail the work outside or not. I signed up for some college-extension classes in English composition and literature and took a correspondence course in fiction writing. I also joined the staff of the prison magazine, *New Era*.

Until now, I had done everything (except my escape plotting!) within the prison rules. I bent a few regulations, but I didn't break any. I had appealed all the way to Washington, trying to get Dan on my mailing list, but the answer was the same—no.

One night I wrote to my sister Doris in Buffalo, including Dan's address in the letter. Because outgoing mail was read as carefully as the arriving letters, I pretended it was the address of a mutual friend she had asked me to send.

I let a couple of days go by, then I wrote a letter addressed to Doris but meant for Dan. Doris promptly forwarded it to Dan in Michigan. No one had to draw Dan a diagram, either. He sent his reply to Doris, and she passed it along to me. From then on, if Dan answered right away, as he almost always did, I had the answer to a question in two weeks. This was better than nothing. Much better.

When I was in The Tombs, I had sent Dan a terrible 5000-word story. He rewrote it, cutting it to 2000 words and making it end with a bang instead of a soft fizzle. He sold it to *Alfred Hitchcock's Mystery Magazine* and split the money with me.

Now that we were in contact again, that was an experience I was anxious to repeat. I continued to send my bland material through the prison censorship mill, but I sent the rest to Dan in letters. He not only told me where I had gone wrong, he showed me. Then, if he could, he would sell the story and split the money with me.

Pulp fiction doesn't earn much, so I'm sure Dan took his portion to keep me from feeling like a charity case and to make me value my writing. The money was a fortune to me, though. At that time, prisoners were allowed to spend only fifteen or twenty dollars a month. I hated to ask anyone outside to send me money, so this gave me a way to earn what I needed. With it, life could be a bit more comfortable; without it, even toothpaste and razor blades became part of the punishment.

I kept improving. I had arrived at Leavenworth in early 1964. By the end of 1966 I had sold my first story. *Alfred Hitchcock's Mystery Magazine* bought it for $42 plus an additional 25 percent for foreign magazine rights. That $52.50 let me cross the invisible line and join the writers who get money for their work. It also kept me in fresh fruit and coffee for over threee months.

I had written and sold the story without sending it to Dan for advice. By then I had been trying to write salable fiction for about three years, and I must have written a million worthless words. The story appeared in the February 1967 issue of *AHMM,* and I immediately began to think of myself as a professional.

But it was another year before I sold anything else.

Slowly, my prison situation began to change for the better. The first, and perhaps greatest, improvement was that through our combined efforts Dan and I finally got his name added to my mailing list. We could then correspond directly.

Then some of the censorship was removed. Before, they had been disapproving anything that some bureaucrat decided wasn't "in the public interest." Now, censorship was limited to biography (the writer's or anyone else's) and pornography, and approval of everything else was almost automatic.

There was still the problem of return envelopes and mail-room staples. To overcome that, Dan offered to send stories around for me. I would send material to him, and he would submit it in my name, using his return address. I gave him a power of attorney so he could cash any checks I was lucky enough to receive.

The only deviation from this procedure was when a story might be right for *AHMM*. Dan and I were both well-known there, so the editor didn't require the usual return envelope from me. I sent stories directly to *AHMM*, and the editor sent his rejection or acceptance to Dan. As it turned out, return envelopes wouldn't have been used very often anyhow. *AHMM* bought almost everything I submitted.

There was another reason for having Dan handle my submissions: I was able to conceal my success. Once when I received $100 from a Sunday supplement for a humorous short story, the associate warden at Leavenworth became hostile. It irritated the hell out of him for a convict to make money while in prison. I was there to be punished, not pampered. It wasn't a good idea to be envied by other prisoners, either. But, at the same time, I had to show the officials that I was learning and growing.

To solve this problem, Dan submitted anything that might earn a check of $100 or more. I submitted to the cheaper markets directly. This way, I received enough money through the mail room to demonstrate a modest proficiency and to take care of my monthly purchases in the prison commissary.

Somewhere early in our correspondence, Dan began sending me carbons of his work in progress. At first, all I could do was marvel. But after I had sold a few stories on my own, I got bolder. In fact, I became a real know-it-all.

And he loved it. If he had to know something about guns, locks, explosives, or whatever, he would ask me. I didn't know everything, but there was usually someone a few cells away who would give me any information I didn't have. For instance, if Dan had an impossible burglary scene, I'd tell him how it should have gone down. If being factual didn't hurt the dramatic impact of his story, he would change the scene before sending the manuscript to his publisher.

For years I had been after Dan to write a sequel to *The Name of the Game Is Death*, the book I had read and called him about from Philadelphia. Finally, I wrote about fifty pages in one last effort to convince him. I analyzed the main character, devised a simplified possible plot for the new book, and even invented a name, Earl Drake, which his hero hadn't had. I must have done something right because I convinced him. He wrote *One Endless*

Hour in about six weeks, and his Earl Drake series was off and running.

My prison number at Leavenworth was 81332. Dan often used it in his books when an airplane registration or telephone number had to be given. Also, he let me get my thoughts, if not my fingers, into most of his series books.

When Dan mentioned that he was doing book reviews for a Detroit newspaper, I had to try that, too. I bought a new book, wrote a review, and sent it to several newspapers. *The Boston Globe* and the *Detroit Free Press* both used it, so I became a free-lance book reviewer. At the peak, there were about fifty newspapers using my reviews with some degree of regularity.

But it was hard to forget who was the student and who was the teacher. Whenever I started getting too cocky, something would happen to open my eyes. For instance, I once asked Dan to send me copies of his short stories that hadn't sold. The idea was, I would rewrite and sell his stories just as he had done with mine while I was learning. Dan promptly sent me a stack of unsold stories, and I rewrote them. But not one of the reworked pieces found a buyer.

Dan was as generous with his friends as he was with his time. He spent a summer in San Francisco, getting background for one of the Drake series. While there, he attended meetings of the Northern California Chapter of the Mystery Writers of America. He mentioned some of the writers he met there in his letters, especially Bill Pronzini and Joe Gores, a pair of prolific storytellers we had been enjoying for years. He even began to pass along the chapter's monthly newsletter when he got finished with it. When he left San Francisco to return to Michigan, he put me in touch with Pronzini and Gores and I had two new correspondents.

I went up for parole after serving six years and eight months. That wasn't until 1970 because the sixteen months I had spent in jail prior to sentencing was deducted from the end of the sentence, not the beginning. Predictably, I was turned down. They gave me a three-year set-off, which meant I wouldn't be considered again until 1973.

I left Leavenworth and was transferred to the U.S. Penitentiary at Marion, Illinois, the prison constructed to take the place of Alcatraz when it was closed. I continued to write and correspond, and I applied for parole again in 1973. I was denied in record time and given another three-year set-off.

I tried to appeal, but I was denied without a hearing. Then in August 1975, prior to the expiration of the three years specified in 1973, I was given a surprise hearing. The courts had been requiring the parole board to give specific reasons for denials, and I think this hearing was to keep me from taking that issue to court. I was denied again, however, with the new hearing set for September 1976, the same date that had been set back in 1973.

I filed an appeal of this most recent denial with the board of parole. I also filed a petition in federal court, claiming I had never been given a meaningful parole hearing in violation of the terms of my sentence. The parole appeal was scheduled first. I was told I could be represented at the hearing if I wanted to be. I told them, yes, I wanted to be, and that Dan J. Marlowe had agreed to appear for me.

The headquarters of the parole board is Washington, D.C.; Dan lived sixty miles north of Detroit, and I was in southern Illinois. I was notified that the hearing would be held outside of San Francisco. It would have been hard to find a more distant spot and remain in the continental United States. Dan and I both figured that was the idea.

Dan wasn't able to make the trip and asked them if he could appoint someone else. They told him he couldn't, but I could. He wrote to me and said I should write the parole board and tell them that Joe Gores would appear for me.

Joe and I exchanged a letter or two, discussing what he would try to emphasize. I think he worked harder preparing for the hearing than I worked in helping him to prepare. He thought I might have a chance. I didn't.

Then I was given a hearing in federal court on my complaint against the parole board. The hearing lasted almost an hour, but the judge made no decision. I didn't feel very optimistic about my chances there, either.

As it turned out, I had underestimated Joe Gores. If anyone ever says writers can't talk, it will have to be someone who has never met Joe. When the parole appeal hearing was held in late January 1976, he won me a parole. They set my release date for July 1, slightly more than six months away.

You'd think my problems were over, but they weren't. I had to find a city whose parole people would accept supervision of me, and which was also a place I wanted to go. I chose Los Angeles because I had nowhere to go back to and the West Coast seemed like a perfect place to make a fresh start. The parole office in L.A. promptly turned me down. They refused supervision. I was told that it might be possible to force myself on them, but it wouldn't be a good idea. If I did, they would probably violate my parole on some pretext.

My caseworker at Marion wrote to New York City to see if they would accept me there. In the meantime, I wrote to the people in L.A. myself, asking them to reconsider. New York refused to accept me, but Los Angeles did an about-face and said they would take me after all.

The whole thing took four months, but at the end of April I transferred to a halfway house in Los Angeles. Joe Gores arranged for me to talk to a television producer who gave me a job. I wrote a script and was paid for it. It hasn't been shot, however, and it probably won't be. The producer is no longer with the show, and the script wasn't very good.

The "Catch-22" of television writing is that you can't ordinarily get a producer to listen to you or read your material unless you have an agent; and you can't get a Hollywood agent unless you've sold something. This single TV sale added to my 100-odd short-story and article credits enabled me to interest a top agency in handling my work.

Since then I have been doing educational writing (books for slow readers) to keep the wrinkles out of my stomach and using the rest of my time to work on other projects. I did a detailed treatment for a big-caper movie and everyone hated it. I drew up concepts for a few new TV series and sent them around. No takers. I did a pilot for a half-hour comedy show, and the result was the same. I'm not a bit discouraged, though.

I received a copy of the court's order, dismissing my complaint against the federal parole board. To show that I had been paroled and the case was moot, the court had been given a copy of the parole board's voting sheet from my appeal hearing. The court sent a Xerox to me. The seven-member board had divided four to three.

I *know* I'm lucky. Very lucky. It's just a matter of time before some of that luck spills over onto my more ambitious writing projects.

AL NUSSBAUM is a contributor to mystery magazines and writer of television plays.

Yellow Kid Weil, Con Man

William T. Brannon

LONG BEFORE WE MET, I was intrigued by the crafty exploits of a roguish character named Joseph Rene Weil, but better known as the Yellow Kid. He was known far and wide for his uncanny ability to separate wealthy (and greedy) men from substantial portions of their opulence.

I was puzzled that nobody had written a book about him and I resolved to tackle the job myself after the Kid had completed his last stretch in Atlanta Federal Penitentiary where he had been sent for mail fraud. I then was, and still am, a staff writer for *True Detective*, which had been edited from its inception by John Shuttleworth.

When I told Shuttleworth I planned a book on the Kid, he said he would run it serially and suggested that I send each chapter as it was completed.

The immediate problem was to find the Kid. Earlier I had agreed to give some talks on fact crime writing at the Midwestern Writers Conference. I had to leave for the Conference, so I sent my secretary to police headquarters to try to find out the Kid's address.

But his latest rap was a federal offense and the Chicago police didn't have his address. She talked to a grizzled veteran who said, "I don't see why you want to fool with him, lady. Them stories has been wrote and wrote."

During the course of one of my talks at the Midwestern Writers Conference I mentioned that I hoped to write a book about the Yellow Kid. I'd hardly finished when a man named Ben Abramson came to meet me. He was a friend of writers, operated the Argus Book Store, and published about a dozen books a year under the Argus imprint.

"You're just the man I've been looking for," he said. "I want a book on the Yellow Kid."

We went to a coffee shop and he offered me a contract. Fine—but I still was faced with the problem of finding the Kid.

I knew he had a brother. I found the brother's address in the phone book. On a bitterly cold night in December, I went to the brother's home on the far south side. A woman who talked to me through the door said in a harsh voice that she didn't know where the Kid could be found and she wouldn't tell me if she did.

A young lawyer who lived in our building told me that the Kid's brother was a Municipal Court bailiff. I wrote him a letter, enclosing one to the Kid, in which I asked the Kid to get in touch with me.

A month passed and the Kid phoned me.

It turned out he lived within walking distance of my apartment.

An appointment was made and the Kid was there right on the dot. He was a dapper little man in a homburg and a dark suit tailored in Bond Street, London. He wore yellow spats and a yellow scarf.

A soft-spoken man, he could be very charming when he chose to be. The Kid talked about the weather, the walk from his apartment to mine, and various timely topics—about everything except the reason for his visit. He charmed my wife and me for almost two hours.

Finally he said, "You wanted to talk to me about something, I believe."

I told him about the proposed book and the arrangement for serial publication in *True Detective*. I explained he would have to sign a by-line release. He said that was okay with him. (I later learned he would sign anything if it would bring money.)

"How often would you want me to come to see you?" he asked.

"Can you come once a week?"

"I think so," he replied. "There's just one thing. I'm a bit short of money and I wonder if you could give me the fifty dollars after I tell you a story."

"I can't do that unless the editor wants the story," I told him. But he took the rebuff in good spirit; he'd tried.

Thus my long series of interviews with the Kid began. He told me how he became a con man, of his marriage to the only wife he ever had and the details of his early chicanery. I made notes.

The Kid told me the stories he was relating never had been told before. "There's a statute of limitations on what I'm telling you," he said. "I don't tell you about a case until the statute of limitations runs out."

"That's fine with me," I said. "It may prevent lawsuits."

In his first story, which we titled *Early Adventures in Chicanery,* he told of having been born on the edge of what now is known as the Chicago loop. "When were you born?" I asked him now.

He said he was born on June 30, 1873. It now was January 1944. "That would make me seventy now, wouldn't it? Well," he said, "let's hope I live long enough to tell you enough stories to fill a book."

At the time the life-expectancy of the American male was sixty-one years. The Kid already had outlived that by almost ten years. This surprised him because he was convinced he had a serious heart condition.

I introduced the Kid to other writers, many of them members of Mystery Writers of America. After being invited to give a talk at one chapter meeting the Kid became a regular visitor.

The slogan of MWA is "Crime Does Not Pay—Enough." After he had heard that, the Kid adopted it as his own catch-phrase. He attended the meetings for a number of reasons: inevitably some member would pay for his supper and buy him drinks. At a propitious moment, he would corner me and ask for a loan—anywhere from five to twenty-five dollars. He usually got it.

It was absolutely amazing how many times and how many places the Kid managed to run into me in a big city like Chicago, presumably by accident. I don't recall any of these meetings when the Kid didn't put the bite on me.

This was in addition to the by-line payments I gave him every week. He continued to tell me stories and I continued to get one to the editor every Tuesday. This went on for twenty-eight weeks, after which the book was completed.

When the Kid learned that Ziff-Davis was to publish the book he hurried to the Loop, where their main offices were located. The Kid charmed everybody in the book department and finally got around to asking for an advance of his share. Although I owned all rights, I had decided it was only fair to divide the royalties fifty-fifty with the Kid.

But that wasn't enough. In time he became a nuisance at Ziff-Davis, because his requests for advances became more and more demanding. When Ziff-Davis finally called a halt to his advances, he dreamed up another scheme. He made a deal with a Hollywood producer for a movie about his exploits. Of course, he had no contractual right to do that and Ziff-Davis had to threaten legal action against the producer if he went ahead with the project. The producer quickly saw the folly of the project and withdrew. However, he effectively prevented the book from being sold to the movies. (I learned this from Andrew Stone, a noted Hollywood producer. "I don't think you have a chance," he said frankly. "The word around Hollywood is that if you buy that book you buy a lawsuit.")

An anthology using a chapter from the book about the Kid was published and he received a royalty check that wasn't large enough to suit him. He took it to a lawyer—he had an amazing faculty for getting the free services of lawyers. The lawyer, who didn't know much about publishers' rates, wrote to the anthology publisher and threatened a suit for a fabulous figure.

The president of the publishing firm phoned the lawyer. The lawyer learned some of the facts of life about rates paid to authors.

All the Kid could do was cash the check, and complain that he could have done better.

In the years that followed about a dozen anthologists used excerpts from the book. The Kid's barroom cronies managed to convince him that he was being victimized while I was getting rich on the fees for these anthologies. Actually, in most cases, rather than have a hassle with the Kid, I simply endorsed the anthology checks over to him. He looked at these checks and fell back on his usual remonstrance: "I could have done better."

"Anytime you can make a better deal, Mr. Weil, I won't stand in your way," I told him. Throughout the thirty-four years of our association he always addressed me as Mr. Brannon and in turn I called him Mr. Weil. We never became more familiar than that.

One day he said, "Did I ever tell you about my rubber road invention?"

"No, but I'd like to hear it."

"It happened before my last sojourn in Atlanta," he said. "I was posing as Dr. Walter H. Weed, a noted scientist. I had obtained a book he had written and had turned it over to a printer in Chicago. Dr. Weed's picture was the frontispiece and the printer removed it, substituted my picture, captioned Dr. Walter H. Weed. Then he bound it in the front of the book and I carried it with me wherever I went.

"I had a rubber square which was my latest invention. One day as I was riding a train east I began conversing with a man I had spotted as a probable sucker. I had a rather uncanny knack for recognizing wealthy men who were so greedy they wanted more money.

"This man I'll call Mr. Rogers. I told him I was on my way to Harrisburg to dicker with the Governor about my rubber road invention. 'I assume you've heard of it.'

" 'No I haven't, but I'd like to,' he replied.

"I reached into my briefcase and removed the rubber square. As I started to close the briefcase, in what appeared to be a clumsy motion, although it was intentional, the book containing my picture fell out. The cover had flipped open and Mr. Rogers couldn't help but see my picture. 'Do you write books too, Dr.

Weed?' he asked. 'Occasionally,' I replied and made a deliberate
effort to appear modest. All this impressed him, as I had intended
it should. 'Let's see your rubber road invention,' he said eagerly.

"I showed him the square and explained that the squares were
designed to be placed between the cracks in concrete roads to provide smoother riding. 'How would that help?' he asked. I explained that the rubber inserts would expand or contract, depend-
ing on the weather. 'Regardless of the weather,' I said, 'the driver
of a motor car would have a smooth ride.' (To the Kid, an automobile always was a motor car.)

" 'Yes, I understand now,' said Mr. Rogers. 'It sounds like a
great idea. Have you sold it in Pennsylvania?'

" 'I expect to,' I replied. 'The Highway commission awards the
contract. That's why I'm going to see the Governor. He has a lot
of influence with the commissioners.' I almost could hear the
wheels going around in his head: how could he get in on what obviously was going to be a money-maker? He kept glancing at my
picture in the book by Dr. Weed. It was clear he was impressed."

"How did you get him to join you—as I suppose he did."

"I really didn't," the Kid replied. "I let him sell himself. I encouraged him by asking, 'Did you ever meet the Governor?' He
said he'd never met this or any other Governor. 'Would you like
to?' I asked.

" 'I sure would,' he replied enthusiastically.

" 'I think I can arrange it. What hotel are you stopping at?' He
named one.

"I had been in Harrisburg before and was acquainted with the
hotels. I said I was staying at another hotel. 'I have a suite,' I told
him. 'I expect to entertain the Governor and the best is none too
good.'

"My confederate, Fred 'the Deacon' Buckminster, was occupy-
ing one of the rooms and I made sure that the hotel I chose was
not in walking distance of where Mr. Rogers was stopping. I didn't
want him walking into our hotel and finding Buck there, because
he was to play an important role in the scheme.

"The Deacon was a tall, portly, impressive-looking man especially when he wore his best suits. It was not difficult to believe
that he was the Governor—the role he was to play. Just to make
sure Mr. Rogers did not know what the Governor looked like, I

maneuvered the conversation around so that I could say what a fine-looking man the Governor was. 'A little portly perhaps,' I said, 'but he's tall and I think a little extra weight is becoming to him.' Mr. Rogers said, 'I've never seen him, but I'm sure you're right.' This was enough to reassure me that he wouldn't recognize the man I would introduce to him as the Governor. We conversed on other subjects and at the station in Harrisburg we parted after arranging to meet at 10:00 A.M. in front of the State Office Building the next day."

A rather quaint characteristic of the Kid was his diction. For example, he seldom talked to anyone; almost invariably he "conversed." More often than not, a minister or clergyman was a "pulpiteer."

Continuing his story about the rubber road invention the Kid said, "I arrived at the building where the Governor had his office at ten o'clock and found Mr. Rogers waiting. I don't know how long he'd been there but I suspect he came early so that he wouldn't miss me—and more important the opportunity to meet the Governor.

"We took the elevator to the floor on which the Governor's office was located. Almost half of the floor was devoted to the Governor's suite. On one door across the hall, a legend was painted on the frosted glass top; it read: OFFICE OF THE GOVERNOR. 'Maybe you'd better wait out here until I go in and see the Governor,' I told Mr. Rogers and indicated an inconspicuous spot along the wall on the side across from the Governor's suite.

"It was a place I had picked deliberately; the way the door opened he couldn't see inside the office I entered. I didn't want him to see the interior because it was nothing more than a large waiting room, where many people sat. Several had appointments with the Governor, others hoped to be able to see him. The Governor himself was in another room which was marked PRIVATE.

"I entered the waiting room, stayed a few moments, and came out. 'The Governor's in another office,' I told Mr. Rogers. 'We may have to wait a few minutes.' Mr. Rogers said that was all right with him. We had only a short time to wait. Soon a tall, well-dressed, slightly stout man left another office—also a waiting room—and walked briskly to the waiting room I had just left.

"I caught up with him just as he was grasping the doorknob.

His face lighted up immediately. 'Dr. Weed!' he exclaimed. 'What brings you to Harrisburg?' This warm greeting by a man he thought was the Governor was not lost on Mr. Rogers. Actually he was The Deacon Buckminster.

" 'Before I answer your question,' I said, 'I'd like you to meet my good friend Jack Rogers.'

"Buck beamed and gave Mr. Rogers his brightest smile and a hearty handshake. 'I'm glad to meet you, Mr. Rogers,' the supposed Governor said. 'Any friend of Dr. Weed's is a friend of mine.' Then he turned back to me. 'What else did you want to see me about, Dr. Weed?'

"I glanced furtively around the corridor. 'I think it is something we should discuss in private.' Then I outlined my invention briefly. 'You're right,' the Governor said. 'Where are you stopping, Dr. Weed?' I named the hotel and told the suite number which, of course, he knew because he shared it with me. But Mr. Rogers knew none of this.

"The Governor said he would be there at eight o'clock.

" 'Do you mind if Mr. Rogers comes, too?' And when he hesitated, I added, 'I will vouch for Mr. Rogers' discretion.'

"The Governor looked relieved. 'In that case,' he said, 'it will be quite all right.'

"We arranged to meet at eight o'clock at the hotel, then parted, Buckminster entering the door to the Governor's suite, where he joined the others who were waiting to see the real Governor.

"I invited Mr. Rogers to have lunch with me and he accepted. After lunch we went our separate ways, but not until Mr. Rogers had assured me he would be at my hotel at eight o'clock. When I got back to the hotel, Buck was there. He agreed with me that Mr. Rogers looked like an easy mark.

"We spent the afternoon resting, had Room Service send up our dinner about six o'clock, and about seven-thirty Buck left to avoid a possible meeting with Rogers, who showed up ten minutes early. Buckminster came promptly at eight.

"We discussed the rubber inserts for some time and finally the Governor said he was convinced of their worth. As ex-officio chairman of the Highway Commission, he anticipated no trouble in having the inserts approved for use on selected state highways.

'I presume you realize that the initial outlay will be rather expensive.'

"I hesitated just the proper length of time, then replied I thought I could finance the project. My main cost would be for the building of a plant and the purchase of the necessary raw materials, as well as the salaries of workers until we began to realize some income from the contract with the road commission. At least, that was my story.

"Mr. Rogers could hardly wait to get in his word. 'Do you suppose I could help?' he asked.

" 'In what way, Mr. Rogers?'

" 'I'd like to invest in your project,' he replied.

"I glanced at Buckminster, who said, 'I have no objection.'

"We conversed more about the rubber inserts and the Governor said he could have the necessary papers ready by Thursday. He left after we had agreed to meet at the same time and place on Thursday evening. It then was Monday evening.

"Mr. Rogers remained behind and we conversed more about the project. I convinced him that $50,000 would be required to set up the plant and get it going. We agreed there was no need to wait until Thursday and if we went ahead the following day, we would be that much ahead. Before he left, he gave me a check for $25,000 to bind the bargain and I assigned him the task of buying some rubber and having the necessary casts made. He left after we had agreed to be at my suite when the Governor arrived with the contracts on Thursday evening.

"I'm sure he must have been stunned when he came back Thursday evening only to find that we had checked out on Tuesday morning. He learned there was practically no resemblance between Buckminster, an imposing figure, and the real Governor, who was an ordinary-looking man.

"But probably what shocked him most was that I had cashed his $25,000 check only a short time after the bank had opened on Tuesday morning. I'm sure he soon learned that his greed had cost him $25,000 at the hands of the notorious con men, 'Yellow Kid' Weil and 'the Deacon' Buckminster."

"What did you do after that?" I asked.

"We didn't linger in Harrisburg. We took the first train to Chicago."

"You always went back to Chicago. Why was that?"

"It was our haven. After the early years, we never worked a con game in Chicago, keeping that as a place we could go back to. The police had nothing on us and didn't bother us."

That was the last friendly talk I ever had with the Kid. I sold nonexclusive rights to the book to three different detective magazines. The Kid was paid but he remained unhappy and became very hard to get along with. When the publisher, Grosset & Dunlap, asked me for permission to use a Yellow Kid story in an anthology, *The Fine Art of Swindling,* I gave them the Kid's address and they wrote to him. In his reply, the Kid accused the editors and me of conspiracy to cheat him. The story wasn't published, and once again perversity cost the kid an honest dollar.

Apparently he believed that many others were conspiring against him. From the mid-fifties to the late sixties he filed endless lawsuits charging libel or invasion of privacy against nearly anyone who even mentioned his name in print.

I read of the suits in the newspapers but never knew the outcome of any of them. I rather suspect he was paid off for the nuisance value of each suit.

For years the Kid, who had an apartment on Lake Shore Drive, walked to the Chicago Loop, usually at a very brisk pace. This continued until he was about ninety-five and had to slow down. Within a few years after that he was too feeble to take care of himself and a conservator was appointed for him. He was moved to a convalescent home where he received professional care.

The Kid lived on until his 102nd year. In February 1976 he died. I haven't seen his grave, but often have wondered if it bears the epitaph his late wife composed:

> Joseph Weil lies under the ground;
> Don't jingle any money while walking around.

WILLIAM T. BRANNON's books include *The Lady Killers, The Crooked Cops,* and of course *Yellow Kid Weil.*

Coppolino Revisited

John D. MacDonald

HERE IS a direct quote from the testimony of Doctor Charles J. Umberger, Toxicologist with the office of the Chief Medical Examiner in New York City. He and the late Dr. Milton Helpern had gone to Naples, Florida, in April of 1967 to testify for the Prosecution in the trial of Carl Coppolino, anesthesiologist, at which he was convicted of second-degree murder for killing his wife with an injection of succinylcholine chloride, a paralyzing compound used to stop the patient from breathing on his own during major surgery on the lungs or heart.

With the glazed eyes of the jurors upon him, Umberger said, "Now this case was treated as a general unknown, and when the analysis was started, tissue was set up to cover all categories. For example, one of the first things that was done was to take a piece of kidney. The kidney was ashed and a sample was put on a spectrograph. The purpose of the spectrograph is to determine whether there were any metal compounds. With the spectrographic plate, all but three of the metals can be excluded. Another sample was subjected to what we call a digestion, using an old-fashioned Reinsch Test, plating out the metal on copper. Arsenic, antimony, and mercury, along with silver and bismuth plated out on copper, and from that one can subject the copper plate to an X-ray fluorescent machine and determine whether any of those three metals are there. That is necessary, because in spectrographic analysis there is what is called the volatile metals and these distill out of the crater or the arc and would not produce the spectrum. . . ."

As if that wasn't enough, a little further along he got into the procedures by which his lab had isolated and identified the components of the succinylcholine chloride which had killed Carmela Coppolino.

He said, "The one [test] depends upon the formation of what we call ferric hydroxamic imides. That happens to be what we call a generic test for esters, which is another type of organic structure. Succinic acid is an acid and shouldn't react with this reagent. In working with it, what we discovered is if the succinic acid is sublimed at ordinary atmospheric pressure that as a result of that heating it is turned into the anhydride. In other words the two acid groups kind of lock together and water is lost, and then subsequent to that we found that if we put in a little phosphorous pentoxide in that tube and carried out sublimation we could convert the succinic acid without a lot of manipulation over the anhydride."

What sort of people were soaking up all this great information?

The jury was composed of twelve men—a retired naval officer, a refrigerator repairman, a construction-crew foreman, two motel owners, a retired clothing salesman, a furniture salesman, a mortgage broker, a maintenance engineer, a fisherman, an air-conditioner serviceman, and a semiretired plumber.

F. Lee Bailey brought on his team of experts to refute the testimony of Helpern and Umberger. I quote from the Naples newspaper the following weekend: "One of the most fascinating and immediate impressions received by all was the paradox of conclusions reached by these highly qualified scientists in their efforts to determine what happens to the drug after it is injected into a muscle or vein of the human body."

A Dr. Moya, Chairman of the Department of Anesthesiology at the University of Miami, had testified, in just as much stupefying detail as Umberger, that Umberger's experiments were flawed and his conclusions improper. He said that the compounds found in

Carmela Coppolino's body were there in normal amounts and had been released for measurement by the embalming fluid.

The newspaper item ends: "You pays your money and you takes your choice. And a man's life rests on the choice made by the 12 good men and true who listened intently all week from the jury box."

What do we have then, in this and in other trials where contemporary expert testimony is given by both sides? Not one of those twelve jurors knew diddly about anesthesiology, toxicology, biochemistry, and pharmacology. They could *not* follow and comprehend the expert testimony. The prosecution lawyers and the defense lawyers knew that the jurors could not follow the expert testimony and evaluate it upon its scientific merits. The experts knew this also.

So it is a charade.

Recognizing the fact of charade, one realizes that the jurors will side with that expert who has the best stage presence, who radiates a total confidence in his grasp of the subject at hand, who speaks crisply, with dignity, confidence, and charm, who is neatly and properly dressed and has no distressing mannerisms.

In short, the expert must be precisely the sort of person an advertising agency would select to talk about a new deodorant on national television.

The expert who mumbles, slouches, grimaces, stares into space, and keeps ramming his little finger into his ear and inspecting what he dredges up *might* be a far better scientist than the television commercial chap. But there is no real correlation here. The impressive presence is more likely to be the result of the number of appearances as an expert than the result of academic credentials.

In January of 1977 Melvin M. Belli, sometimes known as the King of Torts, published a syndicated defense of the jury system which appeared op-ed in scores of newspapers.

He wrote:

After arguing hundreds of cases, both civil and criminal, I do not believe that I have ever seen a jury that did not give the case under submission its honest judgment and deliberation. Contemporary jurors are not swayed by old-fashioned oratory or legal theatrics; thus jury trials have become a precise, orderly business.

Today, jurors take detailed notes during testimony and ask probing questions about the facts and the law. Frequently they will return from their deliberations and ask the judge to have crucial testimony reread or to repeat his instructions on the applicable statutes. Juries do not want to make mistakes—and seldom do.

The question is obvious. How can jurors make honest judgments about a body of knowledge beyond their capacity to comprehend? Are they going to take notes on the ferric hydroxamic imides, and come back out to ask what a Reinsch Test might be?

Trial by jury, using expert witnesses to clarify the testimony of others and add to the body of the case, worked beautifully in a world which was far simpler in all technologies. In a village culture a scout could be called in to testify as to the origin of the arrow which struck the deceased, showing to the jury those points of difference in fletching and notching which indicated the tribe where it had been made.

In a world more compartmentalized, knowledge becomes increasingly impossible to communicate to anyone who has not had a substantial background in the discipline at hand.

A friend of mine has spent most of his life in pure mathematics, in abstractions as subtle as music. He tells me that up until perhaps fifteen years ago it was still possible to explain what he was doing, in rather rough outline, to a bright layman, using analogy, models, little drawings, and so on. But now he tells me that he cannot explain to me where he is and where he is going. He has gone beyond analogy, beyond models and drawings and comprehensible statements. Think of that. What he is doing is out of my reach. And yours. Other disciplines are becoming ever less easy to explain. Computers are playing an ever more active and forceful role in the designing of computers. IBM had a computer exhibit in New York City long ago, a big room full of winking tubes and chuckling sounds. You can hold in one hand a computer that will do everything that one did, and faster.

We have all become that Naples fisherman, wondering at the difference between an ester and an oyster.

Jury trials are becoming ever longer. In notorious trials, the jurors are sequestered for weeks and months. Deadlocked juries are more common. Giving expert testimony has become a profession for scientists who have reason to be disappointed in the rewards from their career alone.

It is possible that the jury system could be saved from its own excesses by a revision of the expert-testimony folkdance.

When it appears that medical or scientific testimony will be a key factor in any case, I would suggest that the prosecution select a single expert to present its side, and the defense do the same. These two gentlemen would then select a third man in their field, satisfactory to both of them. After the third man had listened to the scientific evidence and had a chance to read the documentation and do whatever research might be necessary, there would be a meeting between the experts, the judge, and the attorneys for both sides. The selected expert would give his opinion, and it would be binding on both sides. If, for example, in the Coppolino case, the selected expert backed Umberger's procedures and said that he believed that it had been proven that succinylcholine chloride had been injected into the upper outer quadrant of the left buttock in sufficient quantity to cause death, then the defense would be forced to stipulate that this was indeed so, and it would then be up to the defense to change the plea, or try to show that it could not have been done by the defendant.

If such a procedure were to be instituted in civil and criminal trials we would see trials of less duration. Juries would be more prone to reach agreement on the verdicts. Expenses to both the state and the accused would be dramatically reduced in criminal cases, and reduced for the plaintiff and defendant in civil cases.

I would imagine it would make Mr. Belli's court appearances of far less duration and hence not quite so burdensome to the insurance companies and to the patients of the doctors who must pass along the high malpractice premiums to their patients in the form of higher charges for office visits.

I have taken my samples of expert-witness jargon from the Coppolino trial only because I happen to have a complete transcript in my files, and not because I have any feeling that Coppolino was done any disservice by this oppressive conflicting testimony. At this writing he has been a prisoner of the state of Florida for over ten years.

By the time the long days of scientific testimony and the direct and cross and redirect examinations of the seven or eight expert witnesses had gone droning on and on, the twelve jurors had already decided that it was of no moment to them whether or not the succinylcholine chloride was detectable or not.

Here is how that state of mind came about. During the prosecution's direct examination of its leading expert, Dr. Milton Helpern, there came an opportunity to project onto a large white wall behind and to Judge Lynn Silvertooth's right, some very sharp-focus slides taken by the Medical Examiner's office. The courtroom was darkened. There were a dozen of these slides. The very first one brought a sick gasping sound from the spectators and press. It showed, in about a five-by-eight-foot projection, Carmela Coppolino, clothing removed, face down, full length, after three and a half months in a New Jersey cemetery.

Successive slides moved in closer and closer, focusing on the left buttock, then on the upper outer quadrant of the left buttock to show a tiny crater and, near it and below it, the dark stains of five bruise marks. States Attorney Frank Schaub had asked Dr. Helpern, "Could they be the type consistent with the use of human force, the fingers? Could they be caused by a hand pressing down on the body?" In his quiet clinical voice Helpern testified that they could be consistent, and testified as to how he had proven through micro-examination that the bruises had been inflicted shortly before death.

The final slides showed magnified photographs of the incision Helpern had made adjacent to the crater, showing that it was indeed a puncture wound along with a needle track deep into the subcutaneous fat of the buttock.

Now then, because Helpern had testified that he could find no other cause of death, and because the defense offered no plausible alternative reason for the needle track, and because the jurors could readily believe that Coppolino as a nonpracticing anesthesiologist would have access to the substance in question, and because a reasonably satisfactory motive and a provable opportunity had been established by the State, the jurors did not care whether or not the presence of that suck-something could be proven beyond the shadow of a doubt. They had seen the unforgettable pictures, the fingermark bruises, and the needle track, and nobody had stepped up to show she had died of anything else.

And so they drowsed through a lot of it.

So let us imagine a similar case where there is no needle track, no pitiful and ghastly slides of the slim dead lady, a case where it really *does* hang on the technical evidence presented.

Want to be a defendant? Want to take your chances in a forum where charm rather than fact is the persuader? Want to pay an additional $50,000 to $150,000 for the transportation, housing, fees, and sustenance of your team of experts, plus the additional legal costs of the preparation and the additional days in court?

Or will you choose arbitration?

Final question. *If* it is known that arbitration of conflicting expert testimony *is* available, and the defendant elects to finance a battle of the experts, will it be more difficult to preserve the presumption of innocence?

JOHN D. MACDONALD is the author of the Travis McGee novels and *Condominium*.

The Nut Letter Desk

Thomas M. McDade

AS AN FBI AGENT I had been working in different field offices around the country and had been transferred to FBI headquarters in Washington as a supervisor. This was strictly a desk job with the duty of reviewing reports on different types of crimes, but among my assignments was handling the Miscellaneous Desk. To this desk came all the complaints, queries and suggestions not classifiable into one of the regular crime categories, each of which had a separate supervisor. In practice, this desk was the catchall for all the queer, maudlin, or vituperative letters usually requiring not action but destruction. At Bureau headquarters, it was known as the "Nut Letter Desk."

I recall quite vividly the first letter I read on my new assignment, and my feeling that something must be done about it and quickly. A woman boardinghouse keeper in Altoona, Pennsylvania, was writing the FBI that one of her roomers was trying to poison her with arsenic and that the poison she had already taken had caused her toenails to drop off. In proof of this assertion, there were enclosed with the letter some blackened pieces of cartilage which I did not recognize and which I, with all FBI thoroughness, was prepared to send to the laboratory for analysis. After a second and third reading of this letter I decided from internal evidence that the writer was probably crazy but, as I could not be sure, some reply was required. I therefore advised her, in official language, that the jurisdiction of the FBI was strictly limited to the investigation of crimes arising under some Federal law; that murder or attempted murder, except when committed in places under Federal jurisdiction such as post offices, lighthouses, or U.S. bird sanctuaries, was not a Federal crime; and that she was therefore referred, most courteously, to the police authorities in her local city.

At this point in my Bureau career, I had had no instruction in the handling of the mentally deficient. I had had only one case, the outcome of which had taught me little but wariness.

A year before, I had been working in the Charlotte, North Carolina, office when I was called to the office one fair Sunday morning. A Mr. Hurst had just telephoned (collect) from Asheville to say that he could help us locate Gorden Vining, a fugitive of some ten years' standing. A wanted notice (known as an IO—for identification order) containing Vining's photograph and fingerprints had been distributed and it was a matter of pride to an agent to catch a fugitive for whom an IO had been issued. The brief message Hurst had given the clerk on duty did not tell what he knew of Vining's whereabouts, but to the Agent-in-Charge it seemed best that the lead be covered immediately.

The three-hour drive to Asheville was uneventful. Calling at the address Hurst had given, I was told by a thin and slatternly woman, who was sitting on her porch washing her hair, that he had driven off to a place he had "up in the country." It was seventeen miles from Asheville. I sped up there and found Hurst bent over the wreck of an old car which obviously would never run again. He was one of those thin sticklike men who moved in quick jerky movements. He looked sixty, but his eyes were a bright clear blue in mocking contrast to his mouth which had fallen in over his gums.

"Oh, yes," he said, after I'd introduced myself. "I'm glad you've come. I'll be with you in a minute." His hands flew as he rapidly gathered up his tools and put them into a box on the defunct Ford and presented himself to me.

"I'm ready," he said, "let's go," moving to get into the front seat of my car.

"Where to?" I asked him. He explained to me that he would first have to go back to his house in Asheville. I didn't quite understand the necessity for this, but we started back and, on the way, glancing at him out of the corner of my eye, I tried to learn what he knew of Vining. His answers were disturbingly vague and my sense of anticipation turned into one of distrust. He seemed to be trying to conceal something but, since he himself had volunteered the information about Vining, I couldn't see any point in it.

We were turning into his street in Asheville when he said, "If you'll just drive up to the house, I'll go in and get it."

"Get it? Get what?" I asked him.

"The machine," he said, turning those too blue eyes of his on me reproachfully and using a tone that clearly implied I ought to know what he was talking about.

"Machine? What machine?" And while I asked the question, the suspicion lurking in the back of my mind, and till then unidentified, overtook me. I still couldn't admit to myself the horrible nature of the idea which I knew his reply was going to confirm.

"Why, the machine to locate Vining!" He looked at me very earnestly. "You know, the FBI ought to have one like it. Perhaps they'll be interested in buying mine."

All I could say was, "Bring it out."

It was an extraordinary-looking contraption with dials, levers, and wheels and, though it was unlike anything I'd ever seen before, I recognized some radio parts and the key to a sardine can sticking through a hole in the side. We eyed each other over the contraption and, I don't know why, my impulse was to try to keep the disbelief from showing on my face.

Strangely enough, my feeling of exasperation was outweighed by the desire not to add my disappointment and scorn to what I knew he must have already experienced at the hands of the rest of the world. I made some feeble attempt to keep the subject alive.

"How does it work?" I asked.

His childlike eagerness to demonstrate it was pathetic. From his coat pocket he whipped out our IO on Vining, which he had probably taken off some post-office bulletin board, and sticking one end in a part of the machine he turned a wheel and it was drawn

out of sight like a typewriter pulling in a sheet of note paper. He
gazed at it intently, running his fingers through his sparse gray hair
and then, gesticulating with long bony fingers, confided in me the
secret of the machine's magic.

"You see," he said, "this coil is very sensitive. It picks up the
man's scent from his picture. Then, this dial (demonstrating)
points in the direction where he is. You only have to keep following where it points until you find him."

During the drive back to Charlotte that night, I wondered
whether my attitude had been right. I had refused his generous
offer to sell the machine to the FBI, though I said that J. Edgar
Hoover would be mighty pleased that he had offered it to us, but
(and when I told him this I swore him to secrecy) I had confided
to him that we had developed in our laboratory one of our own
machines just like his and hoped he would keep his a secret; otherwise the underworld would certainly try to get it and use it for illegal purposes.

My new job as Supervisor of Nut Letters had one great drawback;
I was never personally to meet the nuts. But even so, they added a
sort of dream quality to the solid reality of the reports of cases
which poured across my desk.

I was fascinated by a chap who wrote in from San Francisco,
saying that he was being controlled by a radio operated by an
enemy of his in Council Bluffs, Iowa. He described in graphic detail the tortures to which he was put nightly by the waves sent out
against him and which made him do things which he considered
unmentionable. In discussing the case with an older associate, I
was surprised to learn that the delusion of my San Francisco correspondent was so common, and had been the subject of so many
complaints from different people, that an unwritten but almost
standard procedure had been devised for handling them. I dropped
a note to the San Francisco office and in a few days the nut would
get a phone call from them telling him that the Des Moines office
had taken care of his radio assaulter—they had smashed his radio.
We did not dare write him direct; after all, he might show the
reply to anyone and they might properly ask "Who's crazy now?"

I was somewhat disappointed to discover that nuts, even in their madness, follow conventional patterns, even as you and I. It had seemed to me that, freed from reason, fancy would roam freely and generate all kinds of imaginative hallucinations. It seems, however, that there were scores of virtually identical radio fiends attacking helpless victims miles away; innumerable people were being slowly poisoned to death by secret, invisible, unidentifiable drugs; the neighbor next door was not really Joe Schultz but Judge Crater, Charlie Ross, or Dracula—and Somebody Ought To Do Something About It.

I would not say that too-frequent exposure to such a vast and fruitful supply of the deluded made me blasé; let us say, it made me more critical—more selective in my choice of favorites to report to my friends who asked, "What's new with the nuts?"

Naturally I developed favorites. There was one woman in Dodge City, Kansas, who regularly sent in packages addressed to J. Edgar Hoover. The first one of these I received had been opened in the laboratory, as was the common practice, and then passed on to the nut desk. The messenger who brought me the mail took from his small hand-wagon a disorderly bundle of brown wrapping paper and placed it on one corner of my desk. He must have known then what it contained for he had a half grin on his face, but he did not wait to see me examine it.

The container was a regular shoe box and, lifting the lid, I found the following: numerous banana peels and apple cores, walnut and peanut shells, two empty match books, about two dozen burned-out wooden matches, three or four crumpled paper napkins, several paper milk-bottle tops, and an assortment of crushed handbills, envelopes, and prospectuses.

It took a few minutes of reflection to recognize the source of this collection: it represented the contents of one or more wastebaskets.

The laboratory had sent with it the brown wrapping paper containing a Fort Dodge cancellation mark; the sender's name I readily discovered from a Bureau file. I noticed one other item: the sender of the package had placed only a three-cent stamp on the box when it was apparently dropped in some parcel-post box. There were postage-due stamps on it for forty-seven cents which had, of course, been paid by our mail room.

I was told that there was in the files a report of an interview with the sender of these packages, an extremely wealthy woman who had somehow combined a belief in reincarnation with the practice of vegetarianism. Just how this induced her to act as she did I never quite fathomed.

My absolute favorite correspondent was a vigorous, prolific, and, in a sense, poetic woman in Joplin, Missouri. I never knew her real name, but the nom de plume with which she closed all her missives was "Princess Angeleus Maria Lamé." Over a period of almost a year there was barely a day that did not include at least one letter from her; on other days there were two or three. Some of these filled eight or ten pages, while others might be only a paragraph. All were written on the stationery of a good hotel in Joplin, and I assumed (mistakenly as I later learned) that she filched her paper from the hotel writing desks. An example of her early style follows:

Gentlemen:
Nine brothers, all somebody else and different nationalities. Am I expected to round them up and convince them, or is there some sane provision being made, for once, from the hatchery?—A woman isn't a parent mother unless she rears her children. I tried to talk to one yesterday, but he still says his family is German, from Germany and wears one name in print and uses another. No wonder people say to me that I was brought up like an animal—handed out like a pup from a kennel.

Sincerely,
Princess Angeleus Maria Lamé

It was the continuity of letters from the Princess that made her an interesting correspondent. In the beginning her letters, while making no sense, at least contained sentences with subjects and predicates. Then came a change; her letters began to be composed for sound rather than sense. I wondered at the time if she had read Gertrude Stein. She wrote:

Gentlemen:
Elizabeth Reitter, writer, a Righter, wrote a righter to lighten and Winnie Lightner mightner sightner. Sit, sot, mote, wrote, kote—emulsion. Sit, sat, sote—remote. Controelle.
Pendicular, Pendulum Olum olive delum odelum oleum ozone zulum olumozne odium odemolum olum sum lumpsome one lump of coal.
O one lump of dirt—sert, kert Kurtz—merit, oyster—zone—Pearl

dishes—slope hope r retigular rectangular—tied ru's it to see it u slope sunny Southern. Ann Southern. South, mouth of the river—rivers, etc., etc.

The third phase of the Princess's writing might be described as her purple nonrepresentational period. Her letters no longer contained words but consisted entirely of lines and dots meandering all over the page in no identifiable pattern. She used purple ink and with what must have been endless patience moved her pen in small twisting lines back and forth across the paper. It was a style which could not be done rapidly and I estimated that some of these letters which contained over a dozen closely filled pages of wiggles and waves must have taken several hours to draw. In the work was more drawing than writing and when she left off using lines, the trails of dots laboriously placed one by one would wander over the sheet always suggesting the outline of some object but never in fact looking quite like anything identifiable.

One day the correspondence stopped short and I never heard from the Princess again.

In my mind I had an image of a spinsterish old maid who lived alone in a house full of cats and was regarded by the neighborhood as an eccentric. I was wrong. When Burke, our resident agent in Joplin, was in the office one day shortly after she ceased writing, I asked him if he knew of the Princess. He did. Almost eighteen months before, when she had first begun to deluge the Bureau with letters, the local field office had been asked to see who she was and stop her if possible. Burke made some inquiries and discovered she actually lived at the hotel from which she was writing and, further, was married to a prominent tradesman in town. He spoke to the husband first who acknowledged that his wife wrote all kinds of letters during the day when he was in his store and there was little he could do about it. Burke asked if he thought it would make any difference if he, Burke, were to talk to her, and the husband said that he might try.

He took Burke up to their apartment in the hotel and, introducing him to his wife, said, "Dear, here is a man from the FBI who wants to talk to you about some letters." Burke was surprised to find himself looking at a rather attractive woman in her middle thirties, well dressed and groomed; quite the contrary from what he had expected from the confused letters he had in his pocket.

The woman stared at him for quite a few seconds, seemingly trying to make up her mind about him.

Then she said only, "You son of a bitch," and with that turned and walked out of the room.

The Bureau made no more attempts to see her.

She must have harbored no hard feelings from Burke's visit because for the next year she poured a cascade of letters into Washington.

In time I was transferred from the Washington headquarters to the New York field office and, not without regrets, I ended my association with the Nut Letter Desk. It was perhaps just as well for the sheer volume of correspondence was making me cynical about the sanity of my fellow men.

The change, however, did not remove them entirely from my life for, as I was a supervisor in the New York office, and my previous association with the Nut Letter Desk was known there, all the queer, odd, and pixilated visitors were passed on to me for interview. Now, for the first time, I began to see some of the kinds of people who had been my correspondents, for instead of writing, they came to the office in person.

One of the earliest of these proved to be a lean bony man of indeterminate age with an enormous Adam's apple which announced his nervousness to the world.

"I think I can help you solve that double killing on Long Island," he announced.

"What double killing?" I asked.

"The one where the fella and girl parkers were shot and the fella who did it marked their foreheads with red circles." The rapid rise and fall of his larynx was very distracting.

"Have you mentioned this to the police?" I asked, this being a case outside our jurisdiction.

"Oh, no," he said. "I didn't want to get mixed up with them. They don't understand my work."

"Your work?" I asked.

"Yes, my work. How I find out who committed these crimes."

"Then you don't know who committed them?" I asked.

He shook his head.

"No, but I think I can find out. Just give me a trial. I think I can do it. I've found out all kinds of things!"

He had lost my interest and I was waiting for a spot to break off the conversation and still save his face. I pushed my chair back. "How would you go about finding out?" I asked.

He bent toward me, placed a hand on the sleeve of my coat and, in a conspiratorial whisper, made ridiculous by the bobbing Adam's apple, he said, "I'm an automatic writer."

Then he sat back in his chair and stared at me, waiting for the full effect of that revelation to reach me.

I could only repeat his remark, "An automatic writer?" and he took up the refrain again.

"An automatic writer."

I didn't want to crush his self-assurance with my ignorance of what he meant.

"Forgive me," I asked, "but what is an automatic writer?" I may have looked incredulous, but he knew he had my interest; and it occurred to me fleetingly that he had been through this kind of query many times before and knew precisely the effect it created.

"Automatic writers are very rare. They are usually gifted people possessed of a sense like second-sight. It occurs most frequently in seventh sons. It can't be taught or acquired."

He recited this in the flat voice one reserves for reading from museum catalogues. I thought to myself, I've come this far, I might as well hear the end of it.

"How does it work?" I asked. He leaned forward again in his conspirator's role.

"I just sit down at the table with a pad and pencil and let myself go into a kind of trance. While I'm asleep I write. I get the answers to all kinds of questions I ask myself. I'm sure I could find out who killed that couple in Long Island."

I thanked him and took his name. We would consider his offer, I said; in the meantime, I suggested he hold our little talk in confidence. I let him know it was better that it didn't get about that there were people who possessed such powers as his. I tried to look as secretive as he and he departed with enormous confidence and self-importance.

New York proved to have its full share of people controlled or tormented by radio, poisoned by strange gases piped through the walls by fiendish neighbors, or followed interminably by strange

pursuers who never lost sight of their victims. Most of these were
unhappy, harassed, and bedeviled people for whom there seemed
no asylum and to whom I could only listen with sympathy while
expressing no opinion as to whether I believed their delusions.

As I said, most of these were very unhappy people, but not Miss
Larkin.

From experience, the girl receptionists quickly learn to separate
the daft from the sane and can usually divert the most obvious
cases. One day, Miss Callaghan phoned me from the reception desk
to ask if I would see a Miss Larkin. To my question as to what she
wanted, Miss Callaghan wasn't sure. Miss Larkin, apparently experienced with receptionists, was holding out for someone more important to talk to.

"Is she a nut?" I asked her.

"She may be; I'm not sure," was Miss Callaghan's reply.

So I suggested that instead of bringing her to my desk, I would
meet her in the corridor so that getting rid of her would be easier.

In the hall, Miss Callaghan introduced me to Miss Larkin. We
shook hands cordially and I asked her to sit down on the long
bench.

In appearance she was so strikingly like an elderly teacher of
mine in the sixth grade that I had to reassure myself by asking,
"You are Miss Larkin?"

Yes, she said, she was.

The one first sure impression one got on seeing Miss Larkin was
her size; she was quite tiny: five feet tall and certainly she weighed
less than a hundred pounds, but she had the sweetest, gentlest smile
I have ever seen. She sat on the edge of the bench, very erect, her
hands in her lap and the softest of brown eyes looking out from a
creamy complexion. There was still a trace of an Irish accent in
her speech.

"I'm sorry if you had to wait," I said. "We're a little short-
handed in the office."

"Oh, that's all right," she said as she removed her black lace
gloves. "At my age there isn't much reason to be in a hurry." She
turned her smile full upon me.

"How old are you, Miss Larkin?" To myself I put her age at
seventy, but I was wrong.

"I've just passed my seventy-ninth birthday. Old enough so that

I find myself hoping people will ask me. I don't think I look my age, do you?"

I assured her she didn't; then I asked her where she lived.

"In Brooklyn, with my sister, on Columbia Heights. Do you know Brooklyn?" I said I did and she began to describe Brooklyn of fifty years before.

"I taught high-school history for forty years and kept promising myself that when I retired I would go to California to live. I tried it," she said, shaking her head, "but after six months I came back. I missed the city too much."

By this time, I had given up trying to guess what might have brought her to our office.

"By the way, Miss Larkin," I finally broke in, "I'm rather busy now. Could you tell me what you wanted to see us about?" She smiled her best smile.

"Why, of course, it's so silly of me to run on like this when you have so many important things to do." The smile then vanished and she immediately became brisk and businesslike. I could see the little history teacher calling her class to order. She looked me full in the face.

"A very dangerous situation exists," she said, speaking with the utmost earnestness. "Something should be done about it right away." Her head took on a slight tremor as she sat staring at me.

"What situation, Miss Larkin?"

She bent toward me.

"Why, the invasion," she said, her mouth now a straight line and her head moving continuously. "The United States is being invaded invisibly."

With this dramatic pronouncement, she stopped and waited for its full effect on me. I tried to picture an invisible invasion but could conjure up no image.

"How do you know this, Miss Larkin?" I asked as gently as possible.

"Why, my goodness," she said in the most matter of fact tone, "I see them all the time."

"Do you see them *now?*" I asked, still in the dark as to who "them" might be.

"Why, yes," she said, "they're all over." The tremor in her   I 34 head became more pronounced and I wondered if I ought to cut short my questions.

"Do you see them on me?" I asked. Somehow I had mentally assigned the size of an insect to them.

"Yes, they are. They're all over." The startling nature of this communication seems not to have impressed Miss Larkin for she gave me a faint smile with her reply.

I was now desperately searching for a place to end the interview without hurting her feelings.

"Do you know where they come from?" I asked.

She never hesitated in her reply. "Oh, yes. They come from China and they are also making them in a paint factory in Clifton, New Jersey."

I got up from the bench and she followed my action. We walked quietly down the hall, she pulling on her gloves again, her head high in the air and her step light but quick.

At the door, I took her hand and held it for a moment. I can't say I was sorry for her as she obviously was not a person one needed to be sorry for.

"Thank you, Miss Larkin," I said. "You may be assured that what you have told me will be kept in the strictest of confidence." Her smile was back and the tremor had disappeared.

"Thank you ever so much. I'm so glad to have talked to you." I opened the gate in the railing and, as she passed out, she gave Miss Callaghan a smile and a hand wave.

"Such a nice visit," she said and passed out of the office. Miss Callaghan looked at me.

"Is she one of *them?*" she asked.

I nodded. As I went back to my office, the receptionist was making out a card for Miss Larkin. If she were to come back, she wouldn't get past her again.

THOMAS McDADE is the author of *The Annals of Murder,* which won MWA's Edgar Allan Poe award.